REMEMBERING TRADITIONAL ꞮꞮꞮꞮꞮ

Remembering Traditional Hanzi

How Not to Forget the Meaning and Writing of Chinese Characters

Book 1

James W. Heisig

Timothy W. Richardson

University of Hawai'i Press
HONOLULU

14 13 12 11 10 09   6 5 4 3 2 1

Library of Congress Cataloging-in-Publication Data

Heisig, James W., 1944-
    Remembering traditional Hanzi : book 1 : how not to forget the meaning and
    writing of Chinese characters / James W. Heisig, Timothy W. Richardson.
    p. cm.
    Includes indexes.
    ISBN 978-0-8248-3324-4 (pbk. : alk. paper)
    1. Chinese Characters. 2. Chinese language--Study and teaching. I.
    Richardson, Timonthy W. II. Title. III. Title: How not to forget the meaning and
    writing of Chinese characters.
PL1171.H45 2008
495.1'07—dc22

                                                  2008033030

The typesetting for this book was done at the Nanzan Institute for Religion and Culture.

Contents

INTRODUCTION

THE AIM OF THIS course is to help you teach yourself, as quickly and efficiently as possible, the meaning and writing of the 3,000 most commonly used Chinese characters. The course is intended not only for beginners, but also for more advanced students looking for some way to systematize what they already know and gain relief from the constant frustration of forgetting how to write the characters. By showing how to break down the complexities of the characters into their basic elements, assigning meanings to those elements, and arranging the characters in a unique and rational order, the method aims to make use of the structural properties of the writing system itself to reduce the burden on memory.

The 55 lessons that make up Book 1 cover the 1,000 most commonly used characters in the Chinese writing system, plus another 500 included either because they are needed to preserve the logical ordering of the material or because they are especially easy to learn at this early stage. Book 2 will add another 1,500 characters for a total of 3,000—all of them selected on the basis of the frequency with which they appear in written Chinese. What you will *not* learn here is how to pronounce any of these characters or how to combine them to form new words. Since this breaks with conventional methods for teaching characters, it is important that you understand the rationale behind the approach before setting out.

To students approaching Chinese from a mother tongue written with an alphabet, the characters represent a forbidding obstacle, one that involves the memorization of thousands of complex configurations, each of which has to be tethered to a particular sound and a particular meaning or function. Focusing for the moment just on what is involved in trying to commit the written forms to memory, imagine yourself holding a kaleidoscope up to the light as still as possible, trying to fix in memory the particular pattern that the play of light and mirrors and colored stones has created. Chances are, your mind is unaccustomed to processing such material and it will take some time to organize the pattern for retention and recall. But let us suppose that you succeed after ten or fifteen minutes. You close your eyes, trace the pattern in your head, and then check your image against the original pattern, repeating the process until you are sure you have it committed to memory.

Then someone passes by and jars your elbow. The pattern is lost forever and in its place a new jumble appears. Immediately your memory begins to scramble. You set the kaleidoscope aside, sit down, and try to draw what you had just memorized, but to no avail. There is simply nothing left in memory to grab hold of. The characters are like that. One can sit at one's desk and drill a number of characters for an hour or two, only to discover on the morrow that when something similar is seen, the former memory is erased or hopelessly confused by the new information. No wonder learners begin to think that they simply don't have a good memory for characters, or decide that learning to write characters is not so important anyway.

In many cases failure to retain what has been learned has much less to do with a lack of ability than with the lack of a method of learning adjusted to the circumstances of the learner. Of course we forget, and some of us forget more than others. But some of this forgetting is due to a simple misuse, even abuse, of our powers of memory, and is therefore preventable. The first step to prevention is to break with certain preconceptions about learning to write Chinese.

UPROOTING BIASES ABOUT CHARACTER LEARNING

One bias circulating among teachers and students of the Chinese language is that a character's *meaning, pronunciation, and writing need to be learned at the same time.* Chinese textbooks typically include all three bits of information for each character or compound term as it is introduced, in addition to supplying details about grammatical function and examples of usage. Of course, these things are important, but to have to learn them all at once places an unreasonable burden on memory. Little wonder that the brain slows down or grinds to a complete halt.

The Chinese themselves are not faced with this problem. As children, they are exposed first to the spoken language, learning how to associate sounds with meanings. When the time comes to learn how to read, they already have at their disposal a solid basis of words whose sounds and meanings are familiar to them; all that remains is to associate those words with written forms. Doing so opens them to printed texts, which, in turn, helps them assimilate new words and characters. Those of us who come to the language as adults can gain a similar advantage by tying each of the character forms to a particular unit of pronunciation and meaning, a "key word" in English, that we already know.

Before you dismiss the idea of affixing English words to Chinese characters out of hand, consider this: all the Chinese dialects, no matter how mutually unintelligible they are when spoken, use the same characters for writing. These characters convey the same meaning, no matter how they are pronounced. What is more, when the Japanese use Chinese characters, they assign them still other pronunciations. In other words, there is nothing in the nature of a character dictating that it must be verbalized one way or another. Unlike students coming to Chinese from an alphabetically written language, the Japanese already know the meaning and writing of a great many of the characters. By the time you finish this course, you will be in a position similar to theirs. Of course, you will eventually need to learn Chinese pronunciations, just as Japanese students do. But adding difficult and unfamiliar sounds to a solid knowledge of character forms is a much more manageable task than trying to memorize meaning, pronunciation, and writing all at the same time.

If some separation of learning tasks seems reasonable, then why not acquire a sizable vocabulary of Chinese pronunciations and meanings first—as the Chinese children do—and then pick up writing later? After all, oral language is the older, more universal, and more ordinary means of communication. Hence the bias that *if anything is to be postponed, it should be the introduction of the writing system.* The truth is, written characters bring a high degree of clarity to the multiplicity of meanings carried by homophones in the spoken language. For example, even an ordinary pocket dictionary of Mandarin lists some 60 characters that are pronounced *yi* in one or another of its tonal variants, with at least 30 distinct characters in the fourth tone alone. Each of these characters carries its own meaning or meanings, which the simple syllable *yi* of itself cannot communicate. Beginning with characters and their meanings greatly reduces this ambiguity.

The idea that writing should come after speaking is bolstered by another, more pervasive bias: *the writing of characters is the most complex part of the language to learn.* In fact, it is a far simpler task than is often supposed, as these books hope to demonstrate. In addition, beginning with the writing leaves the student with solid units of form and meaning to which Chinese pronunciations can then be attached. Even more important, completing what is usually perceived to be the most challenging task first, and in a relatively short period of time, rather than leaving it for later, cannot help but motivate one to carry on with the language. Given high attrition rates among students of Chinese in the West, the role of such positive reinforcement is not to be discounted.

Yet another bias that needs uprooting is the idea that *characters can only be mastered through constant drill and repetition.* Traditional methods for approaching the Chinese writing system have been the same as those for learning alphabets: practice writing the characters one by one, over and over again, for as long as it takes. Whatever ascetic value there is in such an exercise, it is hardly the most efficient way to approach character study. The reason this bias has such a strong hold on students of Chinese is that persons completely ignorant of the Chinese writing system naturally rely on teachers who have learned characters from childhood. Surely a pedagogy with many centuries of history behind it and over a billion users demands our respect. Here again, the prevailing wisdom is deceptive.

Native speakers of Chinese are clearly in a position to teach a good many things about their language, but they are not necessarily qualified to answer questions from non-native speakers about how best to learn the characters, for the simple reason that they themselves have never been in the situation of having to ask such a question. Having begun their study as children, in whom the powers of abstraction were not yet developed and for whom rote memory was the only option, they cannot be expected to fully grasp the learning potential an adult brings to the study of the characters. As children, we were all good *imitators*, with few habits to get in the way of our absorption of new skills. But we did not become good *learners* until we had the ability to classify, categorize, and organize discreet bits of information into larger blocks. This is precisely what young children cannot do with character forms and why they have no choice but to rely on imitation and repetition. Whatever educational and social advantages there may be to having an entire school population study Chinese characters by writing them again and again from an early age, for the adult approaching the language from the outside it amounts to little more than a gigantic waste of time. A touch of irreverence towards current pedagogical conventions, along with a little rethinking of the way the characters are studied and the order in which they are learned, can produce far better results than simple reliance on methods designed for the teaching of children.

The approach followed in these pages incorporates important elements of all three broad areas into which cognitive learning strategies are thought to fall—organization, elaboration, and rehearsal—and entails a strong reliance on memory techniques or "mnemonics." The very word is sure to tap into predispositions against the use of mnemonics in general, and for the learning of Chinese characters in particular. Here, too, the biases run deep, and we can do little more in these introductory remarks than try to identify them and offer a brief response.[1]

For some, reservations about mnemonics are grounded in the image of disreputable charlatans who hype expensive memory-training courses as the key to a better job and a better life. It is true that exaggerated claims have been

---

1. For more developed arguments making a case for mnemonics, see K. L. Higbee, *Your Memory: How it Works and How to Improve it* (New York: Prentice-Hall, 1988); see also T. W. Richardson, "Chinese Character Memorization and Literacy: Theoretical and Empirical Perspectives on a Sophisticated Version of an Old Strategy," in Andreas Guder, Jiang Xin, and Wan Yexin, eds., 对外汉字的认知与教学 [The cognition, learning, and teaching of Chinese characters] (Beijing: Beijing Language and Culture University Press, 2007).

made, but empirical studies over the last several decades have clearly demonstrated that well-conceived mnemonic devices can be very useful for certain memory tasks. This has lead many scholars to recommend them as legitimate learning strategies.

These scholarly developments also help address another concern: *mnemonics are simply too bizarre or too silly to use.* Actually, they can be quite sophisticated and elegant. Surely the more important question is whether they work or not. The whole range of possibilities, from the silly to the sophisticated, leaves ample room for personal taste or preference in determining what best facilitates learning.

Still another apprehension some may have is that *mnemonic devices clutter the mind and separate the learner from the matter to be learned.* On the contrary, insofar as such devices provide meaning and organization that would not otherwise exist, they actually unclutter the mind. Besides, once recall for a particular item has become automatic, the mnemonic initially used to fix that item in memory usually falls away of its own accord.

The dominant bias against the use of mnemonics for learning Chinese characters is that *it is inappropriate to overstep the boundaries of current etymological knowledge, even more so when these liberties are taken without drawing attention to the fact. To do so is not to communicate the "truth" about the characters.* This complaint speaks directly to what you will meet in these pages. On one hand, much of the course is grounded in scholarly consensus on the history of the characters. On the other, we have not hesitated to ignore established etymologies whenever doing so seemed pedagogically useful. In fact, the course relies heavily on fictions of our own invention. At least two reasons support this choice. For one thing, even the most comprehensive account of how particular characters were formed may be far from the whole "truth" concerning them. Much remains speculative or unknown. For another, however reliable the etymological information may be, for most learners of Chinese it is not as crucial as finding relief for memory—which is what we have tried to provide here. Should a student later turn to etymological studies, the procedure we have followed will become more transparent, and the fact that we did not indicate each departure from an established etymology should not cause any obstacle to learning. With this, we lay the question of mnemonics to rest.

Two final and related biases require brief comment: (1) *the learning of individual characters in isolation from compound words and grammatical patterns is mistaken*; and (2) *a single key word is often inadequate to cover a character's meaning.*

We acknowledge that effective reading requires a knowledge of compound words and grammatical patterns; however, we concur with those who stress the value of learning individual characters well in order to solidify "the network of possible morphemes upon which all dual and multi-character words are built."[2] Similarly, we are aware that one-word definitions are of limited use; however, we agree with those who see them as a solid starting point for developing a richer and more nuanced understanding. The study of individual characters, each with a distinct meaning, is only a first step towards literacy in Chinese. For the rest, only a broad and prolonged contact with the written language will suffice.

A SHORT HISTORY OF THE COURSE

When James Heisig arrived in Japan some thirty years ago, he came with no knowledge of the language. Travels through Asia had delayed his arrival at the language school where he had been pre-enrolled by his sponsors. He decided to forego classes and "catch up" on his own by working through a stack of books on grammar and structure. Through conversations with teachers and other students he soon realized that he should not postpone the study of the kanji (as the Chinese characters are called in Japanese), which, all were agreed, was the biggest chore of all. Having no idea at all how the kanji "worked" in the language, yet having found his own pace, he decided—against the advice of nearly everyone around him—to continue to study on his own rather than join one of the beginners' classes. He began studying the kanji one month after his arrival.

The first few days he spent poring over whatever he could find on the history and etymology of Japanese characters, and examining the wide variety of systems on the market for studying them. It was during those days that the basic idea underlying the method of these books came to him. The following weeks he devoted himself day and night to experimenting with the idea, which worked well enough to encourage him to carry on with it. Before the month was out he had learned the meaning and writing of some 1,900 characters and had satisfied himself that he would retain what he had memorized. It was not long before he became aware that something extraordinary had taken place.

For himself, the method he was following seemed so simple, even infantile, that it was almost an embarrassment to talk about it. And it had happened as such a matter of course that he was quite unprepared for the reaction it caused. On the one hand, some at the school accused him of having a short-term pho-

---

2. E. B. Hayes, "The Relationship between 'Word Length' and Memorability among Non-Native Readers of Chinese Mandarin," *Journal of the Chinese Language Teacher's Association* 25/3 (1990), 38.

tographic memory that would fade with time. On the other, there were those who pressed him to write up his "methods" for their benefit, which he did. The resulting book, originally titled *Adventures in Kanji-Land* and changed in later printings to *Remembering the Kanji*, has gone through numerous editions and been adapted for German, Spanish, French, and Portuguese.[3]

Timothy Richardson, a language teacher who had studied some Chinese at the university level, came upon a copy of *Remembering the Kanji* in the early 1990s. He quickly became interested in the possibility of adapting the work for students of Chinese. In subsequent doctoral work at the University of Texas at Austin, he focused on the method for his dissertation and subjected it to an extensive examination in terms of relevant theory and research.[4] This required careful consideration not only of the underlying cognitive processes that the method might be expected to involve but also of its reasonableness in terms of prevailing perspectives on vocabulary development and reading. His work also entailed the compilation of a new list of 1,000 high-frequency Chinese characters and their integration into a skeletal Chinese version of Heisig's original book. The results were so encouraging that Richardson sent a copy to Heisig with the suggestion that they join forces on a complete Chinese edition. Thus it was that our collaboration began.

Two immediate problems presented themselves: first, whether to opt for traditional Chinese writing or to follow the simplified forms of Mainland China; and second, how many characters to include, and which ones.

The first problem was eventually resolved with a decision to produce two parallel courses, one for each system of writing. Arguments for a learner's beginning with one or the other each have their points, and it is not our wish to take sides in the debate, even though both of us began with traditional characters. That said, the student should know that certain overlaps in the books would only cause confusion if the two versions are studied simultaneously. If your aim is to achieve fluency in writing both systems, then it is preferable to

---

3. *Adventures in Kanji-Land* (1978), subsequently reissued as *Remembering the Kanji* (Honolulu: University of Hawai'i Press, 2007, 5th edition, 22nd printing). Other language editions include *Kanji para recordar 1: Curso mnemotécnico para el aprendizaje de la escritura y el significado de los caracteres japoneses,* with Marc Bernabé and Verònica Calafell (Barcelona: Editorial Herder, 2005, 3rd printing); *Die Kanji lernen und behalten 1. Bedeutung und Schreibweise der japanischen Schriftzeichen,* with Robert Rauther (Frankfurt-am-Main: Vittorio Klostermann Verlag, 2006, 2nd printing); *Les Kanji dans la tête: Apprendre à ne pas oublier le sens et l'écriture des caractères japonais,* Yves Maniette (2005, 2nd printing); *Kanji: Imaginar para aprender,* with Rafael Shoji (São Paulo: JBC Editora, 2007).

4. T. W. Richardson, *James W. Heisig's System for Remembering Kanji: An Examination of Relevant Theory and Research, and a 1,000-Character Adaptation for Chinese.* Doctoral dissertation, The University of Texas at Austin, 1998.

begin with the traditional. If you are sure you will be content with recognizing the traditional and writing the simplified, then begin with the latter.

The first step to resolving our second problem was to settle on introducing a total of 3,000 most frequently used characters. This number may fall below the 3,500 to 4,500 characters that are generally thought necessary for full proficiency, but it also happens to represent about 99.5% of the characters found in running Chinese texts, as large-scale frequency counts show. What is more, students who have learned to write these 3,000 characters will be equipped with the tools for learning to write additional characters as the need arises. Next, since the top 1,000 entries in our complete frequency list account for approximately 90% of characters in running texts,[5] we decided to include all of them in the first book of both the traditional and simplified sets.

Frequency questions aside, the figure of 3,000 characters also makes available certain "economies of scale" that are possible with the method, which fewer characters would not. In the business world, economies of scale are said to arise when an increase in the scale of production leads to a decline in costs per unit. If we are producing widgets, the production cost per widget goes down as more are produced, because the initial investment in machinery has already been made. Similarly, using the method laid out in these pages to learn 3,000 characters, rather than 1,000, for instance, results in a decrease in learning cost per character, because an investment in basic mental "machinery" is largely made early on. In other words, the return on time and effort expended at the outset yields much better returns as more characters are learned.

When it came to deciding just which characters to include and on what grounds, the challenge proved far greater than we had counted on. Frequency lists compiled by specialists do indeed exist. Some of them list only traditional characters and others only simplified; some of them are more formal and others less so; some of them are more technical and some less so; and so forth. What we wanted, however, was a general-use list of 3,000 characters that would apply to the whole of the Chinese-speaking world. In a strict sense, such a list is not possible. If you were to set two pages of identical Chinese text side by

---

5. Based on three lists we consulted that include such data, the 3,000 most frequently used characters comprise 99.56%, 99.18%, and 99.43% of the total number of characters in their respective databases, while the top 1,000 characters comprise 90.3%, 89.14%, and 91.12% respectively. The three sources, in order, are: 新聞語料字頻統計表——語料庫爲本研究系列之一 [Corpus-based frequency count of characters in Journal Chinese: Corpus based research series no. 1]. Technical Report no. 93-01 (Taipei: Academia Sinica Institute of Information Science, 1993); J. Da, "Modern Chinese Character Frequency List 现代语单字频率列表," Chinese text computing. <http://lingua.mtsu.edu/chinese-computing> (2004); and C. H. Tsai, "Frequency of Usage and Number of Strokes of Chinese Characters." <http://technology.cht-sai.org/charfreq/> (1996).

side, one in simplified characters, the other in traditional, about two-thirds of the characters would have exactly the same form on both sides. In other words, about one-third of characters in common use differ in form from one set to the other. Sometimes the discrepancies are slight, sometimes significant. Occasionally, two or more frequently used traditional characters are reduced to a single simplified character. Taking these and other considerations into account, we assembled a core list that was then adjusted to arrive at 3,000 characters for each of the two courses.

Sparing the reader a full account of the actual mechanics of completing the task, not to mention the many detours and dead-ends encountered along the way, the steps we took were basically these: We compared four major frequency lists, two traditional and two simplified,[6] and supplemented our findings with yet another frequency list.[7] All characters that were included among the top 3,050 on at least three of the four major lists—including those of exactly the same form and those of differing form but equivalent meaning across the traditional/simplified divide—were moved to a master list. Some 2,860 traditional characters, and just under 2,800 of their equivalents on the simplified side, met these criteria, the great majority of them appearing among the top 3,050 on all four lists.

In order to select the additional characters needed to bring this common master list up to 3,000 characters, a variety of other factors had to be juggled. Some characters, for example, clearly met the criteria on two lists and fell just outside of them on the two others, while others qualified on two of the four major lists and yet were given a high ranking on the supplemental list mentioned above. In some cases, items falling just outside of frequency criteria are important as components of other characters or often show up in beginning Chinese textbooks. (The character 餃/饺, which figures as the first half of the compound for "Chinese dumplings," is a clear example of this and has been included in Book 2 of each of the courses.) Taking all these factors into account, we added more than 100 new characters to the master list. Another 14 characters representing useful nouns that did not quite meet the frequency criteria brought the total to 3,000 characters on the traditional side. Completing the simplified list required some 75 characters more to compensate for character amalgamations resulting from the simplification process.

6. In addition to the three lists mentioned in footnote 5, see also 现代汉语频率词典 [Modern Chinese frequency dictionary] (Beijing: Beijing Language Institute, 1986), as cited in J. E. Dew, *6000 Chinese Words: A Vocabulary Frequency Handbook for Chinese Language Teachers and Students* (Taipei: SMC Publishing Inc., 1999).

7. 國家言文字工作委 [National Working Committee on the Written Language], 现代汉语常用字表 [Modern Chinese frequently-used characters list] (Beijing: Yuwen Press, 1988).

The next step was to extract a selection of 1,000 characters that would serve as a foundation for the Book 1 of each of the courses. As part of the research for his dissertation, Richardson had found 580 characters that figured among the top 1,000 characters in five different sources.[8] This was the starting point. Another 199 were included by taking characters that were in the top 1,000 in four of those sources and similarly ranked on either of two frequency lists that had not been consulted in the original research.[9] Another 74 were included by taking characters that occurred in the top 1,000 in three of the original sources and similarly ranked on *both* of the new lists, bringing the total up to 853. An additional 74 characters that had appeared among the top 1,000 items on at least three of the four major lists gave us 927.

At each step of the way, an attempt was made to avoid arbitrariness, but the challenge was to relax frequency criteria only enough to include the number of characters we needed and no more. In selecting the remaining 73 characters of the total 1,000, we felt that pedagogical concerns and personal judgments should be given greater weight, because using frequency criteria alone had generated some anomalies that needed to be addressed. For example, frequency dictated the inclusion of the characters for "winter" and "spring," but not for "summer" and "fall"; for "mama," but not for "papa." We therefore consulted a list of the 969 characters taught in the first four grades of elementary school in the Republic of China (ROC).[10] Of these, 810 were exactly the same as the 927 we had selected based on frequency alone. The remaining 73 characters were drawn from the ROC list, always with an eye on the basic frequency lists. As an added check on the simplified side, we compared our list against one of the original sources, a list of the 1,000 characters most frequently used in textbooks in elementary and high schools in the People's Republic of China (PRC).[11] The two lists had 904 characters in common, confirming the pedagogical value of the final list. Of course, all of the items on both the ROC and PRC lists that did not make it onto our list of the 1,000

8. *Corpus-Based Frequency Count of Characters in Journal Chinese*; M. K. M. Chan and B. Z. He, "A Study of the 1,000 Most Frequently Used Chinese Characters and their Simplification," *Journal of the Chinese Language Teachers Association* 23/3 (1988), 49–68; R. M.-W. Choy, *Read and Write Chinese* (San Francisco, California: China West Book, 1990); *Chinese Vocabulary Cards* (New Haven: Far Eastern Publications, Yale University, n.d.); Tsai, "Frequency of Usage and Number of Strokes of Chinese Characters." Note that Choy's frequency data seem to have been taken from a 1928 study by Chen Hegin.

9. See *Modern Chinese Frequency Dictionary*; Da, "Modern Chinese Character Frequency List."

10. "Target Characters by School Grade: Taiwan," as listed by J. Lau at 黃橋 [Yellow-Bridge] <http://www.yellowbridge.com/language/fc-options.php?deck=tw>.

11. See Chan and He, "A Study of the 1,000 Most Frequently Used Chinese Characters."

most frequently used characters were included elsewhere in the master list of 3,000, many of them appearing among the 500 supplemental characters found in Book 1 of both the simplified and traditional courses.

THE BASICS OF THE METHOD

There is no better way to understand the method followed in these pages than to start using it. Still, readers have a right to know what they are getting into, so a brief explanation seems in order.

To begin with, all the characters are made up of pieces, or "primitive elements" as we shall call them here. These are the basic building blocks out of which all characters are constructed. Over 200 of these have been singled out as "radicals," which are used in the organization of character dictionaries, but there are many others. Individual characters can also serve as primitive elements in other more complicated characters. If one is really determined to learn to write Chinese, and not just memorize a small number of characters to meet course requirements, it makes sense to take full advantage of these component parts by arranging the characters in the order best suited to memory.

This course begins, therefore, with a handful of uncomplicated primitive elements and combines them to make as many characters as possible. More elements are then thrown into the mix, a few at a time, allowing new characters to be learned—and so on, until the entire list has been exhausted. This process has a number of important advantages, not the least of which is that learning new elements and characters also invariably reinforces what has already been learned.

Because we are dividing the course into two books of 1,500 characters each and including the most important 1,000 characters in the first volume, not all of the characters that could be learned at a given point are actually introduced in their logical sequence; some of them are saved for later. In the long run, there is no real reduction in efficiency here. It was just a matter of relegating less frequently used characters to Book 2.

Each primitive element is assigned its own concrete image, after which the images are arranged into a composite picture associated with a definition, a unique "key word," given for each character. The key word is meant to capture a character's principal meaning, or at least one of its more important meanings. It is often concrete and visually suggestive, but it can also be conceptual and abstract. In any event, it is the key word, or its use in a familiar English phrase, that sets the stage for the composition of the elements into a single "story." As you will see, the stories are meant to stretch your imagination and get you close enough to the characters to befriend them, let them surprise you, inspire you, enlighten you, resist you, and seduce you; to make you smile or shudder or otherwise react emotionally in such a way as to fix the imagery in memory.

The whole process employs what we may call *imaginative memory*, by which we mean the faculty to recall images created purely in the mind, with no actual or remembered visual stimuli behind them. We are used to hills and roads, to the faces of people and the skylines of cities, to flowers, animals, and the phenomena of nature associated with *visual memory*. And while only a fraction of what we see is readily recalled, we are confident that, given proper attention, anything we choose to remember, we can. That confidence is lacking in the world of the characters, which generally show a remarkable lack of connection to the normal visual patterns with which we are comfortable. It is possible, however, to harness the powers of imagination to give meaning to character elements that visual memory is admittedly ill adapted for remembering. In fact, most students of the Chinese writing system do this from time to time on their own, devising their own imaginative aids, but without ever developing an organized approach to their use.

The stories and plots you will meet in these pages are all drawn with words; there are no pictures or cartoons to control or limit the way your imagination handles the information provided. There is no correct way of imagining; the sole criterion is that it work for you (though we will make frequent suggestions). The only thing you will be asked to draw are the characters themselves. But what you *see* when you make your drawing will be all yours, and most assuredly different from what scholars and historians see when they analyze the characters. A whole imaginary world will come to life for you out of the primitive elements. The more vividly you can visualize the things that inhabit this world, the less need there will be to review what you have learned. Many, if not most, of the characters can be remembered at first encounter, with no need to drill them later other than through the normal reinforcement of actually using them.

As you come to write more and more of the characters in practice, you will find that they all but write themselves once you have set pen to paper, much the same as the alphabet already does for you. In time you will find, as previously suggested, that most of the imagery and key-word meanings will have served their purpose and recede from active memory. Some, we should warn you, will stay with you forever.

THE DESIGN OF THIS BOOK

You will be guided at every step of the way, but a few things about the design of this book need to be clarified at the outset. Clusters of characters have been arranged into lessons of varying length. Many, but not all, focus on a particular class of primitive elements. Nothing more is intended by this than a way to break up the monotony and give you a sense of your overall progress. Each individual character is given its own frame, as in the example below:

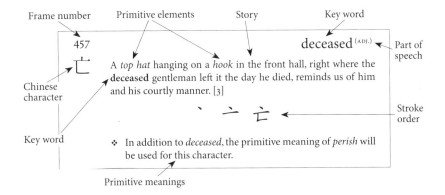

Since the goal is not simply to remember a certain number of characters, but to learn *how* to remember them (and others not included in the course), this book has been divided into three parts. The first, *Stories*, provides a full associative story for each character. By directing the student's attention, at least for the length of time it takes to read the explanation and relate it to the written form of the character, we do most of the work, even as the student acquires a feeling for the method. In the next part, *Plots*, only skeletal outlines of stories are presented, leaving it to the student to work out the details by drawing on personal memory and fantasy. The final part, *Elements*, comprises the major portion of the book, and provides only the key word and the primitive meanings, leaving the remainder of the process to the student.

The stroke order is given in a hand-drawn font. You will notice variations from time to time between the printed form and the hand-drawn form of the same character. This is due to the fact that historical variants of some characters are in common use, especially on the traditional side, and to the fact that there has been no strict standardization of character forms. A given element will occasionally appear in different variations within the same Chinese font. Rather than draw attention to each instance of this, and in order to spare the user unnecessary frustration, we have brought consistency of form to all the characters, except where general usage suggests otherwise. It is best to be aware of these character and font inconsistencies from the start, since sooner or later you will run into them in print and will need to know how to process them. In any case, we recommend that you stick with the hand-drawn forms as a model for writing.

There are five indexes included at the end of each volume; those in Book 2 are cumulative for the whole course. Index I shows all the characters in their hand-drawn form, in the order in which they are introduced in this book. Since discrepancies with the printed form do occur, the student would do well to consult this index in case of doubt. Beneath each character in Index I is its pronunciation, provided here for reference purposes. The list of elements singled out as primitives proper and brought together in Index II is restricted to basic elements that are not themselves characters, or at least not treated as such in this course. Index III organizes the characters in their dictionary order, first according to number of strokes and then according to radical. Index IV arranges the characters according to their pronunciation and is intended to facilitate the search for particular characters. Finally, Index V contains all the key-word and primitive meanings.

CONCLUDING COMMENTS

Before you start out on the course plotted in the following pages, your attention should be drawn to a few final points. First, you must be warned about setting out too quickly. It should not be assumed that, because the first characters are so elementary, they can be skipped over hastily. The method presented here needs to be learned step by step, lest you find yourself forced later to retreat to the first stages and start over. Some 20 or 25 characters per day would not be excessive for someone who has only a couple of hours to give to study. If you were to study them full time, there is no reason why all 1,500 characters in Book 1 could not be learned successfully in four to five weeks. Such a claim is bound to raise more eyebrows than hopes among experienced teachers, but Heisig's own experience with Japanese kanji, and reports from students around the world, bear that estimate out. In any case, by the time the first 200 characters have been studied, you should have discovered a rate of progress suitable to the time available.

Second, the repeated advice given to study the characters with pad and pencil should be taken seriously. While simply remembering the characters does not, you will discover, demand that they be written, there is really no better way to improve the aesthetic appearance of your writing and acquire a "natural feel" for the flow of the characters than by writing them. The method of this course will spare you the toil of writing the same character over and over in order to learn it, but it will not supply the fluency at writing that comes only with constant practice. If pen and paper are inconvenient, you can always make do with the palm of the hand, as the Chinese themselves do. It provides a convenient square space for tracing characters with your index finger when riding in a bus or walking down the street.

Third, the characters are best reviewed by beginning with the key word, progressing to the respective story, and then writing the character itself. Once you have been able to perform these steps, reversing the order follows as a matter of course. More will be said about this later in the book.

Fourth, it is important to note that the best order for *learning* the characters is by no means the best order for *remembering* them. They need to be recalled when and where they are met, not in the sequence in which they are presented here. For that purpose, recommendations are given in Lesson 5 for designing flash cards for random review.

Finally, perhaps only one who has seen the method through to the end can appreciate both how truly uncomplicated and obvious it is, and how accessible to any average student willing to invest time and effort. But while the method is *simple* and does eliminate a great deal of inefficiency, the task is still not an *easy* one. It requires as much stamina, concentration, and imagination as one can bring to it. Of that, too, we are convinced.

ACKNOWLEDGMENTS

We would like to express our gratitude to Robert Roche for the generous assistance he provided that enabled us to complete these books, as well as for the constant stimulus and many useful suggestions he has given us these past several years. A special word of thanks also to the staff and fellows of the Nanzan Institute for Religion and Culture, who provided the facilities and the environment to make a difficult task easier, and to Brigham Young University Hawaii for facilitating our collaborative work at Nanzan during the winter semester of 2007. Among those who lent their expertise to this project, Tsu-Pin Huang and Dr. Yifen Beus were especially helpful and generous with their time. Finally, we wish to acknowledge the support and interest in the project shown by Pat Crosby, Keith Leber, and the editorial team at the University of Hawai'i Press.

Nagoya, Japan
9 August 2007

Stories

LESSON 1

LET US BEGIN with a group of 15 characters, all of which you probably knew before you ever cracked the covers of this book. Each character has been provided with a *key word*—a simple word or phrase—to represent the basic meaning. Some of these characters will also serve later as *primitive elements* to help form other characters, often taking a different meaning, sometimes a purely fanciful invention, in the process. A remark preceded by a special symbol (❖) has been appended to alert you to the change in meaning.

The *number of strokes* of each character is given in square brackets at the end of each explanation, followed by the stroke-by-stroke *order of writing*. It cannot be stressed enough how important it is to learn to write the strokes of each character in proper order. As easy as these first characters may seem, study them all with a pad and pencil to get into the habit from the very start.

Finally, note that each key word has been carefully chosen and should not be tampered with in any way if you want to avoid confusion later on.

1	one

— In Chinese characters, the number **one** is laid on its side, unlike the Roman numeral 1 which stands upright. As you would expect, it is written from left to right. [1]

—

❖ When this character is used as a primitive element, the key-word meaning is often discarded, since it is too abstract to be of much help. Instead, the single horizontal stroke takes on the meaning of *floor* or *ceiling*, depending on its position: if it stands above another primitive, it means *ceiling*; if below, *floor*.

2	two

二

Like the Roman numeral II, which reduplicates the numeral I, the character for **two** is a simple reduplication of the horizontal stroke that means *one*. The order of writing goes from above to below, with the first stroke slightly shorter. [2]

一　二

3	three

三

And like the Roman numeral III, which triples the numeral I, the character for **three** simply triples the single horizontal stroke. In writing it, think of "1 + 2 = 3" (一 + 二 = 三) in order to keep the middle stroke shorter. [3]

一　二　三

4	four

四

This character is composed of two primitive elements, *mouth* 口 and *human legs* 儿, both of which we will meet in the coming lessons. Assuming that you already knew how to write this character, we will pass over the "story" connected with it until later.

Note how the second stroke is written left-to-right and then top-to-bottom. This is consistent with what we have already seen in the first three numbers and leads us to a general principle that will be helpful when we come to more complicated characters later on: WRITE NORTH-TO-SOUTH, WEST-TO-EAST, NORTHWEST-TO-SOUTHEAST. [5]

丨　冂　冂　冏　四

5	five

五

As with *four*, we shall postpone learning the primitive elements that make up this character. Note how the general principle we just learned in the preceding frame applies to the writing of the character for **five**. [4]

6	six

The primitives here are *top hat* and *animal legs*. Once again, we glide over them until later. [4]

7	seven

七 Note that the first stroke "cuts" clearly through the second. This distinguishes **seven** from the character for *spoon* 匕 (FRAME 419), in which the horizontal stroke either stops short or, depending on the font, extends just slightly beyond the vertical stroke. [2]

❖ As a primitive, this form takes on the meaning of *diced*, i.e., "cut" into little pieces, consistent both with the way the character is written and with its association with the character for *cut* 切 to be learned in a later lesson (FRAME 81).

8	eight

八 Just as the Arabic numeral "8" is composed of a small circle followed by a larger one, so the character for **eight** is composed of a short line followed by a longer line that leans towards it without touching it. And just as the "lazy 8" ∞ is the mathematical symbol for "infinity," so the expanse opened up below these two strokes sometimes carries the sense in Chinese of something "all-encompassing."

Note how the printed character on the left and the hand-drawn character below differ somewhat in form. Be sure to imitate the hand-drawn form when you practice writing. [2]

9	nine

九

If you take care to remember the stroke order of this character, you will not have trouble later keeping it distinct from the character for *power* 力 (FRAME 687). [2]

丿　九

❖ When this character is used as a primitive, we shall take it to refer to the game of *baseball,* the meaning being derived from the *nine* players who make up a team.

10	ten

十

Turn this character 45° either way and you have the x used for the Roman numeral **ten.** [2]

一　十

❖ As a primitive, this character sometimes keeps its meaning of *ten* and sometimes signifies *needle,* this latter derived from the character for *needle* 針 (FRAME 264). Since the primitive is used in the character itself, there is no need to worry about confusing the two. In fact, we shall be following this procedure regularly.

11	mouth

口

Like several of the first characters we shall learn, the character for **mouth** is a clear pictograph. Since there are no circular shapes in the characters, the square must be used to depict the circle. [3]

丨　冂　口

❖ As a primitive, this form also means *mouth.* Any of the range of possible images that the word suggests—an opening or entrance to a cave, a river, a bottle, or even the largest hole in your head—can be used for the primitive meaning.

12	day
日	This character is intended to be a pictograph of the sun. Recalling what we said in the previous frame about round forms, it is easy to detect the circle and the big smile that characterize our simplest drawings of the sun—like those yellow badges with the words, "Have a nice **day**!" [4]

$$ｌ\quad 冂\quad 日\quad 日$$

❖ Used as a primitive, this character can mean *sun* or *day* or a *tongue wagging in the mouth.* This latter meaning, incidentally, derives from an old character meaning something like "sayeth" (see FRAME 1499) and written almost exactly the same, except that the latter is more square in shape (日) than *sun* (日). In any case, as a primitive element the shape will alter according to its position in the full character and this distinction will become irrelevant.

13	month
月	This character is actually a picture of the moon, with the two horizontal lines representing the left eye and mouth of the mythical "man in the moon." (Actually, the Chinese see a hare in the moon, but it is a little farfetched to find one in the character.) And one **month**, of course, is one cycle of the moon. [4]

$$丿\quad 刀\quad 月\quad 月$$

❖ As a primitive element, this character can take on the sense of *moon, flesh,* or *part of the body.* The reasons for the latter two meanings will be explained in a later lesson.

14	rice field
田	Another pictograph, this character looks like a bird's-eye view of a **rice field** divided into four plots. Take care in writing this character to get the order of the strokes correct. You will find that it follows perfectly the principle stated in FRAME 4. [5]

$$ｌ\quad 冂\quad 日\quad 甲\quad 田$$

❖ When used as a primitive element, this character's most common meaning is *rice field*, but now and again it will take the meaning of *brains* from the fact that it looks a bit like that tangle of gray matter nestled under our skulls.

15	eye

目

Here again, if we round out the corners of this character and curve the two middle strokes into the shape of an iris, we get something resembling an **eye**. [5]

丨　冂　刀　月　目

❖ As a primitive, the character keeps its sense of *eye*, or to be more specific, an *eyeball*. When placed in the surroundings of a complex character, the primitive can be turned on its side (⺲) and take on the additional meaning of a *net*.

Although only 10 of the 15 characters treated in this lesson are formally listed as primitives—the elements that join together to make up other characters—some of the others may also take on that function from time to time, only not with enough frequency to merit learning them as separate primitive elements and attaching special meanings to them. In other words, whenever one of the characters already learned is used in another character, it will retain its key-word meaning unless we have assigned it a special primitive meaning. Even in these cases, however, the original key-word meaning can be used.

LESSON 2

IN THIS LESSON we learn what a "primitive element" is by using the first 15 characters as pieces that can be fitted together to form new characters—16 of them to be exact. Whenever the primitive meaning differs from the key-word meaning, you may want to go back to the original frame to refresh your memory. From now on, though, you should learn *both* the key word and the primitive meaning of each new character as it appears. Index II contains a complete list of all the primitive elements in the book.

16	ancient

古

The primitive elements that compose this character are *ten* and *mouth,* but you may find it easier to remember it as a pictograph of a tombstone with a cross on top. Just think back to one of those graveyards you have visited, or better still, used to play in as a child, with **ancient** inscriptions on the tombstones.

This departure from the primitive elements in favor of a pictograph will take place now and again at these early stages, and almost never after that. So you need not worry about cluttering up your memory with too many character "drawings." [5]

❖ Used as a primitive element, this character keeps its key-word sense of *ancient,* but care should be taken to make that abstract notion as graphic as possible.

17	recklessly

胡

Everyone knows what a new *moon* is: the first phase when the *moon* is illuminated 0%. So, presumably, an *ancient moon,* like the one in this character, is lit up at 100% wattage. And we all know what that means: people tend to get a little "loony" and start acting **recklessly.** [9]

古　胡

| 18 | I (literary) |

吾

There are a number of characters for the word **I**, but this one is restricted to literary use in Chinese. We need a sufficiently stuffy connotation for the key word, for which the sense of a "perceiving subject" should do just fine. Now the one place in our bodies that all *five* senses are concentrated in is the head, which has no less than *five mouths*: 2 nostrils, 2 ears, and 1 mouth. Hence, *five mouths* = **I**. [7]

一　丁　五　五　五　吾　吾

| 19 | companion |

朋

The first **companion** that God made, as the Bible story goes, was Eve. Upon seeing her, Adam is said to have exclaimed, "*Flesh of my flesh!*" And that is precisely what this character says in so many strokes. [8]

月　朋

| 20 | bright |

明

Among nature's **bright** lights, there are two that the biblical story of creation has God set in the sky: the *sun* to rule over the day and the *moon* to rule the night. Each of them has come to represent one of the common connotations of this key word: the *sun*, the **bright** insight of the clear thinker, and the *moon*, the **bright** intuition of the poet and the seer. [8]

日　明

| 21 | sing |

唱

This one is easy! You have one *mouth* making no noise (the choirmaster) and two *mouths with wagging tongues* (the minimum for a chorus). So when you hear the key word **sing**, think of the Vienna Boys' Choir or the Mormon Tabernacle Choir and the character is yours forever (see FRAME 12). [11]

口　唱　唱

22

晶

sparkling

What else can the word **sparkling** suggest if not a diamond? And if you've ever held a diamond up to the light, you will have noticed how every facet of it becomes like a miniature *sun*. This character is a picture of a tiny *sun* in three places (that is, "everywhere"), to give the sense of something **sparkling** all over the place. Just like a diamond. In writing the primitive elements three times, note again how the rule for writing given in FRAME 4 holds true not only for the strokes in each individual element but also for the disposition of the elements in the character as a whole. [12]

日 　日 　日日
　　　日 　日日

23

品

goods

As in the character for *sparkling,* the triplication of a single element in this character indicates "everywhere" or "heaps of." When we think of **goods** in modern industrial society, we think of what has been mass-produced—that is to say, produced for the "masses" of open *mouths* waiting like fledglings in a nest to "consume" whatever comes their way. [9]

口 　口 　口口
　　口 　口口

24

昌

prosperous

What we mentioned in the previous two frames about three of something meaning "everywhere" or "heaps of" was not meant to be taken lightly. In this character we see two *suns,* one atop the other, which, if we are not careful, is easily confused in memory with the three *suns* of *sparkling.* Focus on the number this way: since we speak of **prosperous** times as *sunny,* what could be more **prosperous** than a sky with two *suns* in it? Just be sure to actually SEE them there. [8]

日 　昌

| 25 | | early |

早

This character is actually a picture of the first flower of the day, which we shall, in defiance of botanical science, call the *sun-flower*, since it begins with the element for *sun* and is held up on a stem with leaves (the pictographic representation of the final two strokes). This time, however, we shall ignore the pictograph and imagine *sun*flowers with *needles* for stems, which can be plucked and used to darn your socks.

The sense of **early** is easily remembered if one thinks of the *sun*flower as the **early** riser in the garden, because the *sun*, showing favoritism towards its namesake, shines on it before all the others (see FRAME 10). [6]

日　旦　早

❖ As a primitive element, this character takes the meaning of *sunflower*, which was used to make the abstract key word *early* more graphic.

| 26 | | rising sun |

旭

The key word here immediately suggests the islands located to the east of China, which would make it, from China's point of view, the Land of the **Rising Sun**, a name easily associated with Japan's national flag. If you can picture two seams running down that great red *sun*, and then imagine it sitting on a *base-ball* bat for a flagpole, you have a slightly irreverent—but not altogether inaccurate—picture of how the sport has caught on in the Land of the **Rising Sun**. [6]

丿　九　九　旭　旭　旭

| 27 | | generation |

世

We generally consider one **generation** as a period of thirty (or *ten* plus *ten* plus *ten*) years. If you look at this character in its completed form—not in its stroke order—you will see three *tens*. When writing it, think of the lower horizontal lines as "addition" lines written under numbers to add them up. Thus: *ten* "plus" *ten* "plus" *ten* = thirty. Actually, it's a lot easier doing it with a pencil than reading it in a book. [5]

一 十 卄 廿 世

| 28 | stomach |

胃

You will need to refer back to FRAMES 13 and 14 here for the special meaning of the two primitive elements that make up this character: *brain* and *flesh (part of the body)*. What the character says, if you look at it, is that the *part of the body* that keeps the *brain* in working order is the **stomach**. To keep the elements in proper order, when you write this character think of the *brain* as being "held up" by the *flesh*. [9]

田　胃

| 29 | daybreak |

旦

The obvious sign of **daybreak** is the *sun* peeking out over the horizon, which is pretty much what this character depicts. If you can imagine the *sun* poking its head out through a hole in your *floor*, however, you will have an easier time remembering this character. [5]

日　旦

We end this lesson with two final pictographic characters that happen to be among the easiest to recognize for their form, but among the most difficult to write. We introduce them here to run an early test on whether or not you have been paying close attention to the stroke order of the characters you have been learning.

| 30 | concave |

凹

You couldn't have asked for a better key word for this character! Just have a look at it: a perfect image of a **concave** lens (remembering, of course, that the characters square off rounded things), complete with its own little "cave." Now all you have to do is learn how to write it. [5]

丨 丨⁻ 凵 凹 凹

31 convex

Maybe this helps you see how the Chinese have no trouble keeping **convex** distinct from *concave*. Note the odd feeling of the fourth stroke. If it doesn't feel all that strange now, by the time you are done with this book, it will. There are very few times you will have to write it. [5]

丨 凵 凸 凸 凸

LESSON 3

AFTER LESSON 2, you should now have some idea of how an apparently complex and difficult character can be broken down into simple elements that make remembering it a great deal easier. After completing this lesson you should have a clearer idea of how the course is laid out. We merely add a couple of primitive elements to the characters we already know and see how many new characters we can form—in this case, 18 in all—and when we run out, add more primitives. And so on, until there are no characters left.

In Lesson 3 you will also be introduced to primitive elements that are not themselves characters but only used to construct other characters. These are marked with a special symbol [❖] instead of a number. There is no need to make a special effort to memorize them. The sheer frequency with which most of them show up should make remembering them automatic.

❖   **a drop of**

ノ

The meaning of this primitive is obvious from the first moment you look at it, though just what it will be **a drop of** will differ from case to case. The important thing is not to think of it as something insignificant like a "drop in the bucket" but as something so important that it can change the whole picture—like **a drop of** arsenic in your mother-in-law's coffee. [1]

ノ   ヽ

❖ In the first examples that follow, this primitive is written from right to left, but there are times when it can be slanted left to right. In addition, as we will see, the handwritten form used here will sometimes be at odds with the printed form. Finally, the *drop* will occasionally be stretched out a bit. (In cases where you have trouble remembering this, it may help to think of it as an *eyedropper* dripping drops of something or other.) If you follow the hand-drawn forms given here, you will never go wrong. Examples will follow in this lesson.

❖

│

walking stick

This primitive element is a picture of just what it looks like: a cane or **walking stick**. It carries with it the connotations of lameness and whatever else one associates with the use of a cane. Rarely—but very rarely—it will be laid on its side. Whenever this occurs, it will ALWAYS be driven through the middle of some other primitive element. In this way, you need not worry about confusing it with the primitive meanings of *one*. [1]

32

自

oneself

You can think of this character as a stylized pictograph of the nose, that little *drop* that Mother Nature set between your *eyes*. The Chinese often refer to themselves by pointing a finger at their nose—giving us an easy way to remember the character for **oneself**. [6]

′　ſ　冂　冃　自　自

❖ The same meaning of *oneself* can be kept when this character is used as a primitive element, but you will generally find it better to give it the meaning of *nose* or *nostrils*, both because it accords with the story above and because it is the first part of the character for *nose* (FRAME 575).

33

白

white

The color **white** is a mixture of all the primary colors, both for pigments and for light, as we see when a prism breaks up the rays of the *sun*. Hence, a single *drop* of *sun* spells **white**. [5]

′　ſ　冂　白　白

❖ As a primitive, this character can either retain its meaning of *white* or take the more graphic meaning of a *white bird* or *dove*. This stems from the fact that it appears at the top of the character for *bird,* which we shall get to later (FRAME 1396).

34 百   hundred

When the Japanese borrowed the Chinese characters, they often played with their shapes to find interesting connections. For example, they came to refer to a person's 99th birthday as the start of the *"white* year" because *white* is the character you are left with if you subtract *one* from a **hundred**. [6]

一 丆 丆 万 苩 百

35 皂   soap

Whatever the color of the **soap** that this character refers to, it does the same trick of *cutting* the grease and grime to make things *white*. That's a bit too abstract and reasonable, though, so you may want to imagine looking at the **soap** under a microscope and seeing little whirling blades *dicing* the blotches of dirt one by one until everything turns *white*. [7]

白 臼 皂

36 中   middle (N./ADJ.)

The elements in this character are a *walking stick* and a *mouth*. The connotation we will associate with the key word **middle** is that period of life known as **middle** age, so called because it is the time in your life when you have trouble with your expanding "**middle**." More often than not, the expansion has to do with eating more and moving around less. This character has the grotesque image of a person with a *walking stick* jammed into his *mouth*, the more easily to shovel food in without the interference of the tedious exercise of opening and closing it. [4]

Note the indicator that the character for **middle** can be used as either a noun or an adjective. Where no part of speech is indicated, assume the most common. In the case of the former frame, for example, *soap* might be taken as a verb, but one's first thought goes to the noun, which is a good place to start for that character. Be aware, though, that even where one part of speech is indicated for a character, other possibilities may exist.

丶 冂 口 中

37 — thousand

千

This character is almost too simple to pull apart, but for the sake of practice, have a look at the *eyedropper* above and the *ten* below. Now put the elements together by thinking of squeezing two more zeros out of an *eyedropper* alongside the number *ten* to make it a **thousand**. [3]

38 — tongue

舌

The characters for *mouth* and *thousand* naturally form the idea of **tongue** if one thinks of a *thousand mouths* able to speak the same language, or as we say, "sharing a common **tongue**." It is easy to see the connection between the idiom and the character if you take its image literally: a single **tongue** being passed around from *mouth* to *mouth*. [6]

39 — liter

升

Think of a one-**liter** carafe (the kind you might serve drinks in) filled not with milk or wine but with a *thousand* sharp *needles*. You may well wonder what they are doing there, but the answer is simple: it's a kind of sports drink for a robot. [4]

40 — rise up

昇

Keeping the image from the last frame, we have here a *liter* carafe with a *sun* above it. Conveniently, the connotation of the key word **rise up** is what the *sun* does in the morning, just before breakfast. Can you actually SEE it **rising up** out of the *liter* carafe of freshly squeezed *Sun*kist orange juice on your breakfast table? [8]

日　昇

---

41   pill

丸

One of the scourges of sports like modern *baseball* has been the use of performance-enhancing drugs, those tiny little **pills** that have helped turn honest competition into cut-throat business. Now look at the character and picture it as a bottle of **pills** hanging on the thigh of a *baseball* player like a PEZ dispenser, ready for the popping as the need arises. [3]

❖ As a primitive, this element takes the meaning of a *bottle of pills*.

We have already seen one example of how to form primitives from other primitives, when we formed the *daybreak* out of *sun* and *floor* (FRAME 29). Let us take two more examples of this procedure right away, so that we can do so from now on without having to draw any particular attention to the fact.

---

42   divination

卜

This is a picture of a divining rod, composed of *a walking stick* and a *drop*, but easy enough to remember as a pictograph. Alternately, you can think of it as a *magic wand*. In either case, it should suggest images of **divination** or magic. [2]

❖ When using this character as a primitive, we will stick with the meaning of a *divining rod* or a *magic wand*.

---

43   tell fortunes

This is one of those characters that is a real joy of simplicity: a *divining rod* with a *mouth*—which are the two ingredients needed to **tell fortunes**.

Note how the movement from top to bottom (the movement in which the characters are written) is also the order of the elements which make up our story and of the key word itself: first *divining rod,* then *mouth.* This will not always be possible, but where it is, memory has almost no work at all to do. [5]

44   above

The two directions, **above** and below, are usually pointed at with the finger. But the characters do not follow that custom, so we have to choose something else, easily remembered. The primitives show a *magic wand* standing **above** a *floor*—"magically," you might say. Anyway, go right on to the next frame, since the two belong together and are best remembered as a unit, just as the words **above** and *below* suggest each other. [3]

45   below

Here we see our famous *magic wand* hanging, all on its own, **below** the *ceiling,* as you probably already guessed would happen. In addition to giving us two new characters, the two shapes in this and the preceding frame also serve to illustrate the difference between the primitive meanings for *ceiling* and *floor:* it all depends on whether the single horizontal line stands above or **below** the primitive element to which it is related. [3]

46   card

The key word **card** can stand for all sorts of things, but let's settle on a credit **card** for our image. Perhaps the first thing that comes to mind is the picture of a shopkeeper sliding your credit **card** up and down (from *above* to *below* and back again) in the reading machine to record your transaction. Now imagine her doing it fast and furiously, again and again, with increasing impatience until your poor **card** is whittled away to a small strip of plastic. [5]

ㅣ　ㅏ　上　卡　卡

---

47   eminent

卓   The word **eminent** suggests a famous or well-known person. So all you need to do—given the primitives of a *magic wand* and a *sunflower*—is to think of the world's most **eminent** magician as one who uses a *sunflower* for a *magic wand* (like a flower-child who goes around turning the world into peace and love). [8]

ㅏ　占　卓

The final two characters of this lesson are a good example of how a primitive element can be used to form a new character, which in turn becomes a new primitive for another character. This will happen often, so it is good to pay attention to it from the start.

❖   mist

   Here is the first of many examples of primitives composed of other primitives but not treated as characters themselves. At the bottom is the primitive (also a character) for *early* or *sunflower*. At the top, a *needle*. Conveniently, **mist** falls *early* in the morning, like little *needles* of rain, to assure that the *sunflower* blooms *early* as we have learned it should. [8]

---

48   dynasty

朝   It is easy to imagine one of the great **dynasties** of China in all its glory. Now all we have to figure out is what the elements *moon* and *mist* have to do with it.

    Picture a great palace with a powerful emperor seated on a throne in its innermost court. To keep the Wizard-of-Oz illusion that this power is beyond question and beyond the understanding of the masses, the whole complex is kept permanently shrouded in *mist*. How do they do it, you ask. On one side of the throne is a servant pulling on a cord to wave a gigantic fan back and forth. On the other, a servant with a long cord hooked on a corner of the quarter *moon*. When he pulls on it, the *moon* tilts over and spills out a month's supply of *mist* that keeps the myth of the **dynasty** alive. [12]

十　卓　朝

49　　　　　　　　　　　　　　　　　　　　　　　　ridicule [v.]

嘲

If you read off the elements in the character, you have something like "*mouthing* off at the *dynasty*." When we think of what we commonly **ridicule** in civilized society, one of the oldest and most universal targets is the ruling elite. Who better to deride than one's leaders? Again, the explanation is too rational, so turn it into a story that has you **ridiculing** a particular *dynasty's* court with particular buffoonery. [15]

口　嘲

Lesson 4

At the risk of going a little bit too fast, we are now going to introduce five new primitive elements, all of which are very easy to remember either because of their frequency or because of their shape. But remember: there is no reason to study the primitives by themselves. They are being presented systematically to make their learning automatic.

❖

animal legs

Like the four that follow it, this primitive is not a character in its own right, though it is said to be derived from 八, the character we learned earlier for *eight*. It usually comes at the bottom of the primitive to which it is related. It can mean the **legs** of any kind of **animal**: from the massive legs of an elephant to an octopus's tentacles to the spindle shanks of a spider. (The one animal not allowed is our friend homo sapiens, whose legs figure in the next frame.) Even where the term "legs" will apply metaphorically to the legs of pieces of furniture, it is best to keep the association with **animal legs**. [2]

❖

儿

human legs

Notice how these **human legs** are somewhat shapelier and more highly developed than those of the so-called "lower animals." The one on the left, drawn first, is straight, while the one on the right bends gracefully and ends with a hook. Though they are not likely to suggest the legs of any human you know, they do have something of the look of someone out for a stroll, especially if you compare them to *animal legs*.

If you had any trouble with the character for the number *four*, now would be the time to return to it (frame 4). [2]

丿　儿

wind

This primitive is actually a character meaning "small table," but for etymological reasons too involved to go into here, it can also mean *wind*, whether in the same shape as above or with the final stroke more shortly "hooked" (几). We will meet the full character for *wind* only in FRAME 483. We will also have at least one occasion to use the primitive meaning of a *small table*.

This primitive can serve as an "enclosure"—an element within which other elements can be drawn—but it can also be compressed together so that there is no room for anything in it. Examples appear in this lesson. [2]

bound up

Like *wind*, the element meaning **bound up** is also an enclosure that can wrap itself around other elements or be compressed when there is nothing to enclose. When this latter happens—usually because there is not enough room—and it is set on top, the little hook at the end is dropped off, like this: ⌐.

The sense of **bound up** is that of being "tied and gagged" or wrapped up tightly. If you have trouble remembering when it serves as an enclosure (with the hook) and when not (without the hook), you might think of the former as a **chain** and the latter as a **rope**. [2]

horns

This primitive element USUALLY appears at the top of the element to which it is related, and is usually attached, or almost attached, to the first horizontal line to come under it. The **horns** can never simply be left hanging in the air. When there is no line available, an extra horizontal stroke (like a *one*) is added. The final character of this lesson gives an example.

The meaning of this element is wide enough to embrace the **animal horns** of bulls, rams, billy goats, and moose, but not the family of musical instruments. As with other elements with such "open" meanings, it is best to settle on one that you find most vivid and stick with that image consistently. [2]

丶　丷

50

只

only

When we run across abstract key words like this one, the best way to get an image is to recall some common but suggestive phrase in which the word appears. For instance, we can think of the expression "it's the **only** one of its kind." Then we imagine a barker at a side-show advertising some strange pac-man like creature he has inside his tent, with **only** a gigantic *mouth* and two wee *animal legs*. [5]

口　只

51

貝

shellfish

To remember the primitive elements that make up this character, an *eye* and *animal legs*, you might be tempted to think of it as a pictograph of a **shellfish** with its ridged shell at the top and two little *legs* sticking out of the bottom. But that might not help you recall later just how many ridges to put on the shell. Better to imagine a freakish **shellfish** with a single, gigantic *eye* roaming the beaches on its slender little *legs*, scaring the wits out of the sunbathers. [7]

目　貝

❖ When this character is used as a primitive, in addition to *shellfish*, the meanings *shells*, *oysters*, and *clams* will often come in handy.

52

貼

paste (v.)

Think here of brushing on an adhesive, as when you **paste** something on a billboard. Here we have an *oyster* **pasting** a poster on his back to advertise his services in the dubious occupation of one who *tells fortunes*. Try to imagine the problem he would have reaching his back with the brush to **paste**, and then see him strutting around and calling out, "Fortunes to tell! Fortunes to tell!" [12]

貝　貼

53

貞

chaste

You have heard of Diogenes running around with his lamp looking for an honest man. Here we have an image of the famous *shellfish*, Oysterogenes, running around with his *divining rod* looking for a **chaste** man. We leave it to you to decide which one has the better luck in his quest. [9]

ㅏ　貞

54

員

employee

How do we get a *mouth* over a *shellfish* to mean an **employee**? Simple. Just remember the advice new **employees** get about keeping their *mouths* shut and doing their jobs, and then make that more graphic by picturing an office building full of white-collar workers scurrying around with *clams* pinched to their *mouths*. [10]

口　員

55

見

see

The elements that compose the character for **see** are the *eye* firmly fixed to a pair of *human legs*. Surely, somewhere in your experience, there is a vivid image just waiting to be dragged up to help you remember this character.... [7]

目　見

56

元

beginning

"In the **beginning**..." starts that marvelous shelf of books we call the Bible. It talks about how all things were made, and tells us that when it came to humanity the Creator made *two* of them, man and woman. While we presume *two* were made of every other creature as well, we are not told as much. Hence we need only *two* and a pair of *human legs* to come to the character that means **beginning**. [4]

二　元

57　　　　　　　　　　　　　　　　　　　　　　　　　　　page

頁

What we have to do here is turn a *shellfish* into a **page** of a book. The *one* at the top tells us that we only get a rather short book, in fact a book of only *one* **page**. Imagine a title printed on the shell of an *oyster,* let us say "Pearl of Wisdom," and then open the quaint book to its *one* and only **page**, on which you find a single, radiant *drop of* wisdom, one of the masterpiece poems of nature. [9]

一　　一　　厂　　丆　　丏　　百　　百
頁　　頁

❖ As a primitive, this character often takes the unrelated meaning of a *head* (preferably one detached from its body), derived from the character for *head* (FRAME 1067).

58　　　　　　　　　　　　　　　　　　　　　　　　　stubborn

頑

This character refers to a block*head,* a persistently **stubborn** person who sticks to an idea or a plan just the way it was at the *beginning,* without letting anything that comes up along the way alter things in the least. The explanation makes "sense," but is hard to remember because the word *"beginning"* is too abstract. Back up to the image we used two frames ago—Adam and Eve in their Eden—and try again: The root of all this goes back to the *beginning,* with two brothers each defending his own way of life and asking their God to bless it favorably. Abel stuck to agriculture, Cain to animal-raising. Picture these two seeking the favors of heaven, one of them with an unusually **stubborn** grimace on his face. No wonder something unfortunate happened! [13]

元　頑

59 凡   ordinary

While we refer to something insignificant as a "*drop in the bucket*," the character for **ordinary** shows us a "*drop in the wind*." To make the image stick as clearly as water dropping into a bucket, stop and think of something really **ordinary** and then say, "It's just a *drop* in the *wind*"—and imagine what that might actually look like. [3]

60 肌   muscle

One of the more common ways of testing the strength of one's **muscles** is to lock hands with a local hulk on a *small table* top and arm wrestle. This is the image here, depicted by the elements for *part of the body* and *small table*. The **muscle** is, therefore, the *part of the body* you test by literally bringing it to the *small table*. [6]

61 負   defeated

Above we have the condensed form of *bound up*, and below, the familiar *shellfish*. Now imagine two *oysters* engaged in *shell*-to-*shell* combat, the one who is **defeated** being *bound and gagged* with seaweed, the victor towering triumphantly over it. The *bound shellfish* thus becomes the symbol for anyone or anything that has been **defeated**. [9]

62 勺   uniform (ADJ.)

The two primitives *bound up* and *two* (clearer in the hand-drawn form) combine to give the meaning of **uniform**. One of the real challenges for primary school teachers is to keep students from scattering every which direction. If you think of the final touch to a school outfit, the shoes, and then recall the childhood jingle, "One, two, buckle my shoe," the solution is near at hand. Instead of having children buckle their shoes, they can be taught to tie their shoelaces together by changing the lyrics to read "One, two, *bind up* my shoes." This keeps them from straying very far from the group and helps teachers provide a **uniform** education. [4]

ク 勺

| 63 | sentence [N.] |

勾

By combining the two primitives *bound up* and *mouth*, it is easy to see how this character can have the meaning of a **sentence**. The *mouth* suggests it is a spoken **sentence**. To be more precise, it is a cluster of words *bound up* tightly and neatly so that they will fit in your *mouth*. [5]

| 64 | decameron |

旬

There simply is not a good phrase in English for the block of ten days which this character represents. So we resurrect the classical term **decameron**, whose connotations the tales of Boccaccio have done much to enrich. Actually, it refers to a journey of ten *days* taken by a band of people—that is, a group of people *bound together* for the *days* of the **decameron**. [6]

ク 句

| 65 | ladle |

勺

If you want to *bind up drops* of anything—water, soup, lemonade—you use something to scoop these *drops* up, which is what we call a **ladle**. See the last *drop* left inside the **ladle**? [3]

66

的

bull's eye

The elements *white bird* and *ladle* easily suggest the image of a **bull's eye** if you imagine a rusty old *ladle* with a **bull's eye** painted on it in the form of a tiny *white bird*, who lets out a little "peep" every time you hit the target.

This is the most frequently used character in Chinese, serving a number of common grammatical functions. But—it ALSO means **bull's eye**. [8]

67

首

heads

Reading this character from the top down, we have: *horns . . . nose.* Together they bring to mind the picture of a moose-head hanging on the den wall, with its great *horns* and long *nose.* The plural form is used to stress the frequent metaphorical use of the term to refer to various kinds of **heads**, including **heads** of state. It might help to see a number of the latter lined up on the den wall alongside the moose, each fitted out with *antlers* and a whopper of a *nose.*

Here we get a good look at what we mentioned when we first introduced the element for *horns*: that they can never be left floating free and require an extra horizontal stroke to prevent that from happening, as is the case here. [9]

丶　丷　䒑　首

LESSON 5

THAT IS ABOUT all we can do with the pieces we have accumulated so far, but as we add each new primitive element to those we already know, the number of characters we will be able to form will increase by leaps and bounds.

If we were not separating into two volumes the 3,000 characters to be treated in this course, there are any number of other characters that we could learn at this time. Just to give you an idea of some of the possibilities (though you should not bother to learn them now), here are a few, with their meanings: 吋 *(English inch),* 罩 *(envelop),* 咒 *(curse),* 咱 *(we, inclusive),* and 囂 *(hubbub).* While many of the stories you have learned in the previous lessons are actually more complex than the majority you will learn in the later lessons, they are the *first* stories you have learned, and for that reason are not likely to cause you much difficulty. By now, however, you may be wondering just how to go about reviewing what you have learned. Obviously, it won't do simply to flip through the pages you have already studied, because the ordering of the characters provides too many hints. The best method for many people is to design a set of flash cards that can be added to along the way.

If you have not already started doing this on your own, you might try it this way: Buy heavy paper (about twice the thickness of normal index cards), unlined and with a semigloss finish. Cut it into cards of about 9 cm. long and 6 cm. wide.

On one side, make a large ball-pen drawing of one character in the top two-thirds of the card. (Writing done with fountain pens and felt-tip pens tends to smear with the sweat that comes from holding them in your hands for a long time.) In the bottom right-hand corner, put the number of the frame in which the character appeared.

On the back side, in the upper left-hand corner, write the key-word meaning of the character. Then draw a line across the middle of the card and another line about 2 cm. below it. The space between these two lines can be used for any notes you may need later to remind you of the primitive elements or stories that you used to

45

BELOW

ʍoꞁǝq puɐʍ
ɔᴉƃɐɯ ɥʇᴉʍ ɹooꞁɟ

remember the character. *Only fill this in when you need to, but make a card for every character* as soon as you have learned it.

The rest of the space on the card you will not need now; but later, when you study the pronunciation of the characters, you might use the space above the double lines. The bottom part of the card, on both sides, can be left free for inserting character compounds (front side) and their readings and meanings (back side).

A final note about reviewing. You have probably gotten into the habit of writing a character several times when memorizing it, whether you need to or not; and then writing it MORE times for characters that you have trouble remembering. There is really no need to write a character more than once, unless you have trouble with the stroke order and want to get a better "feel" for it. If a character causes you trouble, spend time clarifying the imagery of its story. Simply rewriting the character will reinforce any remaining suspicions you still have that the "tried and true method" of learning by repeating is the only reliable one—the very bias we are trying to uproot. Also, when you review, REVIEW ONLY FROM THE KEY WORD TO THE CHARACTER, NOT THE OTHER WAY AROUND. The reasons for this, along with further notes on reviewing, will come later.

We are now ready to return to work, adding a few new primitives one by one, and seeing what new characters they allow us to form. We shall cover 23 new characters in this lesson.

---

68   **straight**

直

Think of the first two elements, *ten eyes*, as referring to a group of five scientists working together on a top-secret, million-dollar project to draw a **straight** line on the *floor* without the aid of special equipment. In the end, all *ten eyes* verify that it is **straight**, leaving no doubt that the use of government funds was fully justified. Time to apply for another grant.

Note how the first two strokes of the element for *eye* are made a little longer so that they can touch the final stroke. The same thing will happen in the following three characters, and later on as well, so pay particular attention to the stroke order below. [8]

一　十　广　市　市　肖　肖　直

69   set up

置

Think of having to **set up** the *net* for a badminton or volleyball game. One of the main problems is how to keep the *net* in a *straight* line so that it doesn't sag in the middle. Which is just what this character shows us. [13]

     ヽ   𠃍   𠃌   罒   四   置

❖   tool

六

Although this primitive is not very common, it is useful to know, as the following examples will show. It is usually drawn at the very bottom of any character in which it figures. The first stroke, the horizontal one, is necessary to distinguish **tool** from *animal legs*.

The sense of the element is a carpenter's **tool**, which comes from its pictographic representation of a bench with legs (make them *animal legs* if you need a more graphic image), so that any element lying on top of it will come to be viewed as a **tool** in the hands of a carpenter. [3]

     一   宀   六

70   tool

具

Here is the full character on which the primitive of the last frame is based. If you can think of a table full of carpenter's **tools** of all sorts, each equipped with its own *eye* so that it can keep a watch over what you are doing with it, you won't have trouble later keeping the primitive and the character apart. [8]

     丨   冂   冂   月   目   且   具   具

71   true

真

Here is an example of how there can be different ways of identifying the primitive elements that make up a character. The most obvious is *straight* and *animal legs*, but the character could as well be analyzed into *ten* and *tool*. Let's choose the latter.

How do you know if something is **true** or not? What if there were a kit of *ten tools* you could count on to run a test? Well, at least when it comes to asking whether people are really **true** to themselves, the *ten* commandments are a good start. [10]

❖

by one's side

This primitive has the look of *ten*, except that the left stroke is bent down toward the left. It indicates where one's hands (all *ten* fingers) fall when the arms are relaxed: **by one's side**. [2]

一 ナ

72

work (N.)

工

The pictograph of an I-beam, like the kind that is used in heavy construction **work** on buildings and bridges, gives us the character for **work**. [3]

一 丁 工

❖ Since the key word can be too abstract when used as a primitive element, we will often revert to the clearer image of an *I-beam*.

73

left (N./ADJ.)

左

By combining the last two frames and reading the results, we get: *by one's side ... work*. Conveniently, the **left** has traditionally been considered the "sinister" *side*, where dark and occult *works* are cultivated and carried out. [5]

一 ナ 左

74

right (N./ADJ.)

右

When thinking of the key word **right**, in order to avoid confusion with the previous frame, take advantage of the double meaning here. Imagine a little *mouth* hanging down *by one's* *side*—one's **right** side, of course—like a little voice of conscience telling one the "right" thing to do. [5]

ナ　右

---

75   **possess**

有

The picture here is a slab of *flesh* dangling *by one's side*, perhaps from a belt or rope tied around the waist. While we normally think of things that we have and **possess**, we also know that there are things that can have and **possess** us. Such cases might be likened to an evil spirit **possessing** one's soul. This character suggests a way to exorcize it: hang a slab of fresh *flesh by one's side* until it begins to putrefy and stink so bad that the demon departs. Take careful note of the stroke order. [6]

ナ　才　冇　有　有

---

76   **bribe** [N.]

賄

To the left we have the primitive for a *shellfish*, and to the right, the character we just learned for *possess*. Keep the connotation of the last frame for the word *possess*, and now expand your image of *shells* to include the ancient value they had as money (a usage that will come in very helpful later on). Now people who are *possessed* by *shells* are likely to abandon any higher principles to acquire more and more wealth. These are the easiest ones to persuade with a **bribe** of a few extra *shells*. [13]

貝　賄

---

77   **tribute**

貢

A **tribute** has a kind of double meaning in English: honor paid freely and money (*shells*) collected by coercion. Simply because a ruler bestows a noble name on a deed is hardly any consolation to the masses who must part with their hard-earned *shells*. Little wonder that this ancient *work* of gathering money by calling it a **tribute** has given way to a name closer to how it feels to those who pay it: a tax. [10]

工　貢

78	item

項

To the right we see a *page* and to the left an element for *I-beam*. The **item** referred to here is not some specific object but an entry on an "itemized" list. Each **item** in the list you have to imagine here is preceded by a little *I-beam*—not a drawing, but an actual iron *I-beam*. Imagine lugging a list like that around the grocery store! [12]

工　項

79	sword

刀

Although this character no longer looks very much like a **sword**, it does have some resemblance to the handle of the **sword**. As it turns out, this is to our advantage, in that it helps us make a distinction between two primitive elements based on this character. [2]

コ　刀

❖ In the form of the character, this primitive means a *dagger*. When it appears to the right of another element, it is commonly stretched out like this ⺉ , and like this ⼑ when to the left of another element. In these cases, it will take the sense of a great and flashing *saber*, a meaning it gets from a character to be introduced in Book 2.

80	blade

刃

Think of using a *dagger* as a razor **blade**, and it shouldn't be hard to imagine cutting yourself. See the little *drop of* blood dripping off the **blade**? [3]

コ　刀　刃

81   cut (v.)

切

To the right we see the *dagger* and next to it the number *seven*, whose primitive meaning we decided would be *diced* (FRAME 7). It is hard to **cut** meat or vegetables with a knife without imagining one of those skillful Japanese chefs. Only let us say that he has had too much saké to drink at a party, grabs a *dagger* lying on the mantelpiece and starts *dicing* up everything in sight, starting with the hors d'oeuvres and going on to **cut** up the furniture and carpets.... [4]

一　　十　　切

82   summon

召

A *sword* or *dagger* poised over a *mouth* is how the character used to **summon** a person is written. Note the immediate—how shall we put it politely?—Freudian implications of the character. (Observe, too, if you will, that it is not at all clear whether the long slender object is **summoning** the small round one or vice versa.) [5]

刀　　召

❖ The primitive meaning remains the same. Just be sure to associate it with a very concrete image, such as a prosecutor at your door with a document that *summons* you to appear in court.

83   evident

昭

Nothing quite works to make something **evident** like "evidence" that backs it up. Here we see a lawyer who *summons* the *sun* down from the noonday sky to stand as a witness and make the facts as **evident** as can be. [9]

日　　昭

84 鬼 rule (N.)

The character depicts a *clam* alongside a great and flashing *saber*. Think of digging for *clams* in an area where there are gaming **rules** governing how large a find has to be before you can keep it. So you take your trusty *saber*, which you have carefully notched like a yardstick, crack open a *clam* and then measure the poor little beastie to see if it is as long as the **rules** say it has to be. [9]

❖ 畐 wealth

To prepare for the following frame, we introduce here a somewhat rare primitive meaning **wealth**. It takes its meaning from the common image of the over**wealth**y as also being overfed. More specifically, the character shows us *one* single *mouth* devouring all the harvest of the *fields*, presumably while those who labor in them go hungry. Think of the phrase exactly as it is written when you draw the character, and the disposition of the elements is easy. [9]

85 副 vice-

The key word **vice-** has the sense of someone second-in-command. The great and flashing *saber* to the right (its usual location, so you need not worry about where to put it from now on) and the *wealth* on the left combine to create an image of dividing one's property to give a share to one's **vice**-*wealth*-holder. [11]

86 丁 fourth

This character is **fourth** in a system of enumeration from first to tenth based on an ancient lunar calendar and referred to as "the celestial stems." What it shows us is someone waiting **fourth** in line, using a giant metal spike as a makeshift chair. [2]

一　丁

❖ When used as a primitive, the character changes its meaning to *nail* or *spike*.

87 　　　　　　　　　　　　　　　　　　　sting (v.)

叮

You know how a bee **stings**, right? It drives the little barbed *spike* in its bottom into your skin and then pulls away. Of course, as we noted way back in FRAME 11, the primitive element for *mouth* can refer to any kind of orifice, but imagine the damage a bee could inflict if it could **sting** with its *mouth* at the same time—a kind of bi-polar attack. [5]

口　叮

88 　　　　　　　　　　　　　　　　　　　can (AUX. V.)

可

To begin with, you will notice that this character is composed of the very same elements as that of the former frame. Only their arrangement is different.

Remember the story about the "Little Engine that **Could**" when you hear this key word, and the rest is simple. See the determined little locomotive huffing and puffing up the mountain—"I think I **can**, I think I **can**..."—spitting railroad *spikes* out of its *mouth* as it chews up the line to the top. [5]

丁　可

89 　　　　　　　　　　　　　　　　　　　older brother

哥

The **older brother** is depicted here as a duplication of the character for *can*. It shouldn't take too much work to imagine him, for whatever reason, as a *can-can* brother. [10]

可　哥

90   crest (N.)

頂   The key word can refer to the summit or **crest** of a mountain,
      but the **crest** of the *head* works better here. The immediate
      image this conjures up is the *head* of a rooster with its comb
      or a cockatoo with its crest feathers. And from there it is but a
      short step to think of the punk hairstyles that imitate this look
      by shaping the hair into a row of brightly colored *spikes*. So a
      spike-head becomes a **crest**. [11]

丁   頂

LESSON 6

THE LAST GROUP OF primitives took us pretty far, and probably forced you to pay more attention to the workings of imagination. In this lesson we shall concentrate on primitives that have to do with people.

Remember that even those characters that are given special meanings as primitives may also retain their key-word meaning when used as primitives. Although this may sound confusing, in fact it turns out to be convenient for making stories and, in addition, helps to reinforce the original meaning of the character. We will see an example in this short lesson which focuses on a few new persons and family members.

91	second [(ADJ.)]

乙

This character belongs to the same series of "celestial stems" as that in FRAME 86 of the last lesson. The **second** person in line is seated in what looks like a rocking chair (much better situated than the *fourth* seat). [1]

乙

❖ Since this is also a pictograph of a *hook* or *fishhook*, let us take these as primitive meanings. Its shape will rarely be quite the same as that of the character. When it appears at the bottom of another primitive, it is straightened out, almost as if the weight of the upper element had bent it out of shape: ∟. When it appears to the right of another element, the short horizontal line that gets the shape started is omitted, and the whole character is stretched out and narrowed—all for reasons of space and aesthetics: ∟.

92	child

子

This character is a pictograph of a **child** wrapped up in one of those handy cocoons that Indian squaws fix to their backs to carry around young **children** who cannot get around by themselves. (Incidentally, this is why English has taken over the word "papoose" from the Algonquin language to refer to the device itself.) The first stroke is like a wee head popping out for air; the second shows the body and legs all wrapped up; and the final stroke shows the arms sticking out to cling to the mother's neck. [3]

⁻ 了 子

❖ As a primitive, this character retains the meaning of *child,* though you might imagine a little older *child,* able to run around and get into more mischief.

---

93   cavity

孔

A **cavity** is really just a small hole, but the first thing we think of when we hear the word is that little pothole that shows up in a diseased tooth. The Chinese may not use the character in this sense, but what's to stop us?.

Probably the one thing most *children* fear more than anything else is the dentist's chair. Can you remember the first time as a *child* you saw your dentist hold an x-ray up to the light and pronounce the ominous word "**cavity**"? Even though you were not likely to know that the word meant that you have an extra hole in your head until you were much older, it did not take long before the sound got associated with the drill and that row of shiny *hooks* the dentist uses to torture people who are too small to fight back. [4]

子 孔

---

94   roar [v.]

吼

A *mouth* and a *cavity* combine to create the character for **roar**. It shouldn't tax your memory banks too much to think back to how you howled and **roared** the first time you had a *cavity* drilled by a doctor poking around inside your *mouth* with his weapons of dental destruction. [7]

口 吼

| 95 | -ed |

了

This character is most frequently used as a grammatical particle. Since it can indicate completion of an action, it is here assigned the key word -**ed**. Learn this character by returning to FRAME 92 and the image given there. The only difference is that the "arms" have been left off (actually, only tuck-**ed** inside). Thus a *child* with its arms wrapp-**ed** up into the backsack is the picture of a job successfully complet-**ed**.

Incidentally, you should be aware that this grammatical particle has generated a great deal of debate among specialists. [2]

フ 了

| 96 | woman |

女

You have probably seen somewhere the form of a squatting **woman** drawn behind this character, with two legs at the bottom, two arms (the horizontal line) and the head poking out the top. A little farfetched, until you draw the character and feel the grace and flow of the three simple strokes. Remembering the character is easy; being able to write it beautifully is another thing. [3]

く 乡 女

❖ The primitive meaning is the same: *woman*. It will help if you have a particular person in mind.

| 97 | good |

好

The sense of **good** carried by this character is very broad in range. And what better image for this than a *woman* holding her *child*. [6]

乡 好

| 98 | be like |

如

Pardon us if we revert to the venerable old Dr. Freud again, but his eye for symbolism is often helpful to appreciate things that more earthy imaginations once accepted more freely but that we have learned to cover over with a veneer of etiquette. For instance, from ancient times things like the *mouth* of a cave have served as natural ritual substitutes for the opening through which a *woman* gives birth. This is just one example of the way in which one thing can **be like** another in a metaphorical sense and can therefore help unlock the hidden meanings of ritual and symbolism. [6]

---

99   mother

Look closely at this character and you will find the outline of the character for *woman* in it, the second stroke of which has been expanded to make space for the two breasts that help a **mother** be a **mother**. [5]

乚 刁 刁 毋 母

❖ As a primitive, this character will take on the added meaning of *breasts* in accord with the explanation given above. Take careful note of the fact that the form is altered slightly when this character serves as a primitive, the two dots joining together to form a longer stroke: 毌. An example follows in the next frame.

---

100   pierce

If one is asked to think of associations for the word **pierce**, among the first to come to mind is that of **piercing** one's ears to hold earrings, a quite primitive form of self-mutilation that has survived into the twenty-first century. The character here is read, top to bottom: *mother . . . oyster*. All you need to do is imagine **piercing** an ear so that it can hold a *mother*-of-pearl you have just wrested from an *oyster*. [11]

乚 口 毌 毌 貫

| 101 | elder brother |

兄

The difference between "older brother" (FRAME 89) and **elder brother** is ever so slight in English, the latter sounding just a bit less colloquial. The same is the case in Chinese.

By now characters like this one should "look like" something to you even though it is more of an "ideogram" than a "pictograph." The large *mouth* on top and the *human legs* below almost jump off the page as a caricature of **elder brother**, the one with the big *mouth* (or if you prefer a kinder image, the one who "has the say" among all the children). [5]

❖ As a primitive this character will take the meaning of *teenager*, in accord with the familiar image of the big *mouth* and the gangling, clumsy *legs*.

| 102 | overcome (v.) |

克

In this frame we get a chance to use the character we just learned in its primitive meaning of *teenager*. The *needle* on top indicates one of the major problems confronting the *teenager* growing up in today's world: drugs. Many of them will fall under the shadow of the *needle* at some time during those tender years. Only when a whole generation rises up and declares, "We Shall **Overcome**," will the *needle* cease to hang over their heads as it does in this character. [7]

LESSON 7

IN THIS LESSON we turn to primitive elements having to do with quantity. We will also introduce the first of many "roofs." These overhead "enclosures" come in a variety of shapes, each of which will given its own unique meaning. But let us begin slowly and not get ahead of ourselves: it is only after you have mastered the simple forms that the apparently impenetrable complexities of later primitives will dissolve. The primitives we give here will immediately suggest others, on the basis of what we have already learned. Hence the somewhat haphazard order among the frames of this lesson.

103	small

小

The sense of **small** in this character is actually of three **small** *drops*, the first of which (the one in the middle) is written larger so that the character has some shape to it. The point of writing it three times is to rub the point in: **small, small**, nothing but **small**. [3]

亅　小　小

❖ The primitive meaning remains the same, *small*. Written above a horizontal line, its form is slightly altered, the last two strokes turning inwards like this: .

104	few

少

First we need to look at the fourth stroke, the *drop* at the bottom that has been extended into a longer diagonal stroke leaning left. This happens because a single, isolated drop will NEVER appear beneath its relative primitive in its normal size, for fear it would drop off and get lost. As for the meaning, let the *drop* indicate a further belittling of what is already *small*—thus making it a **few** of something *small*. [4]

小　少

❖ Note that when this character is used as a primitive element that is placed UNDER another element, the third stroke is omitted, giving us . We will not meet an example of this until FRAME 354.

---

105   **noisy**

吵

You might think that **noisy** should be associated with many people talking at once, but the idea in this character is much more philosophical than that: What happens when things get **noisy** is that people's vocabulary shrinks to a more neolithic level the higher the volume is turned up. And so it is that **noisy** becomes associated with the very *few* things a *mouth* can say when it is talking loudly. Try to picture people quoting Shakespeare to each other in a shouting match, and you will see how right this character is. [7]

口　吵

---

106   **large**

大

Here we have a simple pictograph of a person taking up the space of an entire character and giving it the sense of **large**. It should not be too hard to locate the two legs and outstretched arms. [3]

一　ナ　大

❖ When used as a primitive, this character needs a different meaning, since the element representing the human person will come up later. Therefore, this shape will become a *large dog* or, if you prefer, a *St. Bernard dog*. In FRAME 225 we will explain why this choice was made.

---

107   **tip** (N.)

尖

The **tip** this character refers to is the tapered point of something like a pen or a pagoda. The composition of the elements, *small* and *large,* is perfectly suited to the image of a *small* **tip** at the end of something *larger.* [6]

小　尖

| 108 | evening |

夕

Just as the word **evening** adds a touch of formality or romanticism to the ordinary word "night," so the character for **evening** takes the ordinary looking *moon* in the night sky and has a cloud pass over it—partially hiding it and hence eliminating the final stroke. [3]

丿　勹　夕

| 109 | many |

多

"**Many** *moons* ago," begins much of Amerindian folklore—a colorful way of saying "Once upon a time" and a great deal of help for remembering this character. Here we have two *moons*. (three of them would take us back to the beginning of time, which is further than we want to go.) [6]

夕　多

| 110 | enough |

夠

"**Enough** is **enough**." Who has not been scolded with these words in their youth by a parent or teacher who has run out of patience! Now if you can conjure up the memory of a particular time you yourself blasted those words out at someone who was trying your patience, imagine that short *sentence* becoming an uncontrollable obsession, as you walk off into the sunset muttering it *many* times—over and over and over again. [11]

多　夠

| 111 | outside |

On the left, the primitive for *evening*, and on the right, that for the *magic wand*. Now, as every magician worth his abracadabra knows, bringing your *magic wand* out into the *evening* air makes your magic much more powerful than if you were to stay indoors. Hence, *evening* and *magic wand* takes you naturally **outside**. [5]

夕 外

112

名

name [N.]

Perhaps you have heard of the custom, still preserved in certain African tribes, of a father creeping into the tent or hut of his newborn child on the night of the child's birth, to whisper into its ear the **name** he has chosen for it, before making his choice public. It is an impressive "naming" custom and fits in tidily with the way this character is constructed: *evening . . . mouth*. At *evening* time, a *mouth* pronounces the **name** that will accompany one throughout life. [6]

夕 名

厂

cliff

This primitive means precisely what it looks like: a steep **cliff**. You can certainly imagine someone standing at the top looking down into the abyss below. [2]

一 厂

113

厚

thick

When we refer to someone as **thick**-skinned or **thick**headed, we are often quick to add—even if only under our breath—something about their upbringing. Perhaps it is because deep down we cherish the belief that by nature people are basically tender and sensitive.

Be that as it may, the Chinese character for **thick** depicts a *child* abandoned out on the wild *cliffs*, exposed to the heat of the *sun*, and thus doomed to develop a head and skin as **thick** as the parent who left it there. [9]

厂 厈 厚

114		stone

石

With a *mouth* under a *cliff*, what else could we have here but the entrance to a secret cavern, before which a great **stone** has been rolled so that none may enter? Perhaps it is the hiding place where Ali Baba and his band of thieves have stored their treasures, in which case that magic word known to every school child who ever delighted in the tales of the *Arabian Nights* should be enough to push the **stone** aside. But take care—the *cliff* is steep, and one slip will send you tumbling down into the ravine below.

This is the first of two occasions (for the other, see FRAME 902) on which the second stroke in *cliff* will reach over slightly to the right beneath the horizontal stroke. If you think of the edge jutting outwards (in keeping with the story above), the problem should be taken care of. [5]

❖ The *stone* is a quite common primitive element, which is not restricted to great boulders but is used for *pebbles* or *rocks* of any size or shape.

115		gravel

In this character a *few stones* take on the meaning of **gravel**. Imagine ordering a wheelbarrow of *stones* from your local quarry and having them dump an entire truckload on your garden path. Imagine how annoyed you would be: "I said a *few stones*, a little **gravel** for my walkway—not a blooming mountainside!" [9]

石   砂

116		wonderful

The primitive for *woman* is on the left (there and at the bottom of another primitive is where you will always find her), and to the right the element for *few*. When we refer to a *woman* as **wonderful**, we mean to praise her as the sort of person we meet but *few* of and far between. [7]

女　妙

117

肖

resemble

The word **resemble** should suggest, among other things, a son who **resembles** his father. A "chip off the old block" is the way we often put it, but the character is more simple. It speaks of a *small* bit of *flesh*. [7]

丿　⺍　⺌　肖

❖ When this character is used as a primitive, its meaning changes to *sparks* or *candle*.

118

削

peel (v.)

For want of a kitchen knife, you decide to **peel** an apple with a *saber*. You strike a warrior's pose, toss the apple into the air, and with a guttural shout, brandish your trusty *saber* in the air with lightning speed. Can you see the *sparks* flying and the peelings falling to the ground? [9]

肖　削

119

光

ray

There are really only two primitives here, *small* and *human legs*. The fourth stroke that separates them is added for reasons of aesthetics. (If that doesn't make sense, try writing the character without it and see how ugly the results look, even to your beginner's eye.)

　Now if you have wondered what those little particles of "dust" are that dance around in the light **rays** that come through the window and fall on your desk, try imagining them as *small* and disembodied *human legs*, and you should have no trouble with this character. [6]

⺌　⺍　光

120   overly

太

All right, you are wondering, **overly** "what"? Given the legendary temperament of the *St. Bernard dog,* we may suppose that it is being **overly** affectionate. Hence the large *drop* of slobber—yuck. [4]

大 太

---

121   economize

省

When we decide it's time to **economize**, we take it for granted that we will need to trim back our appetites a bit. If one's *eyes* can be too big for one's stomach, they can also be too big for one's pocketbook. Or, as this character suggests, too many. Imagine yourself with *eyes* all over your head, so that in order to **economize** you will have to pluck most of them out until only a *few* remain. [9]

少 省

---

122   strange

奇

The elements we are given to work with here are *St. Bernard dog* and *can.* Lots of phrases pop to mind to attach these words to the key word, but they end up being too abstract because of the word *can.*

   It is helpful in such cases (and there will be a number of them as we go along) to stick closely to the more basic elements, in this case, *mouth* and *nails.* Now all we need do is create a fictitious "**Strange** But True" column in the Sunday funnies, featuring a *St. Bernard dog* whose *mouth* has been sealed shut with a row of *nails* because he was hitting the brandy keg around his neck too hard. [8]

大 奇

Lesson 8

FOUR BASIC ELEMENTS, it was once believed, make up the things of our universe: earth, wind, fire, and water. We have already met the element for *wind,* and now we shall introduce the others, one by one, in a somewhat longer than usual lesson.

Fortunately for our imaginative memories, these suggestive and concrete primitives play a large role in the construction of the characters, and will help us create some vivid pictures to untangle some of the complex jumbles of strokes that follow.

123	stream [(N.)]

川

A **stream** of water flows pretty much like the character you see in this frame. The reason there are no wavy lines is simply that the Chinese characters no longer use them. [3]

$$) \quad)| \quad)||$$

❖ As a primitive, this character will denote a *stream* or a *flood.* Note, however, that there are certain small changes in the writing of the element, depending on where it appears relative to other elements:

        on the left, it is written 川
        on the top, it is written 巛
        on the bottom, it is written 川

124	state [(N.)]

州

Here we see *drops of* land (little islets) rising up out of a *stream,* creating a kind of sandbar or breakwater. Ever wonder how the **state** line is drawn between **states** separated by a river? If there were little *drops of* land as in the character, there'd be nothing to it. [6]

$$, \quad) \quad 小 \quad 州 \quad 州 \quad 州$$

125 obey

順

In the language of the primitives, this character would read *stream . . . head*. This turns out to be convenient for remembering its meaning of **obey**. Either one **obeys** the person who is *head* of an organization or else **obeys** by following the *stream* of opinion ("current" practice, we call it). Both these senses come together in this character. [12]

川　順

126 water (N.)

水

This character, which looks a bit like a snowflake, is actually a pictograph of **water**—not any particular body of water or movement of water, but simply the generic name for **water**. Should you have any difficulty remembering it, simply think of a *walking stick* being dropped vertically into the **water**, sending *droplets* out in all four directions. Then all you need to learn is how to write it in proper order. [4]

亅　기　水　水

❖ As a primitive, this character can keep its form, or it can be written with three drops to the left of another primitive, like this: 氵. This latter, as we will see, is far more common. It can also be written stiffly, in five strokes, as 氺, in which case we will take it to mean a *snowflake*. An example will follow shortly. Finally, as we will see later in FRAME 380, in the printed form, the *snowflake* element can be straightened out to give .

127 eternity

永

This character also uses the full form of *water*, though its meaning seems to have nothing at all to do with it. Remember what William Blake said about seeing "infinity in a grain of sand and **eternity** in an hour"? Well, reading this character from top to bottom, we see "**eternity** in a *drop of water*."

Note how the introduction of the drop requires that the first stroke of *water* begin with a short horizontal "starter line." Try leaving it out and you will see how reasonable this is. [5]

` 丁 永

128	request ^(v.)

求

Let the key word suggest a formal invitation that begins, "Mr. and Mrs. Snow **request** the honor of your presence at the wedding of their beloved daughter *Snowflake* to Drip*drop*, the son of Mr. and Mrs. Leak…." The only stroke remaining to account for is the *one* that runs between and "unites" the happy couple together until death (or sunlight) do them part. [7]

一 丁 丁 丈 丈 求 求

129	spring ^(n.)

泉

Call to mind the image of a fresh, bubbling **spring** of *water*, and you will probably notice how the top of the **spring** you are thinking of, the part where the "bubbling" goes on, is all *white*. Happily, the *white* is just where it should be, at the top, and the *water* is at the bottom. [9]

白 泉

❖ We will keep this image of a *spring* when using this character as a primitive, but not without first drawing attention to a slight change that distinguishes the primitive from the character. The final four strokes (the element for *water*) are abbreviated to the three small *drops* that we learned earlier as the character for *small,* giving us: 泉.

130	flatlands

原

🎼 "The **flatlands** are alive, with the sound of muuusic…." 🎵 Well, they are in this case anyway, though the setting is a rather grisly one. Watch Schwester Maria as she skips along merrily, dodging in and out of the *springs* that pop up like landmines until she comes to the edge of a *cliff* and loses her balance. Listen to her words echoing as she falls and this character should be yours forever. [10]

厂 㕠 原

131　　　　　　　　　　　　　　　　　　　　wish (N.)

願

Flatlands and a *head* are all we are given to work with in the character for **wish**. Since the key word already suggests something like a formal request made of some higher power, let us imagine a gigantic Wizard-of-Oz *head* located in the middle of the flowery *flatlands* we saw in the last frame. Then just picture people kneeling before it, each with a **wish** they hope to have fulfilled. (The scarecrow wanted brains, the lion courage, and the tin man a heart. What about you?) [19]

原　願

132　　　　　　　　　　　　　　　　　　wash away

沖

Imagine a few innocent looking *drops of water* creeping up on you to **wash** you **away** out into the *middle* of the ocean. Impossible, you say? Not if *drops of water* have drifted in from the Bermuda Triangle where they have had a lot of practice at **washing away** everything from yachts to ocean liners. In any case, this character gives a completely new meaning to the danger of "drowning in a teaspoonful of *water*." [7]

氵　沖

133　　　　　　　　　　　　　　　　　　swim (V.)

泳

On the left we see again the primitive for *drops of water*. To the right, we see the character for *eternity*. Knowing how much children like to **swim**, what could be a better image of an *eternity* of bliss than an endless expanse of *water* to **swim** in without a care in the world? [8]

氵　泳

134	continent
洲	If *states* are separated by smaller bodies of *water*, **continents** are separated by great oceans. The *drops of water* to the left of *state* fill this function. [9]

氵　洲

135	marsh
沼	Unlike the *flatlands* with their cliffs, the **marsh**lands are low and near a source of *water* that feeds them until they get soggy through and through. Why certain land becomes **marsh** is probably due to the fact that it feels thirsty, and so tries its best to *summon* the *water* over to its side. But, like so many temptations, the last state of the victim is worse than the first. Hence the slushy **marsh**. [8]

氵　沼

136	sand (N.)
沙	Learn this character in connection with that for **gravel** from FRAME 115. The difference between **sand** and gravel is one your feet know very well from walking along the beach. The **sand** is finer and the gravel cuts into the skin. Hence the element for *stone* figures prominently in gravel, whereas that for *water* (which, after all has done the work of grinding away at the stone for centuries) shows up here in **sand**. [7]

氵　沙

137	Yangtze
江	China's equivalent to the Mighty Mississip' is the **Yangtze**. In fact, the character in this frame, although generically meaning river, can be used as an abbreviation for the **Yangtze**, much the same as the "River" of "Ole Man River" is for those who live on the banks of the Mississippi. The elements that make it up show *water* and an *I-beam*. Actually, the heavy metal *I-beam* is being launched as a raft by some mentally challenged Huck Finn hop-

ing to cruise on the **Yangtze**. If you see him shoving off and imagine what happens afterwards, it could help fix the elements in your mind. [6]

氵　江

138　　　　　　　　　　　　　　　　　　　　　　　　juice^(N.)

汁　This is not just any ordinary **juice**, but a brew of *water* and *needles*. Its distinctively sharp taste cuts your thirst by distracting it with excruciating pain as the **juice** passes down your throat. [5]

氵　汁

139　　　　　　　　　　　　　　　　　　　　　　　　　　tide

潮　Before we get to explaining this character, take a look at it and see if you can figure out the primitive elements on your own.... On the left is the *water*—that much is easy. On the right we have only one primitive, the character for *dynasty* learned back in FRAME 48. See how an apparently complex character falls apart neatly into manageable pieces?

　To get the meaning of the key word **tide**, just think of the ebb and flow of a *dynasty's* fortunes—literally. Watch as all the wealth of the empire flows into the emperor's court at high **tide**, and note how everything there empties out back into the populace when it is at low **tide**.

　By the way, if you missed the question about the number of primitives, it is probably because you forgot what we said earlier about characters becoming primitives, independently of the pieces that make them up. As a rule, look for the largest character you can write and proceed from there to primitives stranded on their own. [15]

140 source

源

With the advice of the last frame in mind, it is easy to see *water* and *flatlands* in this character for **source**. Both in its etymology (it has a common parent with the word "surge") and in popular usage, **source** suggests the place *water* comes from. In this character, it is under the *flatlands*, where we earlier saw it breaking the surface in those bubbly little springs. [13]

氵　源

141 lively

活

When we speak of a **lively** personality or a **lively** party, we immediately think of a lot of chatter. This character depicts the idea of **lively** by having *tongues* babble and splash around like flowing *water*. [9]

氵　活

142 extinguish

消

Among the many things *water* can do is help **extinguish** fires, and that is just what we have here. First of all, take the *water* at the left as the *drops of water* that are used to depict *water* in general. In the best of all possible worlds, the most efficient way to **extinguish** a fire would be to see that each *drop of water* hits one *spark* of the conflagration. An unthinkable bit of utopian fire fighting, you say to yourself, but helpful for assigning this key word its primitives. [10]

氵　消

143 situation

況

What we have here is "an awkward **situation**." The *teenager* of the family has used up all the *water* for his bath, and there is nothing left to make tea. What the hey, it's all in the family, you say, and rather than throw out the bath*water*, you decide to keep the **situation** secret and make the tea anyway. Little do the guests know, as they sip their tea daintily, that the tea is not the only thing in the hot *water*. [8]

氵 況

---

144 river

河

The character in this frame represents a step up from the *stream* we met in FRAME 123: it is a full-sized **river**, just like the character in FRAME 137 for *Yangtze*. The *water* to the left tells us what we are dealing with, and the *can* at the right tells us that our "little engine that *could*" has now become amphibious and is chugging down the Yellow **River** (which is written using this character) like a regular old **river**boat. [8]

氵 河

---

145 lake

湖

Rather than use the character for *recklessly* from FRAME 17 as a primitive element, let us take the elements one by one: *water* . . . *ancient* . . . *flesh*. You have heard of legends of people being abandoned in the mountains when they had become too *ancient* to work. Well, here is a legend about people being set adrift in the *waters* of a stormy **lake** because their *flesh* had gotten too *ancient* to bear the burdens of life. [12]

氵 湖

---

146 fathom (v.)

測

Connoting the measurement of the depth of water, the key word **fathom** begins with the *water* primitive. To its right, we see the character for *rule* (FRAME 84) which we learned in the sense of "gaming *rules*." Now when we measure the depth of *water*, we have to follow a different set of *rules* than those we use to measure the fish we pull out of it. We **fathom** it; that is, we measure it in units of six feet. Picture yourself **fathoming** a body of *water* several hundred feet deep according to official *rules*, which stipulate that you must use a government-approved tape measure and avoid the use of electronic equipment. [12]

氵 測

---

147   soil ^(N.)

土

We don't like it any more than you do, but this character is not the pictograph it is trumped up to be: a mound of **soil** piled on the ground. All we can recommend is that you memorize it as it is. Anyway, it will be occurring with such frequency that you have almost no chance of forgetting it, even if you try. [3]

一　十　土

❖ When this character is used as a primitive, the sense of *soil* is extended to that of *ground* because of its connection with the character for the same (FRAME 478). From there it also takes the added meanings of *dirt* and *land*.

---

148   equal

均

The idea of making things **equal** is pictured here at its most basic: land reform. It provides *soil* in *uniform* portions to everyone. To help with the association, we may recall the famous line of Napoleon the Pig in George Orwell's *1984*: "All animals are **equal**, but some animals are more **equal** than others." Picture one of those suspicious *land* reforms going on in the barnyard and led by one group of animals (the pigs) who apportion the largest parcels to themselves and ration out among everyone else *uniform* slivers of *land* too small to live on. [7]

圡　均

---

149   belly

肚

Here we see a *part of the body* that looks like a mound of *soil*. What else could it be but that large compost pile that over-eaters carry around where their waistlines used to be? Happily, the key word **belly** already suggests something bell-shaped. [7]

月　肚

150   fill in

填

When you **fill in** a form, it is expected that the information be *true*. That said, most people are less concerned with full and *true* disclosure than with protecting their privacy, whereas those who make the forms are often more interested in getting the *dirt* on them. If you can imagine **filling in** some of the blanks with shovelfuls of actual *dirt* to give them what they want, you will keep the metaphor more concrete. [13]

土   填

151   spit (v.)

吐

We have here a rather small *mouth* (it is always compressed when set on the left) next to a much larger piece of *dirt*. It is not hard to imagine what you might do if you got a *mouth* full of *dirt*. As least we know what we would do: **spit** it out as fast and far as we could! [6]

口   吐

❖   bricks

The two characters for *soil* piled on top of one another give us the primitive element for **bricks**. Given the fact that **bricks** are mostly made of *soil* and that they are made to be piled on top of one another, it should not take much effort to remember this element. [6]

土   圭

152   waaah!

哇

The shrill cries of a bawling infant can be more piercing than any noise an adult makes, which is why they are so hard to ignore. In this character, we see the sounds of that cry, **Waah!**, likened to a *mouth* spitting out *bricks* to shatter the silence of our sleep. [9]

口   哇

153 寸   Chinese inch

This character stands for a small measurement used prior to the metric system, a little less than 1⅓ English inches in length and one-tenth of a *Chinese foot* (which we will meet later, in Book 2). The character, appropriately, represents one *drop* of a *ten* (with a hook!). [3]

❖ When this character is used as a primitive, we shall use it to mean *glue* or *glued to*. There is no need to devise a story to remember this, since the primitive will appear so often you would have to struggle hard NOT to remember it.

154 封   seal (v.)

Think of the key word **seal** in connection with a letter you have written and are preparing to close. Instead of using the traditional hot wax to **seal** the document, you *glue* a *brick* on the outside—a love letter SWAB (**sealed** with a *brick*). A romantic thought, but the postage will bankrupt you. [9]

155 寺   Buddhist temple

You have heard of people "attaching" themselves to a particular sect? Here is your chance to take that metaphor literally and imagine some fellow walking into a **Buddhist temple** with a fervent resolve to attach himself to the place. Since there is plenty of unused *land* around the precincts, he simply picks out a suitable patch, brushes the soles of his feet with *glue*, steps down firmly, and so joins the **Buddhist temple** as a "permanent member." [6]

156   time (N.)

時

"What is **time**?" asked St. Augustine in his memoirs. "Ask me not, and I know. Ask me, and I cannot tell you." Here we have a curious answer to that perennial riddle. **Time** is a *sun* rising over a *Buddhist temple*. It sounds almost like a Zen kōan whose repetition might yield some deep secret to the initiated. At any rate, imagining a monk seated in meditation pondering it might help us remember the character. [10]

日   時

157   fire (N.)

火

Just as sitting before a **fire** enlivens the imagination and lets you see almost anything you want to in the flames, this character is so simple it lets you see almost any sort of **fire** you want to see. It no longer makes a good pictograph, but we invite you to take a pencil and paper and play with the form—first writing it as shown below and then adding lines here and there—to see what you can come up with. Everything from matchbooks to cigarette lighters to volcanic eruptions to the destruction of Sodom and Gomorrah have been found here. No doubt you, too, will find something interesting to bend your memory around these four simple strokes. [4]

丶   丷   少   火

❖ Although the generic meaning of *fire* can be carried over as a primitive meaning, it is usually best to keep to the meaning of *flames* or *fireplace*. Another primitive element for *fire*, based on this one, is written 灬 and will mean *cooking fire*.

158   ashes

灰

The character for **ashes** naturally includes the primitive for *fire*, or more specifically, a *fireplace*. Now what do you do with that bucket of **ashes** you have just cleaned out of the *fireplace*? You strap it to your belt and walk around with it *by your side* until the wind scatters them, with distributive justice, over everyone else's property. [6]

一 ナ 灰

159

煩

vexed ^(ADJ.)

When people are **vexed** about something, they often refer to themselves as "really burned" about it. In this character, the person's *head* is on *fire*, raising the metaphor to new heights. [13]

火 煩

160

炎

inflammation

A *fire* belongs IN the *fireplace*, not OVER it. When the *fire* spreads to the rest of the house, we have an **inflammation** of the house. As with any **inflammation**—including those that attack our bodies—the danger is always that it might spread if not checked. This is the sense behind the reduplication of the element for *fire*, one atop the other. [8]

火 炎

161

淡

thin ^(ADJ.)

You may not think there is such a thing as **thin** *water* or **thin** *fire*, but when you mix *fire* and *water*, the one does make the other **thin**. When you see this key word, think not of "slender" but of **thin** in the sense of pale, diluted, or weak. Paint **thin**ner makes paint **thin** in this way (though we do not recommend mixing it with *fire*, unless you want a REAL *inflammation*). [11]

 淡

162

災

disaster

Of all of nature's **disasters**, this character picks out two of the worst: *floods* and *fires*. To recall the disposition of the elements, think of nature's solution to nature's own problem: a great *flood* pouring down over a great forest *fire*. [7]

巛   災

163 illuminate

昭

Although the range of possible meanings that the character for **illuminate** can have is about as rich as the connotations of the English word, we need to focus on just one of them: to make something obscure *evident*. If you glaze a pot and put it into the oven to "fire" it, you in fact **illuminate** it. Hence the character for **illuminate** makes a connection between the character for *evident* and the primitive element for *cooking fire*. [13]

164 fish (N.)

魚

Breaking down this character give us three elements, which we list in the order of their writing: *bound up ... rice field ... cooking fire*. Not much to work with at first sight. But we can join them together by thinking of a three-part story: first a **fish** is caught and *bound up* on a line with its unfortunate schoolmates; when the fisherman gets home, he cuts off the head and tosses it, with the entrails, out into the *rice field* for fertilizer; and the rest he sets in a skillet over a *cooking fire* for his supper. [11]

 鱼 魚

165 fishing (N.)

漁

To the story we have just made about *fish*, this character for the profession of **fishing** adds yet another element BEFORE the others: namely the *water*, where the *fish* was happily at home before being caught, disemboweled, and eaten. Be sure to get a clear image of the *water* when you put it all together to create a picture of **fishing**. [14]

We conclude this lesson by introducing a character that could have been learned earlier, but which we left for now to show two examples of its use as a primitive element. The character itself typically falls just outside the 3,000 most frequently used, but since we need it as a primitive, we might as well learn it as a character, too. We will do this a few more times, as the need arises.

---

166   Yao

堯

This character, used as a family name, is best associated with the legendary sage king **Yao**, who lived around 2300 BCE and became a model for rulers in ancient China. One fact about this king, which can help us remember the writing of the character, is that he is said to have invented the board game of Go as a way to sharpen the brain of his dim-witted son. Here we see the son as simply a *pair of human legs* (no brain attached), playing Go on the *floor* with little clumps of *dirt* (instead of the customary stones). [12]

❖ Used as a primitive, this character will be associated with the image of that unforgettable character in the Charlie Brown cartoon strips, *Pigpen*. Or, if you prefer, some particularly memorable slob from your high-school days. The association should be obvious: *dirt, dirt* everywhere and a *pair of human legs.*

---

167   fever

燒

Picture little *Pigpen* as "running a **fever**." Can you see the *fire* chasing after him as he runs away, kicking up even more dust than he usually does? [16]

---

168   dawn (N.)

曉

When you think of the **dawn**, imagine the *sun* rising up over the horizon, drenching the landscape in a golden color. Imagine little *Pigpen* sitting in the middle of a field, getting scrubbed up all spic-and-span as the *sun* passes over him, his hair neatly combed and parted, his trousers pressed, and his shirt fresh and white. Until he stands up, that is, and starts walking around, at which point the dirt starts whipping up around him again. [16]

LESSON 9

ALTHOUGH completing the presentation of the four basic elements in the last lesson brought us a lot of new characters—46 in all—we have only scratched the surface as far as *water, earth, wind,* and *fire* are concerned. Perhaps by now it is clear why we said at the beginning of this lesson that we are lucky that they appear so frequently. The range of images they suggest is almost endless.

In this lesson our focus will be on a few new "roof" and "enclosure" primitives. But first, a character that we might have included in the last group but omitted so as not to be distracted from the four elements.

169	*li*

里

That's right—a *li*. Don't bother looking it up in your English dictionary; it's a Chinese unit of distance. One *li* is about a half kilometer. The character depicts how the measure came to be used. Atop we see the *rice field*, and below the element for *land*. Think of those four sections you see in the *rice field* (and which we made mention of when first we introduced the character in FRAME 14) as blocks of *land*. Thus, a *land* division based on the size of a *rice field* would be a *li*. [7]

丶　冂　冂　日　旦　甲　里

❖ To get a more concrete primitive meaning for this character, we shall refer to it as a *computer*, a meaning deriving from the character for *logic,* which we will meet in LESSON 12. To remember the meaning, it might help to think of the alternative meaning of the primitive at the top: *brains.*

170	quantity

量

Think of **quantity** as having to do with measuring time and distance, and the rest is simple: you have a **quantity** of time in the new day that begins with *daybreak,* and a **quantity** of distance in the rural *li.* [12]

旦 量

---

171   bury

埋   When we **bury** something (or someone, for that matter), we
      usually mean putting it under *ground*. Only here, we are **bury-
      ing** our beloved *computer* that has served us so well these past
      years. Behind us a choir chants the "Dies irae, dies illa" and
      there is much wailing and grief among the bystanders as they
      pass by to shovel a little *dirt* into what will be its final resting
      place. R.I.P. [10]

土 埋

Before going any further, we might pause a moment to look at precisely WHERE
the primitive elements were placed in the character of the last frame: the *ground*
to the left and the *computer* to the right. Neither of these is an absolutely fixed
position. The character for *spit* 吐 (FRAME 151), for instance, puts *ground* on the
right, and that for *wild* 野 (FRAME 939) will put the *computer* on the left. While
there is no reason to bother memorizing any "rules," a quick glance through a
few general guidelines may help. Use them if they help; if not, simply adjust the
story for a problem character in such a way as to help you remember the position of the elements relative to one another.

    In any case, here are the guidelines that follow from the characters treated
up to this point:

1. Many characters used regularly as primitives have a "strong" position or
   two from which they are able to give a basic "flavor" to the character. For
   example, *ground* at the left (or bottom) usually indicates something to do
   with earth, soil, land, and the like; *fire* at the bottom in the form of the
   four dots, or at the left in its compressed character form, usually tells us
   we have to do with heat, passion, and the like; a *mouth* at the left commonly signifies something to do with eating, coughing, spitting, snoring,
   screaming, and so forth. Where these elements appear elsewhere in the
   characters, however, they do not, as a rule, have the same overall impact
   on its meaning.

2. Some primitive elements ALWAYS have the same position in a character.
   We saw this earlier in the case of the primitive meaning *head* 頁 (page
   43) and in the three drops of *water* 氵 (page 70).

3. Enclosures like *cliff* 厂 (page 65) and *bound up* 勹 (page 40) are always set above whatever it is they enclose. Others, as we shall see later, "wrap up" a character from the bottom.

4. All things being equal, the element with the fewer strokes (usually the more common element) has first rights to the "strong" position at the left or bottom. (Note that the left and bottom cannot both be the dominant position in the same character. Either one or the other of them will dominate, usually the left.) The characters for *gravel* 砂 (FRAME 115) and *sing* 唱 (FRAME 21) illustrate the point.

---

172   **black**

黑

Three frames ago we noted that it might help to think of the top part of the primitive for *computer* as *brains*. In this character you will see why. Note how the third stroke, ordinarily written as a single horizontal line, is here broken up into a pair of *animal horns* right in the middle of the element. Think of this as a brain impaled (literally) on the *horns* of a dilemma.

That done, there is no problem with this character. Like most things electrical, a *computer*, too, can overheat, and often this happens because its *brain* is caught on the *horns* of a dilemma. Now look closely with your imaginative eye and you can see the *horns* sprouting out of the CPU and *flames* pouring out of the *computer* to char the keyboard, the monitor, and your desk a sooty **black** color. [12]

丶 冂 冂 冂 回 里 甲 里 黑

---

173   **spot** (N.)

點

When Madam Cheng **tells fortunes**, she not only tells you about the bright and beautiful things that await you but also about the dark, *black* misfortunes that menace your future like **spots** on a white background. Look into the crystal ball and you can see these *black* **spots** peppered here and there. And if you zoom in, you will see that each **spot** is a particular place that bodes ill for you. These are, literally, the *black* **spots** in your future. [16]

黑 點

174

墨

black ink

Besides meaning **black ink**, this character also appears in the word for an inked string that is pulled taut and snapped to mark a surface, much the same as a carpenter doing repair work in your home might use a chalked string. Here it is used to mark the *dirt* on a baseball diamond with a long, heavy piece of string soaked in **black ink**. [15]

❖

冂

hood

In addition to the basic meaning of **hood**, this shape can be used for a **glass cover**, such as that used to serve "pheasant under glass." Note its difference from the element for *wind*: the second stroke is hooked INWARDS here. To help remember this detail, think of the wind as blowing "out" and a **glass cover** as keeping something "in." Among the related images suggested by this primitive are: a monk's **cowl**, a riding **hood**, a **helmet**, and an automobile **hood**. [2]

175

冒

risk (v.)

In order not to **risk** being identified, burglars often wear a mask or something else draped over their face. If you look closely at the character and "read off" the primitive elements, you will end up with a *hood* with *two* slits for the *eyes*. It would almost be worth trying one on if becoming a burglar didn't **risk** a lot more than just being recognized.

Even if you followed the explanation above, it bears repeating that the top four strokes are NOT the same as the primitive for *sun* or *day* or *tongue wagging in the mouth*. The difference is subtle but not to be ignored. [9]

176 同   same

The primitives in this character show us *one* and *mouth* under a *hood*. Let us take the key word to connote the sense in which monks living in community share the **same** life, routine, food, and ideals. We might say they all have the **same** habits, including the "habit" they wear on their backs. Here we see the monk's *cowl*, drawn down over the eyes so that all you can see when you look at him is a *mouth*. But since monks also speak their prayers in common, it is but a short step to think of *one mouth* under a *hood* as the character for everything that is the **same** about monastic life. [6]

❖ When this character is used as a primitive, it will mean *monks* dressed in a common habit.

177 洞   cave

Early hermit-*monks* often lived in **caves** where they prayed and fasted for years on end. The one thing they could not do without was *water*. To fix this image, imagine a *monk* who has filled up his **cave** with *water* neck high, which makes it difficult to sleep but at least protects him from dehydration. [9]

氵　洞

178 向   orientation

This character begins with a mysterious *drop* off in the distance. Then we find a sort of transparent *helmet* with no eyes or nose, but only a prominent *mouth* under it—obviously an extraterrestrial. And what is it jabbering on about with its *mouth* open like that? It has strayed far from its spaceship (the *drop* off in the distance) whose fuel tanks are bone dry. Seeing that the poor creature is completely "disoriented," you offer a first **orientation** to life on earth by handing him a few bucks and pointing the way to the nearest gas station. [6]

179 — esteem (v.)

尚

Above we see the primitive for *small* attached to one of those *glass covers* you might use to display a family heirloom. Its being *small* is important, because what is in fact on display is the shrunken, stuffed, and mounted *mouth* of an ancestor we particularly **esteem**. We may be used to **esteeming** the words our forebears leave behind, but here we also **esteem** the very *mouth* that spoke them. We leave it to you to imagine a suitable place in your room for displaying such an unusual conversation piece. [8]

❖ — house

This extremely useful primitive element depicts the roof of a **house**. You can see the chimney at the top and the eaves on either side without much trouble. It is a "crown" element, which means that it is invariably set atop other things. Examples follow immediately. [3]

180 — character

字

Here is the character for **character** itself. Not just Chinese characters but any written **character** from hieroglyphs to Sanskrit to our own Roman alphabet. It shows us simply a *child* in a *house*. But let us take advantage of the double meaning of the key word to note that just as a *child* born to a Chinese *house* is given **characters** for its name, so it is also stamped with the "character" of those who raise it from infancy on. [6]

| 181 | guard (v.) |

守

If you want to **guard,** the best way is to post a watchman, like the royal soldiers in front of Buckingham Palace or the Pope's Swiss Guard. The whole idea of hiring people to **guard** is that they should stick like *glue* to your *house* to protect it from unwanted prowlers. So go ahead and find a watchman who is really stuck on his job and *glue* him to your *house* to **guard** it. [6]

| 182 | finish (v.) |

完

To start a *house* we lay the foundations; to **finish** it, a roof. This character shows the "finished" product, from the *beginnings* in the foundation at the bottom, to the roof with its chimney at the top. Come to think of it, the same holds true of anything we start and **finish**. [7]

| 183 | reality |

實

This apparently complex character is really simplicity itself. It has only two elements: *house* and *pierce*. The problem is the key word, which, despite its claims to **reality,** is about as abstract as they come. But if you think of a *house* that is really old-fashioned and out of touch with **reality,** then perhaps all it needs is a professional to *pierce* the chimney, or put a couple of studs on the front door. Who knows, maybe there's a career out there somewhere for a "*house* piercer" who goes around the suburbs blaring out over a microphone, "Hey, *houses,* get REAL!" [14]

| 184 | proclaim |

宣

Think of the key word in its religious sense of a missionary preaching: "**proclaiming** the good news to all nations" and "shouting it from the *house*tops" all day, day in and day out. The element for *daybreak* that follows below has an additional stroke at the top. Remembering what we said about the *sun* creeping up over the horizon (the *floor*) at *daybreak* (FRAME 29), the extra stroke can represent the other horizon towards which the *sun* journeys, giving us "*sun*rise, *sun*set." That should be enough to help you remember this simple character, used in fact both for traditional missionary work as well as for one of its contemporary replacements: propaganda. [9]

---

185 — nighttime

宣 Unlike the "evening" (FRAME 108), **nighttime** suggests time spent at night, as in pulling an all-nighter to prepare for an exam when everyone else is fast asleep in bed. The character expresses this by picturing a *house* with a *candle* in it. The reason is obvious: whoever is living there is passing the **nighttime** "burning the *candle* at both ends." [10]

---

186 — peaceful

安 To be told that the place of the *woman* is in the *house* may not sit well with modern thought, but like all cultural habits the Chinese characters bear the birthmarks of their age. So indulge yourself in a Norman Rockwell image of a **peaceful** moment: a weary *woman* of the *house* slouched asleep in the living room chair, her hair in curlers and a duster lying in her lap. [6]

---

187 — banquet

宴 To carry on from the last frame, we note the entire *day* of work that comes between a *woman* and her *house* in preparing for a dinner **banquet**, pictorially "interrupting" her *peaceful* relaxation. [10]

188　　　　　　　　　　　　　　　　　　　　　mail ^(v.)

寄

Now there is nothing particularly *strange* about your normal mailbox, but the one depicted here is a *strange house* that you actually have to enter to drop off your letters. Think of the haunted *House* of Usher that Edgar Allen Poe immortalized, or the enchanted Gingerbread *House* that Hansel and Gretel are heading towards with an armful of letters to **mail**. [11]

189　　　　　　　　　　　　　　　　　　　　　wealthy

富

Here we have the original character on which the primitive element for *wealth* is based. In keeping with the story introduced back then, note how many **wealthy** people get that way through simple inheritance, being born into the *wealth* of their parents' *house*. [12]

190　　　　　　　　　　　　　　　　　　　　　store up

貯

This character shows a family that literally **stores up** its *clams* by hanging them on a large, six-foot *nail* driven into a space under the roof of their *house*. [12]

貝　　貯　　貯

LESSON 10

Of the several primitive elements that have to do with plants and grasses, we introduce two of the most common in this lesson: *trees* and *flowers*. In most cases, as we shall see, their presence in a "strong" position (in this case, to the left and at the top, respectively) helps give a meaning to the character.

191	tree

 This is a pictograph of a **tree**, the main trunk shown in the long vertical stroke and the boughs in the long horizontal stroke and the final two strokes sweeping down in both directions. Although it may look similar at first sight to the character for *water* (FRAME 126), the order in which it is written is completely different and this affects its final appearance. [4]

一　十　才　木

❖ As a primitive, this character can mean *tree* or *wood*. When the last two strokes are detached from the trunk (朩), we shall change its meaning to *pole* or *wooden pole*.

192	woods

 Learn this frame in connection with the next one. A **woods** is a small cluster of *trees*. Hence the simple reduplication of the character for *tree* gives us a **woods**. [8]

才　林

193	forest

森 A **forest** is a large expanse of *trees*, or "*trees, trees* everywhere," to adopt the expression we used in FRAMES 22, 23, and 166. [12]

194

植

plant (v.)

You have no doubt seen how people practicing the Japanese art of bonsai take those helpless little saplings and twist them into crippled dwarves before they have a chance to grow up as they should. The more proper way to **plant** a young *tree* and give it a fair shake in life is to set it into the earth in such a way that it can grow up *straight*. [12]

木 植

195

杏

apricot

Since **apricots** can be eaten just as they fall from the *trees*, picture this *mouth* agape at the bottom of a *tree* (just as the elements have it), waiting for **apricots** to fall into it. [7]

木 杏

196

呆

dim-witted

The **dim-witted** thimblehead in this character is seated in the topmost branches of a *tree* with his mouth agape, waiting for the fruit to fall into it, but the only thing that happens is that nothing happens. [7]

口 呆

197

枯

withered

When a *tree* is **withered** and about to die, it is probably due to a kind of arteriosclerosis that keeps its sap from flowing freely. This character shows us an *ancient* and wrinkled *tree* with poor circulation, **withered** up and whiling away its remaining days in a retirement center. [9]

木 枯

198 村   village

The character for *village* shows a circle of *trees glued* together to measure off the confines of a **village**. [7]

木 村

199 相   one another

The key word **one another** stirs up associations of people interacting. When we read off the elements, *tree . . . eye*, we are given an idea of how to keep this interaction amicable by calling to mind the scriptural proverb about first taking the *tree* trunk out of your own *eye* before helping your neighbors remove the splinters from theirs. [9]

木 相

200 本   notebook

Recalling that **notebooks** are made of paper, and paper made of *trees*, one might think of a **notebook** as a slice of a *tree*. Can you see the "cross-cut" in the trunk of the *tree*? Picture a chainsaw cutting you out a few **notebooks** to take to school. [5]

木 本

201 案   case

The **case** that this key word refers to is the legal kind and the image contrasts the attitudes of the parties involved. While you are in a frazzle, the lawyer answers all your phone calls with, "I'm working on your **case**," when actually she is swaying, relaxed and *peaceful*, in a hammock strung up between the *trees* in her backyard. Imagine that—people actually get paid to take it easy while you do all the worrying. [10]

安 案

202	not yet

未

As the key word suggests, this character has to do with something not quite over and done with. More concretely, it shows us a *tree* that is **not yet** fully grown. The extra short stroke in the upper branches shows new branches spreading out, leaving one with the feeling that the *tree* has a ways to go yet before it reaches maturity. In other words, the character conveys its meaning pictographically, playing on the earlier pictograph of the *tree*. [5]

一　未

203	last ^(N./ADJ.)

末

This character is best learned in connection with that of the previous frame. The first stroke shows a branch that is longer than the main branch, indicating that the tree has reached the **last** of its growth, so that its top branches stop spreading and start drooping downwards. Be sure to keep this imagery in mind, to avoid confusing this key word with synonyms that will appear later. [5]

一　末

204	foam

沫

The **foam** this character refers to is the *last* stage of *water* after it has dashed and splashed against the rocks, spraying in all directions. The **foam** is thus a wave that has run its full course and reached its *last* on the rocky seashore. If you picture it in your mind's eye, this somewhat rare (but oh-so-easy-to-learn) character is yours for good. [8]

氵　沫

205	flavor ^(N.)

味

When a tree has *not yet* finished growing, it produces fruit with a full **flavor**. When the official taster (the professional *mouth* to the left) determines that full **flavor** has been reached, the tree is pruned back so that it remains permanently *not yet* grown. A neat little agricultural trick and an easy way to see the sense of **flavor** hidden in this character. [8]

口　味

206 younger sister

妹　The **younger sister** in the family is the *woman* in the family who, like the newest branch in a tree, is *not yet* old enough or mature enough to do everything the older sister can do (see FRAME 1298). [8]

女　妹

207 investigate

查　To **investigate** is to get to the bottom of something or track something down, which often has you working all through the night, right to *daybreak*. In the case of this character, it is Sir Isaac Newton, who is **investigating** the laws of physics when the appearance of the sun at *daybreak* prompts the *tree* to stretch and welcome a new day. At that, an apple drops from its branches square on Sir Isaac's head, inspiring him to discover the law of universal gravitation. [9]

木　查

208 sediment

渣　This character has you in your scuba-diving gear *investigating* at the bottom of a reservoir to see what has made the *water* go bad. See yourself mucking around the **sediment** and finding remnants of all sorts of garbage and chemical waste. Hopefully, someone will find the "dregs" of society that put it there and bring them to justice. [12]

氵　渣

| 209 | dye (v.) |

染

Take a handful of ash tree seeds, plant them in your backyard, and sprinkle them with *water* mixed with your mother's hair **dye**. If you are patient enough to nurture this little orchard of ash *trees* to full size, you could carve yourself out the first-ever-in-history brunette or platinum-streaked *baseball* bat. [9]

氵　　氿　　染

| 210 | plum |

李

Little Jack Horner has left his corner and his Christmas pie to try out his fortunes with a *tree* in the garden. He sticks in his thumb and out drops a **plum**, which says, "What a weird *child* you are!" [7]

木　　李

| 211 | table |

桌

You have to think here of a group of magicians seated around a magical **table**, which is made out of the stump of a *tree,* and has the image of a large *sun* carved into its surface. The magicians pass the *magic wand* around from hand to hand to see if any of them can make the *sun* shine. At last, one of them succeeds, and the *sun* begins to glow (burning a hole in the **table** in the process). [10]

ト　　占　　桌

| ❖ | flower |

艹

We are not yet equipped with all the pieces necessary to learn the character for **flower**, so shall have to content ourselves here with the first three strokes, which represent the primitive of the same meaning. Concentrate on the actual "bloom" of the **flower**, and keep a particular flower in mind. Try a rose, a tulip, or a daisy, since none of them will have their own character.

Think about it well, since once you have decided on your **flower** of choice, you will be using it in a rather large number of stories later on. [4]

The tendency today is to print the primitive element for **flower** in the form shown in this frame, even though its drawing follows the older, more traditional form:

ㅣ   ㅗ   ㅗㅣ   ㅗㅏ

---

212   **as if**

若

Here we see a *flower* held in the *right* hand, calling to mind the famous story of the Buddha who held up a *flower* with his *right* hand to a small gathering of his disciples. Most of them were perplexed, but Kasyapa smiled and the Buddha handed him the *flower*, **as if** he had understood something that everyone else had missed. To this day it remains a mystery what it was that the Buddha communicated to Kasyapa, but everyone treats the story **as if** it is of pivotal importance. [9]

ㅗㅏ   若

---

213   **grass**

草

Perhaps you know the custom of seeding **grass** randomly or in some particular pattern with the *flower* called the crocus, which blooms for a few days each year in *early* spring. As the **grass** begins to turn green again after winter has passed, these tiny *flowers* dot up here and there. Now just look out your window at a patch of **grass** somewhere and think what a nice idea it would be to have your name spelled out in *flowers* once as a sort of *early* harbinger of spring. [10]

ㅗㅏ   草

---

214   **suffering** (N.)

苦

The picture of **suffering** we are given here is that of a *flower* that has grown *ancient*. When a flower ages, it pales and dries up, and probably even endures a kind of botanical **suffering**. If you think that plants are incapable of such feelings, then ask yourself why so many people believe that talking to their flowers helps them bloom better. [9]

---

215   **wide**

寛   The key word **wide** will suggest a **wide**-angle lens, since that is one of the first expressions likely to pop into mind at the sound of the word. What we are trying to *see* in a single view is an immense green*house* filled with one each of all the *flowers* of the world. Picture yourself trying to *see* the whole thing through the viewer of your **wide**-angle lens, and then focusing on a single *drop* of dew on the tiniest petal of the tiniest blossom. To *see* everything in all its detail may be asking a little much of a single lens, but nothing short of such a vision could ever satisfy the curiosity that comes with the gift of sight. [15]

广　宀　寛　寛

❖   **family tree**

枼   The element we introduce here for a **family tree** is made up of the elements for *generation* and *tree*. At present, we can only use the element to learn one character, but it will prove useful in Book 2. [9]

世　枼

---

216   **leaf**

葉   Two elements we have to work with here are *flower* and *family tree*. Now all of us know what it is to have some rotten fruit on the *family tree*, but let us never forget that it is always possible for even the worst of us to turn over a new **leaf** and burst into *flower* if given the chance. [13]

217

莫

nobody

A rickety old sign with the warning written on it "**Nobody,** but **Nobody** Leaves Here" dangles from a shingle over the entrance to a graveyard. But, contrary to what you expect, this is a thoroughly modern graveyard. Gone are the cobwebs and gnarled trees, the tilted headstones and dark, moonless nights that used to scare the wits out of our childhood imaginations. Instead, we see brightly colored *flowers* placed before the tombstones, the *sun* shining gloriously overhead, and a cuddly *St. Bernard dog* sitting at the gate, making sure that **nobody** tries to leave. [11]

艹 苩 莫

❖ When this character is used as a primitive element, we will replace the abstract key word with the more concrete *graveyard*.

218

模

imitate

Ah, but haven't they made a parody of the modern *graveyard* in trying to **imitate** its classic ancestors! The flowers are plastic, the writing on the stones is unimaginative and cold, and the whole thing looks more like a marble orchard than a right and proper *graveyard*. This character continues with the modernization trend by picturing artificial *trees* in the *graveyard*. But of course, how convenient! They don't need pruning or fertilizing, their leaves don't fall, and they remain the same color all year long. But far from **imitating** the real thing, they end up a cheap "imitation." [15]

木 模

219

漠

desert (N.)

Let this key word suggest to you a mirage in a **desert**. The haze rising up from the **desert** sands creates the illusion of a body of *water* in the distance. In fact, the mirage only recedes as you crawl your way across the surface of what will soon be your *graveyard*. To fix the image, imagine yourself reaching the mirage and finding out that it is in fact a *graveyard*, in which there is a headstone with your name on it. [14]

氵　漠

220

墓

grave

The mounds of *soil* with crude wooden crosses set at their head suggests those Boot Hill **graves** near Tombstone, Arizona, that many of you will remember from cowboy lore. The only odd thing about this character is that the *soil* comes UNDER the *graveyard*, rather than to its left, where we might expect it. Just think of how it looks as you walk toward Boot Hill, with the cross and mound of *soil* in the foreground.

By the way, this is not the first time, nor will it be the last, that we learn a character whose key word is the same, or almost the same, as a primitive element based on it, but whose shape differs somewhat. There is no cause to worry. By using the primitive in a variety of other characters, as we have done here, the confusion will be averted as a matter of course. In most cases, as here, the primitive element is simply one part of the fuller original character. [14]

莫　墓

221

苗

seedling

To avoid confusion with the image of rice seedlings to appear later, we shall take these **seedlings** out of their agricultural setting in the *rice fields* and into the frame of Brave New World surgery, where "ideas" or "values" are being implanted into *brains* like **seedlings** to insure a harmonious society. Then you need only imagine them taking root and breaking out into *flower* right through the tops of the skulls of people walking around on the streets. [9]

艹　苗

❖ When this character is used as a primitive element, we will adjust its meaning to *tomato seedling*.

222   aim (v.)

瞄   In order to **aim** at something through the sights of a rifle, you
fix your *eyes* on the thin crosshairs. In this case, however, the
usual crosshairs have been replaced with the completely useless
serrated leaves of a *tomato seedling*. And not only that, they are
poking out of where the lens should be and keep tickling your
eyeball, keeping you from **aiming** properly. Obviously the sabo-
tage of peacemakers working in a rifle factory. [14]

目   瞄

Lesson 11

Now that we have made our way through well over 200 characters, it is time to pause and consider how you are getting on with the method introduced in this book. While this lesson will be a short one (only 18 new characters) you might want to spend some time reviewing your progress in light of the remarks that follow. In them we have tried to draw out the main principles that have been woven into the fabric of the text from frame to frame and lesson to lesson. We do so by looking at some of the typical problems that can arise:

If you can remember the key word when you see the character, but have trouble remembering the character when you have only the key word to go on...

Probably you did not take seriously the advice about studying these stories with a pad and pencil. If you try to shortcut the process by merely learning to recognize the characters for their meaning without worrying about their writing, you will find that you have missed one bird with two stones, when you could have bagged two with one. Let us repeat: study only from key word to character; the reverse will take care of itself.

If you find yourself having to go back to a character, once you have written it, to make corrections or additions...

Our guess is that you are asking your visual memory to do the work that belongs to imaginative memory. After Lesson 12, you will be given more leeway to create your own images and stories, so it is important that you nip this problem in the bud before going any further. A small step in the wrong direction on a journey of 3,000 characters will land you in deep trouble in no time. Here are the steps you should be following each time you come to a new frame:

1. Read the key word and take note of the particular connotation that has been given it. There is only one such meaning, sometimes associated with a colloquial phrase, sometimes with one of the several meanings of the word, sometimes with a well-known cultural phenomenon. Think of that connotation and repeat it to yourself. When you're sure you've got the right one, carry on.

2. Read through the particular little story that goes with the key word and let the whole picture establish itself clearly.

3. Now close your eyes, focus on those images in the story that belong to the key word and primitive elements, and let go of the controls. It may take a few seconds, sometimes as long as a minute, but the picture will

start to change on its own. The exaggerated focal points will start to take on a life of their own and enhance the image with your own particular experiences and memories. You will know your work is done when you have succeeded in creating a memorable image that is both succinct and complete, both faithful to the original story and yet your very own.

4. Open your eyes and repeat the key word and primitive elements, keeping that image in mind. This will clear away any fog, and at the same time make sure that when you let go you didn't let go of the original story, too.

5. In your mind, juxtapose the elements relative to one another in line with your image or the way they normally appear in the characters.

6. Take pencil and paper and write the character once, retelling the story as you go.

These are basically the same steps you were led through in reading the stories, even though they were not laid out so clearly before. If you think back to the characters that "worked" best for you, you will probably find that each of these steps was accomplished perfectly. And if you look back at the ones you are forgetting, you should also be able to locate which step you skipped over. In reviewing, these same steps should be followed, with the only clue to set the imagination in motion being the key word.

If you find that you are forgetting the relative position of the elements in a character...

Before all else, go back and reread the frame for that character to see if there were any helpful hints or explanatory notes. If not, return to the frame where the particular primitives were first introduced to see if there is any clue there. If this is not the problem, then, taking care not to add any new words or focal points to your story (since they might end up being elements later on), rethink the story in such a way that the image for each element actually takes the position it has in the character itself. This should not happen often, but when it does, it is worth spending a few minutes to get things sorted out.

If you are confusing one character with another...

Take a careful look at the two stories. Perhaps you have made one or the other of them so vivid that it has attracted extraneous elements to itself that make the image of one character melt into that of another. Or again, it may be that you did not pay sufficient attention to the advice about clarifying a single connotation for the key word.

Whether or not you have had all or only a few of these problems, now is the time to review the first ten lessons keeping an eye out for them. Put aside

any schedule you may have set yourself until you have those lessons down perfectly, that is, until you can run through all six steps outlined above for every
character, without a hitch. The most important thing in this review is not really
to see whether you are remembering the characters, but to learn how to locate
problems and deal with them.

One final note before you close the book and begin running your review.
Everyone's imagination works differently. Each has its own gifts and its own
defects. The more you pay attention to how you imagine things, the more likely
you are to find out what works best for you—and more importantly, *why*. The
one thing you must distrust, if the system outlined in this book is to work for
you, is your ability to remember characters just as they are, without doing any
work on them. Once you start making exceptions for characters you "know" or
"have no trouble with" or "don't need to run through all the steps with," you are
headed for a frustration that will take you a great deal of trouble to dig yourself
out of. In other words, if you start using the method only as a "crutch" to help
you only with the characters you have trouble with, you will quickly be limping
along worse than ever. What we are offering here is not a crutch, but a different
way to walk.

That said, let us pick up where we left off. In this lesson we turn from primitive elements having to do with plants to those having to do with animals, four
of them in all.

223	portent

兆　　Here we have a pictograph of the back of a turtle, the two slop-
ing vertical strokes representing the central ridge and the four
short strokes the pattern. Think of reading turtle shells as a way
to foretell the future, and in particular, to suggest a **portent** of
coming evils. [6]

丿　丿　丬　兆　兆　兆

224	peach

桃　　To associate the **peach** with the primitive for a *portent,* recall
the famous Japanese legend of Momotarō, the **Peach** Boy. It
begins once upon a time with a fisherman and his wife who
wanted badly to have a child, but none was born to them. Then
one day the old man caught a giant **peach**, out of which jumped
a healthy young lad whom they named **Peach** Boy. Though the

boy was destined to perform heroic deeds, his birth foreshadowed great misfortune (how else could he become a hero?). Thus the **peach** *tree* is seen as a *portent* of coming evil. [10]

木 桃

225

犬

pooch

We have already learned that the character for *large* takes on the meaning of the *St. Bernard dog* when used as a primitive. In this frame we finally see why. The *drop* added as a fourth and final stroke means that we have to do with a much smaller dog, a **pooch**, which compared to the *St. Bernard dog* is no more than a *drop* in the kennel. [4]

大 犬

❖ As a primitive this character can take two meanings. In the form given here it will mean a very small dog (which we shall refer to as a *chihuahua* for convenience sake). When it takes the form 犭 to the left of a character, we shall give it the meaning of *a pack of wild dogs*.

226

尤

remarkable

We learn this next character here simply because it is the easiest place to learn it. Later it will figure as an element of other, more complex characters.

The only thing that distinguishes this character from the *pooch* is its **remarkable** *human leg*. As the story goes, the poor creature lost its leg in a car accident and hobbled around pitifully, until one day a mad scientist caught sight of it, dragged it into his castle, and fastened on it the severed leg of a local chorus girl (whose leg had mysteriously flown off her chassis in the middle of a performance, striking a French tourist on the head). So there you have it, the altogether **remarkable** Franken*pooch*. [4]

一 ナ 九 尤

❖ As a primitive, this character will keep its meaning of the *Frankenpooch*.

227 silent

默

"But my words, like **silent** raindrops fell...." The famous ode to "silence" from which these words were taken begins with an enigmatic phrase that this character will clear up once and for all: "Hello, Darkness, my old friend...." It has long been assumed that Darkness referred to nighttime, but actually it was the name of a **silent** *black chihuahua* that hung around the set without ever once barking, eventually inspiring the song. [16]

黑　默

228 sort of thing

然

The character in this frame is used as a suffix for certain adverbs and adjectives, and for too many other purposes to capture in a single key word. Rather arbitrarily, we have settled on "**sort of thing**." Reverting to the time when dog was more widely eaten than it is today (see FRAME 230), we see the *flesh* of a *chihuahua* roasting over a *cooking fire*—a "hot-diggity, dog-diggity" **sort of thing**. [12]

丿　勹　勺　夕　狄　然

❖ chatterbox

口口

We introduce this element here even though there is only one character we can use it in at this point, since the other examples will be scattered throughout the book. The two *mouths* naturally come to mean **chatterbox** if you recall Mark Twain's famous line: "If we were meant to talk more than listen, we would have two *mouths* and one ear." It will help here to think of a particular **chatterbox** you know, one of those persons who talk so incessantly that they could keep two *mouths* busy.

Alternatively, you could use the image of a pair of those *wind-up teeth* you find in novelty shops. In any case, we will use the word **chatterbox** throughout to identify it. [6]

口　口口

229

哭

cry [v.]

Here we have a *chatterbox* of a *chihuahua*. Listen to it gabbing away in its high, shrill voice and you have a pretty good idea of what you sound like when you **cry**. [10]

口口　哭

230

器

utensil

The picture in this character is not a pleasant one. It shows a tiny little *chihuahua* lying on a platter all stuffed and stewed and garnished with vegetables, its paws in the air and a cherry in its mouth. At each corner of the table sits an empty but eager *mouth*, waiting for the **utensils** to arrive so the feast can begin. [16]

口　口口　哭　哭　器

231

臭

stinking [ADJ.]

This character is a bit friendlier to the animal world than the last one. Our friend the *chihuahua* is alive and well, its *nose* in the air sniffing suspiciously after something **stinking** somewhere or other. [10]

自　臭

232

狗

dog

This is the generic character for **dog**, indicated by the elements for *pack of wild dogs* and *sentence*. Think of the twenty-six letters of the alphabet as a *pack of wild dogs* that run things down in order to work them into *sentences*. Here they are chasing after your fleet-footed pet terrier. When they catch up with the poor little creature, they circle around it and form themselves into the famous *sentence* that contains all the letters of the alphabet: "The quick brown **dog** jumped over the lazy fox." [8]

犭　狗

233 · detest

厭

Let the key word suggest someone who has come to **detest** everything and everything, for whom all the things of life have become meaningless. We are reminded of a vivid image of despair in Nietzsche's *Thus Spoke Zarathustra* that makes the character simple to remember.

Walking the dark *cliffs* at midnight, Zarathustra hears a dog (the *pooch*) howling. He approaches, and under the pale light of the *moon* he sees a shepherd lad lying on the ground with a thick, black snake hanging out of his mouth (like a long, *wagging tongue*). The snake had crawled in while the lad was asleep, grabbed on to his throat, and held fast. Zarathustra tells the shepherd to bite off the head of the snake and become free of the despair that holds him in tortured captivity, and cease to **detest** the things of life. [14]

厂 戸 肩 厭

234 · pressure [N.]

壓

Too much **pressure** in the classroom not only affects students' ability to learn, but it also has the dangerous effect of leading young children to *detest* time "wasted" on the play*ground*. If you try to picture the **pressure** in a literal, not just a psychological sense, the image will be easier to remember. [17]

厭 壓

235 · COW

牛

Can you see the "doodle" of a **cow** that has just been run over by a steamroller? The small dot in the first stroke shows its head turned to one side, and the next two strokes, the four legs. [4]

丿 𠂉 𠂇 牛

❖ When this character is used as a primitive, the same sense of *cow* is kept. Note only that when it is placed OVER another element, its tail is cut off, giving us 牛. In this case, and when the element appears on the left (牜), the order of the final two strokes is changed.

236   special ^(ADJ.)

特

Let the key word of this frame refer to something in a **special** class all its own—like the sacred *cows* of India that wander freely without fear of being butchered and ground into hamburger. Even though the practice is originally a Hindu one, and in any case no longer followed among the majority of Mahayana Buddhist monks, the Buddha's refusal to take the life of any sentient being makes it only fitting that *cows*, **special** as they are, should be placed on the sacred grounds of a *Buddhist temple* in this character. [10]

丿　ﾄ　牛　牛　特

237   declare

告

Folklore throughout the world tells us of talking animals who show a wisdom superior to that of human beings, and that same tradition has found its way into television shows and cartoons right in our own century. This character depicts a *cow* with a large *mouth* that utters, with oracular wisdom, answers to questions posed to her. She begins each reply by opening her *mouth* wide enough to swallow you whole and stating (in a thick southern drawl), "Aah do **declare**...."

Observe that the stroke order of the *cow* element changes in the abbreviated form it takes here. [7]

丿　ﾄ　牛　生　告

238   vast

浩

The word **vast** almost inevitably suggests an endless body of *water*. Only in the case of this character, it is not located in any of the known bodies of *water* but inside the large *mouth* of the oracular cow. Take a peek inside and see if you can see the waves splashing against her palate. [10]

氵　浩

239 先   before

Take this key word in its physical, not its temporal, sense (even though it refers to both). If you have a *cow* with *human legs,* as the elements show us here, it can only be because you have two people in a *cow* suit. Who would not prefer to be the one standing **before**, rather than the one that holds up the rear and becomes the "butt" of everyone's laughter! [6]

生   𠂯   先

240 洗   wash (v.)

This character is so logical that one is tempted to let the elements speak for themselves: *water . . . before.* Let's see what we can do to make it more memorable.

We all know the parental insistence inflicted on children, "**Wash** your hands *before* you come to the table." At some point, your mom gets so fed up with repeating it that she calls in a plumber to fix a small *water* spigot to the edge of the table in front of each chair. Mom dutifully **washes** her own hands to drop the hint, and everyone does the same in turn. Of course, we would end up with wet laps and *water* all over the floor, but at least everyone's hands would be clean. [9]

氵   洗

Lesson 12

In this the final lesson of Stories we introduce the useful compound primitive for metal and the elements needed to form it, in addition to picking up a number of stray characters that have fallen by the wayside.

---

umbrella

The actual character on which this primitive meaning **umbrella** is based will not show up until Book 2. Think of it as a large and brightly colored beach **umbrella**. If you compare this with FRAME 8, you will notice how the two strokes touch here, while the character for *eight* would leave a gaping leak in the top. [2]

241

introduce

介

The right way to enter a new situation is to have someone politely **introduce** you, so that you don't feel that you are intruding. This character shows a *walking stick* being **introduced** into an *umbrella* frame by someone shoving it into an already occupied slot in the *umbrella* stand at the door. First notice the vertical strokes: on the left is the curved umbrella handle, and on the right the straight *walking stick*. Now try to imagine the two parties tugging at their respective properties like two kids on a wishbone, creating a scene at the entrance of an elegant restaurant. So much for polite "introductions." [4]

242

world

界

Whoever it is that decides to *introduce* the construction of more and more buildings in our cities as "development projects" should be held accountable someday for what a mess we are making of the natural **world**, not to mention the living and working conditions of those who populate them. From a bird's-eye view, this glass-and-cement jungle begins to look more and more like a gigantic checkerboard (replacing the neatly partitioned *rice fields*). If you look closely at the character, you should be able to see a kind of movement taking place as still more buildings are being *introduced* into already cramped spaces. [9]

243	tea

茶

As everyone knows, **tea** is made from **tea** leaves. But the **tea** plant itself has its own *flowers,* which can be quite beautiful and add a special flavor to the **tea**, as the Chinese found out over 4,600 years ago. With the image of a terrace of *flowering* **tea** bushes in mind, picture a number of brightly painted and very l-o-n-g *wooden poles* (FRAME 191) placed here and there in their midst, with an *umbrella* at the top of each of them to shade the delicate-tasting **tea** *flowers.* [10]

meeting

This compound primitive depicts a **meeting** as a massive gathering of people under *one umbrella*. The full character from which this derives will be introduced immediately below. The important thing here is to picture the scene just described and associate it with the word **meeting**. [3]

244	meeting

Here is the full character for the primitive element introduced in the previous frame. The two added elements below, the *brains* impaled on the *horns* of a dilemma (see FRAME 172) and *tongues wagging in the mouths* create a memorable, and accurate, description of a lot of **meetings**. [13]

245 fit ^(v.)

合 The character for **fit** reads literally, top to bottom, as a *meeting of mouths*—which is a rather descriptive way of speaking of a romantic kiss. We all know what happens when there is no meeting of minds and when people's ideas don't *fit* with one another. But this character invites us to imagine what happened to the romance of a certain unfortunate couple whose *mouths* didn't *fit*. [6]

246 ha!

哈 This is a "sound character" for the sound of laughter. Write it twice and it is read—what else!—**ha-ha**. Now nothing *fits* the human *mouth* better than a good laugh, one of the few things that separate us scientifically from other primates. Can it be accidental that the sound of laughter is universal across languages? Another reason to say that it *fits* the *mouth* perfectly. [9]

247 pagoda

塔 On the left we see a mound of *dirt* and on the right, *flowers* made to *fit* together. The two combine to create a great **pagoda** made of *dirt,* with *flowers* by the tens of thousands made to *fit* together for the roofing of each of the layers. Be sure to put yourself in the scene and *fit* a few of the *flowers* in place yourself so that the image works its way into memory with full force. [13]

248   king

王

See what you can do to come up with a pictograph of a **king's** scepter here that suits your own idea of what it should look like. You might even begin with the basic element for *I-beam* and then try to fit the remaining third stroke in. [4]

一   二   王   王

❖ As a primitive, this character can mean either *king* or *scepter*, but it will usually be taken to mean *jewel* or *ball* (from the characters introduced in the following two frames.).

249   jade

玉

Note the *drop* here in the king's *scepter*, which is exactly what you would expect it to be: a gold staff with a large **jade** jewel on the handle, a symbol of his wealth and power. [5]

王   玉

❖ When this character is used as a primitive and retains its original shape, it will keep the original meaning of *jade*. When it appears on the left, however, it will be lacking the final stroke, making it the same as the character in the previous frame, 王. In such cases, its meaning will be *jewel* or *ball*.

250   ball

球

Immediately we introduce the primitive element for *ball* and we meet the full character for **ball** on which it is based. As an aid to remembering it, think of a catcher signaling the pitcher his *request* not for a strike but for a **ball**. As if he was going to throw his glove or his hat. What else can the pitcher throw? Heaven only knows what Alexander Cartwright was smoking when he gave it that name. [11]

251

現

present (ADJ.)

Do not think of a "gift" here, but of the **present** time, as distinct from the future and the past. The character gives us a *ball* in which we see the **present** moment—obviously a crystal *ball* that enables us to *see* things going on at the **present** time in faraway places. [11]

王　現

252

玩

play (V.)

The very first game people **played** dates back to the *beginning* of creation, in the Garden of Paradise. For those who see it as a story of original sin, it went something like the game children **play** called "hot potato." You take a *ball* and pass it around as quickly as possible until someone drops the *ball*, thereby losing. In the case of Adam and Eve, it was a piece of fruit from the forbidden tree. "It's not mine, it's his." "No it's not, she had it first…." In any case, if you see an original sin in all of this, then both of them clearly dropped the *ball* for the rest of us. [8]

王　玩

253

狂

crazy

We sometimes refer to people or ideas that are **crazy** as being "looney," which literally means driven mad by the light of the moon. The most famous of the "looneys" are the legendary lycanthropes or "wolfmen." Sometimes the transformation is only a temporary phenomenon; sometimes it is permanent. In the latter case, the poor chap takes off on all fours to live with the beasts. To remember this character, imagine one of these lycanthropes going **crazy** and setting himself up as *king* of a *pack of wild dogs* that roams about and terrorizes innocent suburban communities. [7]

犭　狂

254   emperor

皇

An **emperor**, as we all know, is a ruler—something like a *king* but higher in status. The *white bird* perched above the *king*, elevating him to "imperial" heights, is the messenger the **emperor** sends back and forth to the gods to request advice and special favors, something that *white birds* have long done in folklore throughout the world. [9]

白   皇

255   resplendent

煌

In this character we see a *fire-emperor*, **resplendent** in his glory. He is not an *emperor* who rules over *fire*, but one made of *fire*. His speeches, his temper, his eyes—everything about him is "fiery." [13]

火   煌

256   submit

呈

The trick to remembering this character lies in associating the key word **submit** with the line from the nursery rhyme about four and twenty blackbirds baked in a pie: "Wasn't this a dainty dish to set before the *king*?" If we think of **submit** as "setting before" or "presenting to," then all we have to do to complete the picture is imagine a *king* with his head thrown back and his *mouth* wide open as twenty-four blackbirds fly in one after the other. Dainty? [7]

口   呈

❖ Note that when this character is used as a primitive, in some fonts the first stroke of *king* is drawn from right to left and slanting downwards, replacing the usual horizontal stroke shown here, drawn left to right.

---

257   **whole**

全

Being **whole** suggests physical and spiritual health, "having one's act together." This character compares being **whole** to "being *king* under one's own *umbrella*," that is, giving order to one's own life. Granted it sounds terribly abstract, but what could be more abstract than the word **whole**? [6]

入   全

---

258   **logic**

理

We first referred to this character back in FRAME 169 to which you might want to return to have a peek. The image of **logic** we are given is something like a central *jewel* in a *computer*, like the *jewels* in old clocks that keep them running smoothly. Try to picture yourself making your way through all the RAMS and ROMS and approaching this shining *jewel*, a chorus of voices and a blast of trumpets in the background heralding the great seat of all-knowing **logic**. [11]

王   理

---

259   **lord**

主

"A man's home is his castle," goes the proverb from an age where it was the male who was **lord** of the household. Fundamentally, it means only that every one of us is a bit (or *drop*) of a *king* in our own environment. As for the positioning of the elements, if you take care to "read off" the primitives in this way, you won't end up putting the *drop* down below, where it turns the character into *jade*. [5]

丶   主

❖ When using this character as a primitive element, we set the key word aside entirely and take it as a pictograph of a solid brass *candlestick* (with the drop representing the flame at the top).

260 pour

注

Picture yourself trying to hold your hand steady as you **pour** *water* from a lighted *candlestick*. What could be more ridiculous, or simpler, as a way to recall this character? [8]

氵 注

261 gold

金

If this were not one of the most common characters you will ever have to write, we would apologize for having to give the explanation that follows. Anyway, we want to depict bars of **gold** bullion with an *umbrella* overhead to shade them from the heat (and perhaps to hide them as well). The bullion is made by melting down all the *scepters* of the kingdom, *drop* by *drop*, and shaping them into bars. [8]

丿 人 人 仝 仝 仝 全 金

❖ When this character is used as a primitive, it means not only *gold* but any *metal* at all.

262 copper

銅

Picture an order of *monks* serving as chaplains for the police force. Their special habit, made of protective *metal*, is distinguished by a row of **copper** buttons just like the "cops" they serve. [14]

丿 ケ ヒ 乍 午 午 余

金 銅

263 go fishin'

釣

The character we learned for *fishing* (FRAME 165) refers to the professional, net-casting industry, while the key word in this frame, **go fishin'**, is related to the pastime or sport. The odd thing is that your "go-fishin'" rod is a *golden ladle* which you are using to scoop *gold*fish out of a river. [11]

金 釣

---

264   needle ^(N.)

針

In FRAME 10 we referred ahead to this full character from which the primitive for *needle* (on the right) derives. Since we already expect that **needles** are made of *metal*, let us picture a set of solid *gold* darning **needles** to complete the character. [10]

金 針

---

265   nail ^(N.)

釘

Here we have the full character for **nail** from which the primitive element of the same meaning derived (see FRAME 86). As long as you picture the **nail** as made of pure *gold* and bending out of shape ever time you try to hammer it, you should have no trouble remembering it. [10]

金 釘

---

266   inscription

銘

Take **inscription** in the sense of the *name* you ask the jeweler to carve on a *gold* bracelet or inside a *gold* ring to identify its owner or communicate some sentimental message. It will help if you can recall the first time you had this done and the feelings you had at the time. [14]

金 銘

---

267   at ease

鎮

The first lie-detector machines of the twentieth century worked by wiring pieces of *metal* to the body to measure the amount of sweat produced when questions were asked. It was discovered that nervousness produced more sweat, indicating subconscious reactions when the *true* facts of the matter were getting too close for comfort. The only way to beat the apparatus is to have complete control over yourself and remain perfectly **at** ease. Picture yourself trying to do it while the examiners ask questions guaranteed to extract buckets of sweat from you. [18]

金　鎮

With that, we come to the end of the first part of this book. Before going on to the next section, it would be a good idea to return to the Introduction and read it once again. Anything that did not make sense at first should now be clear.

By this time, too, you should be familiar with the use of all the Indexes. If not, take a few minutes to study them, since you will no doubt find them useful in the pages ahead.

Plots

LESSON 13

BY THIS TIME, if you have been following along methodically frame by frame, you may find yourself growing impatient at the thought of having to read through more than 3,000 of these little stories. You probably want to move at a quicker pace and in your own way. Take heart, for that is precisely what we are going to start doing from now on. But if you happen to be one of those people who are perfectly content to have someone else do all the work for them, then brace yourself for the task that lies ahead.

We begin the weaning process by abbreviating the stories into simple plots, leaving it up to you to patch together the necessary details in a manner similar to what we did in the previous lessons. As mentioned in the Introduction, the purpose of the longer stories was to impress on you the importance of recreating a complete picture in imagination, and to insure that you did not merely try to associate words with *other words* but with *images*. The same holds true for the characters that remain.

Before setting out on our way again, a word of caution is in order. Left to its own, your imagination will automatically tend to add elements and see connections that could prove counterproductive in the long run. For example, you might think it perfectly innocent and admissible to alter the primitive meaning for *child* to *infant*, or that for *cliff* to *cave*. In fact, these changes would be confusing when you meet the characters and primitives with those meanings later on. You would return to the earlier characters and find that everything had become one great confusion.

You may have experienced this problem already when you decided to alter a story to suit your own associations. That should help you appreciate how hard it is to wipe out a story once you have learned it, particularly a vivid one. To protect yourself against this, stick faithfully to the key words as they are given, and try not to move beyond the range of primitive meanings listed. Where such confusion can be anticipated, a longer story will be presented as a protective measure, but you will have to take care of the rest.

We start our Plots with a group of 20 characters having to do with travel, and the primitives that accompany them: a *road*, a *car*, and a pair of *walking legs*.

❖

road

辶

The **road** envisioned here is a road for traffic, or a path or walkway. The natural sweep of these three simple strokes should be easy to remember, as it appears so often. [3]

丶　氵　辶

268

way

道

The key word carries both the sense of a road or **way** for transit and a **way** or method of doing something. The primitives here read: *heads* and *road*. You've probably heard about companies cleaning house and threatening that "*heads* are going to roll." Well, here is the *road* they are rolling on. If you want, think of it as the **Way** of the Bottom Line. [12]

首　道

269

guide (v.)

導

When we allow someone to **guide** us, we permit ourselves to be *glued* to a certain *way* of doing something, and try to "stick" to it. [15]

道　導

270

speedy

迅

This character shows a **Speedy** Gonzales wanna-be tearing down the highway in his '57 Chevy, only to be brought to an abrupt halt by the highway police who have scattered *hooks* and *needles* across the *road* to puncture his tires. [6]

乙　凡　迅

271

create

造

We sometimes think of **create** as meaning to make something out of nothing. Most of the time, however, there is something there to begin with, and often what is **created** doesn't amount to much of an improvement. Like politicians invoking the right of eminent domain to *declare* that a *road* will be built across the farmland that has been in your family for two hundred years. Some "creation." [10]

告 造

272

巡

patrol ^(v.)

The motorcycle police, exercising their duty to **patrol** the high-ways, are pictured in this character as a virtual *flood* washing down a *road*. [6]

巛 巡

273

逛

stroll ^(v.)

A *crazy* person decides to **stroll** down the middle of a very busy *road* during rush hour. [10]

狂 逛

274

車

car

You may keep the whole range of connotations for this key word, **car**, provided it does not interfere with the pictograph. Look for the front and back axles (the first and last horizontal strokes) and the seat in the carriage in the middle. [7]

❖ *Car, cart, wagon,* and *vehicle* may all be used as primitive meanings.

275

連

one after another

Imagine a convoy of large *vehicles* transporting heavy construc-tion equipment. They are following **one after another** and hog-ging the entire *road* for miles on end. [10]

車 連

276   lotus

蓮

Imagine yourself sitting on the edge of a **lotus** pond in the early morning as the pink and white **lotus** *flowers* softly pop into bloom, *one after another.* Given the subtlety of sound they make, it is no surprise that the opening of the **lotus** *flower* has served Buddhist monks for centuries as an image of the moment of spiritual enlightenment. [14]

❖   butcher

刖

The elements for *flesh* and *saber* here combine to create a compound element for a *butcher* and his trade. [6]

---

277   in front

前

Picture a pair of *horns* (borrowed from a Texas steer) hanging **in front** of a *butcher's* shop. [9]

❖ Following the explanation above, when this character is used as a primitive, the meaning will be a *butcher shop.*

---

278   shears

剪

Here, weld together a pair of *daggers* to make some meat **shears** for use in the *butcher shop.* [11]

前 剪

❖   slaughterhouse

俞

The first three strokes of this primitive, you will remember, are the primitive element for *meeting.* The most common *meeting* place for *butchers* is a **slaughterhouse.** [9]

279 輸 transport (v.)

Usually we employ *vehicles* to **transport** refrigerated meats, but here we have an entire *slaughterhouse* that is being carried across the country on wheels. [16]

車　輸

280 逾 exceed

The *road* to the *slaughterhouse* is a two-lane, one-way highway, crowded with animals of all sizes approaching their doomsday. To accommodate the chickens, the speed limit is set at 2 mph. A motorcycle cop drives up and down warning the buffalo and ostriches not to **exceed** the speed limit. [12]

俞　逾

❖ 夂 walking legs

We call this element **walking legs** because it indicates "legs in motion," whether you want to think of them as jogging or walking in long strides, as the shape seems to suggest. Be careful how you write it, with the first two strokes like a stylized "7." [3]

ノ　ク　夂

281 各 each

"Suum cuique" goes the popular Latin proverb. A certain disease of the English language makes it almost impossible to translate the phrase without gender bias. In any event, here we see someone walking with his/her *mouth* between his/her *walking legs*, giving us an image of "To **each** his/her own." [6]

夂　各

❖ The sense of the proverb should help when using this character as a primitive; otherwise, reduce it to its original elements. But do NOT associate it in any way with the word "every," which we shall meet later in another context.

---

282   **pattern**

格

To *each tree* its own **pattern**. Think of the key word as referring to the **patterns** on an array of Hawaiian shirts that you are dressing up the *trees* in your garden with to give to *each* its own identity and keep them distinct from one another. Take a moment to admire the whole fashion show. [10]

木 格

---

283   **guest**

客

When you are a **guest** in a courteous town, *each house*hold has its own way of welcoming you, and *each house* becomes your home. [9]

宀 客

---

284   **forehead**

額

As Miss Manners will be the first to tell you, out of respect one does not look straight into the eyes of one's *guests* of honor, but focuses on the knots of their neckties. Here, however, you are told to look at the upper part of the *head*, to the **forehead** of your *guest*. [18]

客 額

---

285   **summer**

夏

In the **summer**, fatigued by the heat, you have devised a creative and energy-saving fan: you have hired a couple of racewalking stars in training for the **summer** Olympics, stuck their *noses* to the *ceiling*, and asked them to practice by moving their *walking legs* around quickly in mid-air, giving you a fresh breeze and enhancing their chances of picking up a medal. [10]

一　百　夏

286 L.A.

洛

The key word (the well-known abbreviation of the city of Los Angeles) represents one of the important uses of this character in Chinese, namely, as the first character in the full compound for Los Angeles. How do we get from *each drop of water* to the city of **L.A.**? Think of what happens to the moisture in the air over that city. To *each droplet of water* is added its own particle of pollutant. Hence the gray blanket of smog that hangs over that unfortunate symbol of industrial devastation. [9]

氵　洛

287 fall (v.)

落

One of the worst consequences of the smog in cities like *L. A.* is that the petals of *flowers* exposed to the open air **fall** before their time—good news for the artificial *flower* industry, but bad news for those who prefer the real thing. [13]

艹　落

LESSON 14

THE FOLLOWING group of primitives, around which this lesson is designed, have to do with headgear and lids.

❖

⌐冖

crown

This pictograph of a simple **crown** is distinguished from the *roof* only by the absence of the chimney (the first *drop* at the top). It can be used for all the principal connotations of the word **crown**. We will meet the full character from which this element is derived later on in this lesson (in FRAME 293). [2]

$\prime$　⌐冖

288

兀

superfluous

A *crown* is supposed to be a sign of leadership, wisdom, and nobility. Without those virtues, it is a **superfluous** symbol, as in the case of the royal airhead depicted in this character. You can actually see the *wind* blowing between his ears. [4]

⌐冖　兀

289

沉

profound

See the philosopher lost in **profound** speculation on matters metaphysical, the *drops of water* on his forehead showing the intensity of his concentration, and the accusation of his more pragmatic neighbors that the whole thing is **profound**ly *superfluous*. [7]

氵　沉

290

軍

army

The *crowned vehicle* depicted here is a "chariot," symbol of a Caesar's **army**. [9]

冖 軍

❖ Used as a primitive this character means only *chariot*.

291　　　　　　　　　　　　　　　　　　　　　radiance

輝　Take advantage of the first syllable of the key word to think of the *ray* of light to the left. Now add the glittering *chariot* that is emitting those *rays* and you have **radiance**. [15]

光　輝

292　　　　　　　　　　　　　　　　　　　　　　carry

運　A row of "sweet" *chariots* "swinging low" to our *roads* is a sure sign that, as the old southern spiritual has it, the Lord is "comin' for to **carry** us home." [12]

辶　運

293　　　　　　　　　　　　　　　　　　　　crown [N.]

冠　By having the **crown** pass from one age to the next, a people keeps itself *glued to* its *beginnings*. [9]

冖　冠　冠

294　　　　　　　　　　　　　　　　　　　　dream [N.]

夢　To have a **dream** after going to bed is really the *crown* to a perfect *evening*. The *flower* petals over the *eyes* (instead of the "sand" that Westerners are used to finding there when they awake in the morning) only confirm the image of a pleasant **dream** suggested by the rest of this rather complex character. [14]

艹　苗　苩　夢

❖

亠

top hat

The broad rim and tall top of the **top hat** is pictured graphically here in these two simple strokes. [2]

At this point, by the way, you can revert back to FRAME 6. If you have had any trouble with that character, you now have the requisite elements to make a story: **Six** suggests the number of legs on a bug of some sort. Actually, it's a cockroach standing on its hind *animal legs* and sporting a tall silk *top hat* in a hopeless attempt to pass itself off as a gentlebug. [2]

` 亠

❖

亢

whirlwind

A formal high, silk *top hat* resting atop an eddy of *wind* represents a **whirlwind**. To keep it distinct from *wind*, try to picture the vortex, or tornado-like spinning movement, of a *whirlwind*. The next frame should help. [4]

亠 亢

295

坑

pit (N.)

A *whirlwind* begins to dig its way into the *soil* like a drill until it makes a deep **pit**. [7]

土 坑

296

高

tall

Recalling an image from FRAME 178, first see the *mouth* under the extraterrestrial's transparent *helmet*, and then the *mouth* under the *top hat* of one of his mates who has tried on the *top hat* only to find that this strange earthlings' headgear makes him look much, much **taller** than everyone else. [10]

亠 高 高 高

❖ As a primitive, this character keeps its sense of *tall* and its position at the top of other primitives, but its writing is abbreviated in one of two forms: when drawn with only the

first five strokes (亠), it keeps the generic meaning of *tall,*
but when the next two strokes are added (髙) it will mean a
tall *tiara,* since the element for *hood* is compressed into the
form of a *crown.*

297

享

enjoy

While the other *children* **enjoy** themselves at hopscotch and
jacks, this one, a *tall child*—but a REALLY *tall child,* 11 feet 4
inches and only in second grade—**enjoys** herself at less terres-
trial play: peeping into bird nests, chatting up the giraffes at the
zoo, and high-jumping over the pole-vault bar. [8]

298

熟

ripe

When fruit is **ripe** and in season, we can't get enough of it. The
problem is, we want to *enjoy* the taste of **ripe** peaches and man-
gos all year round. What we have here is a *bottle of pills* distilled
from **ripe** fruit, after stewing for hours over a *cooking fire,* into
"essence of peach" and "essence of mango." *Enjoy* them whenever you want. [15]

299

亭

pavilion

Think of all the **pavilions** at County Fairs or World Expos you
have wandered into or seen advertised in the media, and you
will no doubt see rising up among them the towering *spike* of a
structure with a revolving restaurant at the top—often the only
pavilion to survive the event. The difference here is that the restaurant is in the shape of a high, bejeweled golden *tiara.* [9]

300

亮

shiny

To restore those musty old *tiaras* in the museum back to their
original **shiny** luster, it occurs to you to try an air blaster. Picture

yourself with a tank of compressed air strapped to your back, protective goggles over your eyes, and nozzle in hand. As you approach the row of irreplaceable treasures, you squeeze the trigger and a hurricane-force *wind* sends the whole display flying against the far wall and landing in a heap of junk. [9]

---

301   capital

京

When you think of a **capital** city, think of the *tall*, domed capitol building with swarms of *small* folk gathered around its base, probably demonstrating for their government's attention. [8]

❖ As a primitive element, this character will take the meaning of a *capitol building*.

---

302   cool

涼

Here we see a *capitol building* getting a **cool** shower (the *drops of water*), probably because some politician has done something scandalous again. [11]

氵　涼

---

303   scenery

景

Scenery is depicted as a *sun* rising over a *capitol building*, which is as close as some city dwellers get to natural **scenery** for years at a time! [12]

日　景

---

304   at once

就

The key word **at once** suggests an order to be carried out immediately. In this case, it is our little *Frankenpooch* being summoned to come **at once** to the *capitol building* to testify before a subcommittee on organized crime in the canine world. [12]

京　就

❖

吉

lidded crock

Soil over the *mouth* of a container gives us a piece of clay pottery with its lid. Behold the **lidded crock**. [6]

土　吉

305

周

circumference

Look more closely at your *lidded crock* and you will see little ruler marks along its bottom edge. This is so you can use it to calculate the **circumference** of your motorcycle *helmet*: just begin at a fixed point and turn the *lidded crock* around and around, keeping it flush against the side of the *helmet*, until you come back to your starting point. If you kept track of how many turns and part-turns your *lidded crock* made, you now know the **circumference**. [8]

冂　周

❖ As a primitive, this character can take the added significance of a *lap*.

306

週

week

Picture a circular *road* with seven markers on it, one for each day of the **week**. When you have walked one complete *lap* on this *road*, you shall have completed one **week**. [11]

周　週

307

士

soldier

The shape of this character, slightly differing from that for *soil* by virtue of its shorter final stroke, hints at a broad-shouldered, slender-waisted **soldier** standing at attention. [3]

一　十　士

308   lucky

吉

Here we see a statue of the famous *Soldier* of Good Fortune, G. L. ("Good Luck") Joe, standing on a street with a gigantic open *mouth*. Every day people walk up to and stick their heads down deep inside. As the superstition goes, G. L. Joe will make this their **lucky** day. [6]

士 吉

❖ When this character is used as a primitive, we shall take this shape to mean an *aerosol can*, from the *mouth* and the very tight-fitting *lid* (note how it differs here from the *lidded crock*).

309   buy (v.)

買

We have waited to introduced this character here because it forms a pair with the following frame. Depicted here is a woman at a fish market to **buy** some quality *oysters*. You should be able to see her *eyeball* right down on one of the *oysters*, examining its quality at close range. [12]

丶 冖 冖 罒 罒 買

310   sell

賣

The companion character to *buy* is that for **sell**. The only difference is the *soldier* watching the person eyeing something to *buy*, just to be sure that everything is properly paid for. [15]

 賣

LESSON 15

IN THIS LESSON WE consider a group of primitives associated one way or another with schooling. Be sure to give your stories enough time to come to life in imagination, because your images will need a lot more vividness than these brief "plots" allow for. You know that you are NOT giving enough time when you find yourself memorizing definitions rather than playing with images.

❖   brush

This primitive element, not itself a character, is a pictograph of a writing **brush**. Let the first three strokes represent the hairs at the tip of the **brush**, and the following two strokes the thumb and forefinger that guide it when you write. Note how the long vertical stroke, cutting through everything, is drawn last. This is standard procedure when you have such a stroke running the length of a character. However, as we saw in the case of *cow*, when this primitive appears on top of another primitive, its "tail" is cut off, giving us 聿. [6]

---

311   book^(N.)

The sage talks rapidly with his *tongue wagging in his mouth*, while the *brush* of the scribe runs apace to write down the master's words in a **book** for posterity.

Just as the stroke order changed in the abbreviated form that *cow* took as a primitive (FRAME 235), here, too, the last two strokes of the element for *brush* are drawn in a sequence different from that of the frame above. [10]

312 drawing (N.)

畫

The character for **drawing** begins, logically enough, with a *brush*. But what in heaven's name, you ask, are those *brains* doing lying on the *floor*? We leave the rest of the story of you. [12]

畫 畫 畫

313 scratch (V.)

劃

Remember the game where one child would **scratch** a *drawing* of something on another kid's back to see if she could guess what it was? Here we have a troupe of bored French Foreign Legionnaires playing the game with long, shining *sabers*. [14]

畫 劃

❖ taskmaster

First find the long rod (the first stroke), held in the hand of someone seated (the next three strokes, not unlike the pictograph for *woman*, but quite different from that for *walking legs* introduced in Lesson 13). The only thing left to do is conjure up the memory of some **taskmaster** (or taskmistress) from your past whom you will "never forget." [4]

丿 乚 ㇇ 攵

314 attack (V.)

攻

A foreman, the *taskmaster* at a large construction site, orders his workers to pick up their *I-beams* and **attack** the house of the little old grandmother who refuses to leave the home she has lived in all of her life. [7]

工 攻

315 fail

敗

The *taskmaster* lays the rod to all the *clams* that **fail** to make the grade in Marine School. [11]

貝　敗

316

故

deliberately

To do something wrong **deliberately** is to risk the ire of that most *ancient* of *taskmasters:* the law. [9]

古　故

317

救

rescue [v.]

Usually it is the school *taskmaster* who is *requesting* something or other of us, but here you are drowning in the swimming pool and the only one around is that most dreaded of all your curricular *taskmasters*, your English poetry teacher. You carefully parse your words: "I respectfully *request* that you **rescue** me immediately." [11]

求　救

318

敬

revere

In front of someone you **revere**, you get self-conscious and may try to speak in *flowery sentences*. The *taskmaster* at the right is drilling you in the practice of "polite language." [13]

艹　苟　敬

319

敞

spacious

The leap from *esteem* and *taskmaster* to **spacious** seems huge, but if we associate the key word with the song "America the Beautiful," it becomes but a small step. "O beautiful for **spacious** skies..." begin the well-known lyrics that *esteem* the natural beauties with which the country has been blessed. But then, directly in the second stanza, the song enjoins the country to "Confirm thy soul in self-control," reminding us of the need to be *taskmasters* over our selfish appetites. [12]

尚　敞

320

言

say

Of all the things we can do with our *mouths*, speech is the one that requires the greatest distinctness and clarity. Hence the character for **say** has four little sound waves, indicating the complexity of the achievement. (The hand-drawn form, unlike the printed form, begins with something like a *top hat*.) [7]

丶　亠　言　言　言

❖ When this character is used as a primitive, it will often be given the meaning of *words*.

321

警

police (N.)

For all the negative things some people have to say about the **police**, when they get pulled over on the highway, chances are they bite their tongues and make a special effort to *revere* the officers' *words*, hoping to get off with just a warning. [20]

敬　警

322

計

plan (N.)

Words and a *needle* combine to form the character for a **plan**. Think of the *needle* on some kind of meter or gauge, depending on what kind of **plan** you intend for your story. [9]

言　計

323

獄

prison

Here we have a typical scene in a high-security **prison** for the scum of the canine world: a weak and vulnerable *chihuahua* (doing time for insider trading) surrounded on the **prison** yard by a ferocious looking *pack of wild dogs* (all of them long-timers and hardened criminals). The only thing the *chihuahua* has to protect himself from the pack are his shrill and frightened *words*. [14]

犭　猞　獄

324

討

condemn

Words spoken to **condemn** us stick to us like *glue* in a way no other *words* can. [10]

言　討

325

訓

instruction

The personalism connoted by the word **instruction**, as opposed to "teaching" or "discipline," suits the picture here of *words* guiding one's progress like the gentle flowing of a *stream*. Even the etymology of the word **instruction** suggests the sense of "pouring into". [10]

言　訓

326

話

talk (N.)

That the *words* of the *tongue* should form the character for **talk** is no surprise. Think of the phrase, "He's all **talk**," and a story should not be far behind. [13]

言　話

327

詩

poem

Since silence is treasured so highly at a *Buddhist temple*, the *words* spoken there must be well chosen. Perhaps this is why the records of the monks often read to us like **poems**. [13]

言　詩

328

語

language

Whereas the character for *say* and *talk* (FRAMES 320 and 326) focused on the actual talking, the character for **language** stresses the fact that although it is *I* (remember: the *literary I*) who use them, the *words* of a **language** are not my own. [14]

言　語

---

329 read (v.)

讀

In the age of advertising, most *words* we **read** are out to *sell* some product or point of view. [22]

言 讀

330 tune (N.)

調

A complete **tune** is composed not only of a succession of notes but also of one *lap* of the *words* that go with it. [15]

言 調

331 discuss

談

In attempts to **discuss** an issue, the fervor of one's convictions can come to the surface and create an *inflammation* of *words* (if you will, the "cuss" in **discuss**). [15]

言 談

332 this

這

When you are driving along, you sometimes see *words* written on the *road* before you, usually telling to stop or yield or slow down or watch out for something or other. In this case, we see only the word **This** written in giant white letters. Imagine the scene, and the confusion it would cause you for hours afterwards. [10]

言 這

LESSON 16

IN THIS SHORT lesson of 20 characters we come to an interesting cluster of primitive elements—unique among all those we have met or will meet throughout this book—built up step by step from one element. Be sure to study this lesson as a unit in order to appreciate the similarities and differences of the various elements, which will appear frequently later on.

---

 arrow

Here we see a pictograph of a long and slightly warped **arrow**. By extending the short final stroke in both directions, you should see the **arrow**head without any difficulty. The hook at the bottom represents the feathers at the butt end. When it serves as a semi-enclosure for other primitives, the first stroke is drawn longer, as we shall see in the following frames. [3]

---

333 **style** (N.)

Take **style** in its sense of some fashion design or model. Then let the element *arrow* and *work* stand for the well-known **style** of shirts known as "*Arrow* shirts" because of the little *arrow* sewn on each one. [6]

---

334 **test** (N. / V.)

When a manufacturer produces a new *style* for the market, the first thing that is done is to run a **test** on consumers, asking them to *say* frankly what they think about the product. Never mind the anachronism (the character was there well before our capitalistic market system) if it helps you remember. [13]

335 halberd

戈

A halberd is a kind of lance made up of a long, arrowhead-shaped pike with two curved blades below it. If you don't have one in your closet, you might consult a dictionary. [4]

一 弋 戈 戈

❖ When this character is used as a primitive, we will revert to a friendler meaning. Think of the third stroke as a kind of deocrative tassle fixed to the shaft of an *arrow* to indicate that it is no longer a weapon but a symbol of a *fiesta*.

336 or

或

Unless you were one of those saintly children who always did what they were told, you should have no trouble associating the key word in this frame with the stern warning of a parent or teacher to do something—"**or** else!" Here we see a rather grim depiction of the **or** else: you are lying down with your *mouth* on the *floor* (an inventive substitute to wearing a dunce-cap and sitting in the corner) while everyone else is out enjoying the *fiesta*.

Just as the phrase "**or** else" does not necessarily imply dire consequences but can be used as a simple indication of an alternative, so, too, this character is a simple conjunction. Pay special attention to the stroke order. [8]

一 口 或 或 或 或

337 burglar

賊

From a **burglar's** point of view, a *fiesta* is an occasion to take out the old lock-picking *needle* and break into the unattended safe filled with the family *shells* (the old form of money, as we saw in FRAMES 76 and 77). [13]

貝 貝 財 賊

❖

Thanksgiving

To make this primitive more concrete, we choose the word **Thanksgiving**. The term, as the primitives make clear, refers to a *"land fiesta"* or harvest feast. [6]

338

戋

laden

It is not hard to think of the folks from the Little House on the Prairie riding a *cart* **laden** to overflowing with all the trimmings of a great *Thanksgiving* feast. [13]

339

鐵

iron (N.)

You *submit* a bar of **iron** to the annual *Thanksgiving* contest for the thing for which the town is most thankful. At first, everyone laughs at you, but when the judges stop to think of how important it is for so many of the things we depend on, **iron** wins the *gold* medal. [21]

❖

parade

Note first the order of the writing. The second stroke, which has been added to *fiesta*, gives us a full-fledged enclosure, because of which we should always think of this as a **parade** OF something or other, namely whatever is inside the enclosure. [5]

340

茂

lush

The sense of the key word **lush** is that of something growing luxuriously, though not necessarily in excess—in this case a whole *parade* of weeds (outcast *flowers*). By way of exception, the *flowers* take their normal place OVER the enclosure. [9]

艹 茂

341

成

turn into

Let the phrase "**turn into**" suggest some sort of a magical change. What happens here is that the *parade* marching down main street **turns into** a *dagger*-throwing bout between competing bands. Note how only one stroke has to be added to make the change. [6]

一 厂 厃 成

342

城

city

In this frame, we see a mound of *dirt* that is being *turned into* the walls of a **city** (the way you may have built a sand castle as a child playing on the beach). [9]

土 城

343

誠

sincere

The sure test of how **sincere** you are is whether or not your *words* are being *turned into* deeds. [13]

言 誠

❖

戍

march

As distinct from the *parade*, the **march** points to a formal demonstration, whose emotions are generally a far cry from the happy spirit of the *parade*. The inclusion of the *one* gives a sense of the singlemindedness and unity of the group joined in the **march**. As was the case with *parade,* the primitive inside the enclosure indicates who or what is **marching**. [6]

一 厂 厂 戌 戍 戍

---

344 might (N.)

威

Here we see a *march* of *women* demonstrating on behalf of equal rights, a show of **might** not always welcome to the male chauvinist population. [9]

厂　反　威

---

345 destroy

滅

Picture a *march* of *flames* demonstrating against the Fire Department for their right to **destroy**, but being doused with *water* by the police riot squads. [13]

氵　沪　泜　滅

---

346 everybody

咸

Reading this character off literally, we have *mouths* on the *march*. Now as the song reminds us, "**Everybody** needs somebody sometime." Here, quite literally, the *marching mouths* are desperately in need of some BODY. (For that matter, everyBODY needs a *mouth*.) Imagine them singing the song and you should feel a twinge of pity that will stick this character in memory. [9]

厂　后　咸

---

347 reduce

減

A group of unquenchable *mouths* sets out on a *march* across the country, drinking *water* wherever they can find it, until their imbibitions **reduce** the *water* supply to a trickle, triggering a national disaster. Of course, you are free to create your own image with the primitives *water* and *everybody*. [12]

氵　減

---

348 list (N.)

單

As in the last frame, we are opting to break up the first primitive, *chatterbox*, into its component primitives. Picture yourself going through a **list** of persons you and the captain of the other team have to divide into two teams for a sporting event. The names are not written on a sheet of paper but on the petals of a *sunflower*. The ones you choose you pluck off and pop into your *mouth*; the other captain does the same, putting his choices in his *mouth*.

This is a good example of how it is sometimes helpful to revert a composite primitive element (*chatterbox*) to its component parts. [12]

口　品　單

349　　　　　　　　　　　　　　　　　　　　　war (N.)

戰　Victory in **war** is commonly celebrated as a national *fiesta*—until a knock comes at the door informing your family that the younger brother or son whose return you are awaiting is on the *list* of those who will be returning in a pine box. [16]

單　戰

❖

㦰　The **floats** that are such an important part of a *fiesta* are not just static displays on wheels, but often have a *fiesta* of their own going on—dancers, musicians, acrobats, and so forth. The primitive for **float**, accordingly, shows a *fiesta* atop a *fiesta*. [8]

float

㦰

350　　　　　　　　　　　　　　　　　　　　coin (N.)

錢　Those special *gold*-colored tokens minted each year for the Mardi Gras and thrown into the crowds by people on the *floats* give us the character for **coins**. [16]

金　錢

351   shallow

淺

An entourage of *floats* going from one town to the next must always seek a **shallow** place to cross the *water*. Try to picture what happens if they don't. [11]

352   cheap

賤

When the town tightwad agrees to enter a *float* in the annual parade, he first calculates how many *clams* it is going to set him back and then starts pinching pennies to make it as **cheap** as possible. [15]

Lesson 17

Because of the rather special nature of that last group of primitives, it might be a good idea not to rush too quickly into this lesson until you are sure you have them all learned and fitted out with good images. Here we will take up another set of primitives built up from a common base, though fewer in number and lacking the similarity of meaning we saw in the last lesson.

| 353 | stop (v.) |

止 The character for **stop** is easiest to learn as a pictograph, though you have to take a moment to see it. Take it as a rather crude drawing of a footprint, the track that is left when your foot has **stopped** long enough to make an impression. The first three strokes represent the front of the foot and the last one, the heel. The big toe (the second stroke sticking out to the right) indicates that this is a left foot. [4]

$$| \quad \vdash \quad \text{止} \quad 止$$

❖ Although the meaning of *stop* will be retained, we will return often to the pictographic meaning of *footprint*. When the last two strokes are moved to look like this 止, it means a whole *trail of footprints*, as you might find on the beach. We will not see an example of this until FRAME 973.

| 354 | footstep |

步 *Footprints* that follow one another a *few* at a time indicate **footsteps**. Don't forget what we mentioned back in FRAME 104 about the abbreviation of the element for *few* when it appears under another element. [7]

$$\text{止} \quad \text{少} \quad \text{歩} \quad 歩$$

355

涉

ford (v.)

One way to **ford** a body of *water* is to wade across it on foot. You need to take your *footsteps* one after the other, but unlike a stroll on dry land, you have to be careful to keep your balance and not end up in the *water*. Remember what is feels like to walk gingerly on the slippery bottom of a shallow stream, calculating your every *footstep* as you go. [10]

氵　涉

356

頻

repeatedly

The image of something occurring **repeatedly**, over and over again, is of having one's *head* walked on, a succession of *footsteps* trampling on your cranium. [16]

步　頻

357

肯

agree

Seeing *footprints* on someone's *flesh* indicates a rather brutal way of having persuaded that person to **agree**. [8]

止　肯

358

企

look forward to

Who doesn't **look forward to** *stopping* under a large beach *umbrella* for a day of relaxation and "dolce far niente"? [6]

人　企

359

歲

years of age

The character indicating one's **years of age** pictures a *few footprints marching* along. No feet, just the *footprints*. [13]

止　庐　炉　歲

360 — military (ADJ.)

武

Think of the 24-hour clock, also known as "**military** time," as a watch face whose numbers actually go from 1 to 24, but which has only the hour hand on it (the elements for *one* and *arrow*), due to cutbacks in **military** expenditure. Now all you have to do is find a way to introduce the element that can mean either *stop* or *footprint*. Be sure to retain a **military** flavor in your image. [8]

一　二　正　武　武

361 — levy (N.)

賦

A **levy** can be imposed for any number of reasons, but here it is pictured as a certain number of *clams* (money) collected by the powers that be to offset current *military* expenses—presumably so they can get back the minute hand for watches like the one in the last frame. [15]

貝　賦

362 — correct (V./ADJ.)

正

"A journey of a thousand miles begins with a single step," says the Chinese proverb. Here we see *one footprint*, complementing that proverb with the sound advice that if the first step is not **correct**, the rest of the journey will be off track. This is the ideal that teachers are supposed to have in **correcting** their students, and parents in **correcting** their children. [5]

一　正

363 — politics

政

To the many definitions for **politics** that already exist, this character offers yet another: *correct taskmastering*. When those in **politics** twist this ideal and start maneuvering people to their own advantage, it is time to elect a *correct taskmaster*. [9]

正　政

❖

疋

mending

This primitive differs from the character for *correct* only by the movement added to the last two strokes, the "-ing" of **mending** if you will. But take a more concrete sense, like **mending** holes in socks. [5]

364

定

settle on

To **settle on**, in the sense of deciding on a certain course of action, is likened here to *mending* one's *house*. [8]

宀　定

365

走

walk⁽ᵛ·⁾

To **walk**, we are told here, has the effect of *mending* the *soil*. If you consider what driving an automobile over the *soil* does to it, taking more time off to **walk** might not be a bad idea.

Note that the final stroke of *soil* doubles up with the first stroke of *mending*. Of course, you could also use *soil* and *trail of footprints* as the primitive elements, but if you do, you're on your own. [7]

366

超

transcend

Things that are beneath us tempt us to be satisfied with less than we are capable of. It is the things that **transcend** us that *summon* us to *walk* the path to a higher state.

Note in this and the following frame how the element for *walk* can embrace other elements from below, much the same way as the element for *road* does. In order to do this, the final stroke needs to be lengthened. [12]

367   surpass

越

Here we see two *parades* in competition, each trying to **surpass** the other by *walking* at breakneck pace from one town to the next. Note the little "hook" at the end of the first stroke of the element for *parade*. This is the ONLY time it appears like this in the characters treated in these books. [12]

走 走 赱 越

368   be

是

"To **be**, or not to be: that is the question." Hamlet's soliloquy is a prime example of how memorizing a little Shakespeare can *mend* a *tongue wagging in the mouth*, transforming the broken speech of everyday English into a few minutes of golden eloquence. Like Hamlet, we, too, are riddled with doubt. "To Shakespeare or not to Shakespeare: that **be** the question." [9]

日 是

369   topic

題

The **topic** of your term paper appears at the top of the first *page*. That *be* what your paper's about, dude. [18]

是 題

❖   stretch

辶

The primitive meaning to **stretch** might at first seem similar to that for *road*. Take a moment to study it more carefully and you will see the difference. Like *road*, this character holds other primitives above its sweeping final stroke. [3]

乛 辶 辶

370   **build**

建

To **build** something complex, you first need to draw a set of plans (the writing *brush*) and then *s-t-r-e-t-c-h* your drawing out to scale in reality. [9]

聿　建

---

371   **prolong**

延

To **prolong** something enjoyable, like a vacation, is to *stretch* it out for as long as you can. If you look closely, you can see a stopper (the long *drop*) halting the progress of the *footprints* of time. [8]

ノ　正　延

---

372   **nativity**

誕

The key word, of course, calls to mind the feast of Christmas. As the famous poem at the start of St. John's gospel tells us, the **nativity** we celebrate at Christmas had its origins at the very start of time and governs all of human history. Celebrating the **nativity** *prolongs* the memory of the eternal *Word* in time and space. [15]

言　誕

❖   **ZOO**

疋

To avoid confusion with the animals that will be showing up, this primitive will signify a **zoo**. Except for the downward hook at the end of the first stroke, this element is indistinguishable from *mending*. Perhaps by now you have developed a quick eye for such details. If not, you will before long. [5]

フ　丁　下　疋　疋

373   clear (ADJ.)

楚

If you build a *zoo* in the *woods*, the animals might feel comfortable, but the visitors wouldn't get a **clear** view of anything but the trees. [13]

林   楚

374   foundation

礎

This character depicts a corner*stone*, which was not—as it is today—a decorative slab of marble set in a corner of a finished building. Rather, it was the first *stone* laid as a *clear* guide for all the other *stones* to follow. It was, quite literally, a **foundation** *stone*. [18]

石   礎

LESSON 18

THE THREE GROUPS of characters brought together in this rather long lesson are clustered around three sets of primitives dealing respectively with cloth and clothing, weather, and postures.

375	clothing

衣　At the top we see the *top hat*, and at the bottom a pictographic representation of the folds of a piece of clothing. If you break the four folds into two sets of two strokes, you will find it easier to remember the character for **clothing**. [6]

❖　When this character is used as a primitive element, particular attention has to be paid to the changes in shape that it can undergo. In fact, it is the most volatile of all the characters we shall treat, and for that reason we will assign distinct meanings to each of the variant shapes.

　　When it appears to the left, it looks like this: 衤, and we shall generally take it to mean a *cloak* or *cape*. At the bottom, when attached to the stroke immediately above it, the first two strokes (the *top hat*) are omitted, giving us: 𧘇, which we shall take to mean a *scarf*.

　　On rare occasions, the final four strokes are drawn with the first two strokes slightly repositioned to give us 𧘇. We will refer to this element as a *bandana*. An example will not show up until FRAME 610.

　　Occasionally the element can be torn right across the middle, with the first two strokes appearing at the top and the last four at the bottom of another primitive or cluster of primitives: 衣, in which cases we shall speak of a *top hat and scarf*.

　　And finally, of course, the element can keep its original character shape, along with its original meaning of *clothing* in general.

Note that when any of the above forms have something beneath them (as in FRAME 379), the third from final stroke is "unhooked," like this: 衤.

376 裡   inside

All you need to do is imagine a *computer* sewn to the **inside** of your *clothing*, and you are equipped to begin your career as a spy. [13]

This character can also be written 裏. If you look closely, you will see that it uses the same primitive elements as the story above, but arranges them differently: *top hat and scarf . . . computer.*

377 哀   grief

A drunken sot in a tattered *top hat and* soiled silk *scarf* with a giant *mouth* guzzling something or other gives **grief** to family and friends alike. It sounds like a role W. C. Fields might have played with relish. [9]

亠   吂   哀

378 袁   Yuan

It is used today as a family name, well illustrated by **Yuan** Shikai (1859–1916). As President of the Republic of China and successor to Sun Yatsen, he remains a very controversial figure. The *lidded crock* and *scarf* should be easy enough to associate with a suspicious politician. [10]

吉   袁

379 遠   distant

The **distant** figure on the *road* is *Yuan* Shikai, receding into the annals of suspicious politicians. [13]

380   bad

壊

When we introduced the character for *water* back in FRAME 126, we noted that one of its primitive element shapes (to which we assigned the meaning *snowflake*) often appears one way in block print and another in handwritten or calligraphic form. Here we see an example of just that.

There are a lot of elements to work with here in creating a story for **bad**. It begins with *dirt* and passes on to the *top hat and scarf* which sandwiches two more elements: *eyeball* and *snowflake*. Now, while some people have the capacity to find something good in everything, here we see a pessimistic aristocrat (in *top hat and scarf)* with his *eyeball* fixed on a *snowflake* and looking for the tiniest speck of *dirt* in it to satisfy his macabre view of reality. [19]

土 扩 垆 壊 壊

381   elementary

初

The primitives here take care of themselves: *cloak* and *dagger*. And to whom might those terms apply? "**Elementary**, my dear Watson." [7]

ヽ ヲ ネ ネ 初

382   towel

巾

The basic meaning of this character is a **towel**. Its shape suggests a super-thin fashion model who has just stepped out of the bath and thrown a **towel** over her shoulders. [3]

丨 冂 巾

383   cloth

布

Think of a bolt of terry **cloth** that the maid drags along *by her side,* cutting out new *towels* as they are needed and saving herself the trouble of doing the extra laundry. [5]

一 广 布

384   hat

帽

Because of some *risk* or other (you decide on the details), you tie up a makeshift **hat** out of a dirty old *towel*. [12]

巾 帽

385   curtain

幕

Instead of the usual gates, this *graveyard* has a **curtain** at its entrance sewn together from *towels* that the occupants had stolen from hotels around the world, come back to haunt them after death. So next time you think of slipping that beautifully imprinted *towel* with the logo of a hotel into your suitcase, remember that one day it will be **curtains** for both of you. [14]

莫 幕

❖   white towel

帛

This primitive element is simple to remember. All you need do is read off the elements that make it up: *white towel*. [8]

白 帛

386   cotton

棉

Cotton usually grows on bushes, but here we see it growing on a rather large *tree*. The clumps of **cotton** are big, in fact, the size of large *white towels*. When you get tired of picking, you take one of them and use it to wipe your brow. [12]

木 棉

387   help (v.)

幫

Remembering the little Dutch boy who **helped** save the town from a flood by sticking his thumb in the dike, you **help** save your apartment from an overflowing bath by *sealing* off the bottom of the bathroom door with a *white towel*. [17]

封 幫

---

388   market^(N.)

市

Dressed in nothing but a bath *towel* and *top hat*, one sets off to the **market** in search of a bargain or two. [5]

亠 市

---

389   lungs

肺

One is surprised, strolling through the *market*, to find amidst the *flesh* hung out for sale a slab marked: **lungs**. [9]

月 肺

❖   apron

帀

The *towel* that has edges trimmed with little *crowns* is the cook's **apron**. [5]

冖 帀

---

390   sash

帶

The part of the *apron* where one finds the buckle (represented pictorially by the first six strokes, whose order of writing should be carefully noted) is on the **sash**. It may help if you think of one of those giant flashy buckles on the title belts that professional wrestlers compete for. [10]

一 十 卄 卄 卅 卋 帶

---

391   stagnant

滯

People who have been "*sashed*" to something (whether their mother's apron strings or a particular job) for too long are like *water* that has stopped moving: they become **stagnant**. [13]

氵 滯

❖ belt

冂

This primitive, derived from that for *towel*, is always hung on another vertical stroke, and takes the meaning of a **belt**. [2]

丨　冂

❖ thorn

朿

Here we see a *belt of* **thorns** wrapping itself around a *tree* and choking the life out of it. [6]

一　厂　冂　市　束　朿

392 thorn

刺

The full character for **thorn** differs only by the addition of the *saber* to the right, presumably to indicate how the poor tree feels as it is being cut into by the heartless *thorns*. [8]

朿　刺

393 system

制

This character shows a unique **system** for leading a *cow* to the slaughterer's *saber*: tie a *belt* about its waist and fix that *belt* to an overhead cable, pulling the *cow* up into the air where it hangs suspended, helpless against the fate that awaits it. [8]

丿　ㄏ　ㅌ　片　乍　制　制

394 manufacture [v.]

製

To **manufacture** *clothing* nowadays one needs an international *system* of production and distribution. The label sewn into so many articles of *clothing* indicating their origin from other parts of the planet shows how commonplace it has become to **manufacture** goods on a large scale. [14]

制 製

395 utter

云

This character is meant to make visible that invisible but oh-so-familiar *rising cloud* of hot air originating at the podium of some boring professor you know who **utters** his pet theories while looking off into the distance with an air of self-absorption, completely oblivious of his audience. [4]

一 二 云 云

❖ When used as a primitive element, this character will take the meaning of a *rising cloud* of something or other.

396 rain (N.)

雨

This character, also a primitive, is one of the clearest instances we have of a complex pictograph. The top line is the sky, the next three strokes a pair of clouds, and the final four dots the **rain** collected there and waiting to fall. [8]

一 厂 厂 币 币 币 雨 雨

❖ Used as a primitive this character can mean either *rain* or *weather* in general. To conserve space, it is usually contracted into a crown by shortening the second and third strokes into a *crown* like this: . Note how the four dots are straightened out in this case.

397 cloud (N.)

雲

Here is the full character for **cloud** from which the primitive for a *rising cloud* derives. **Clouds** can begin with *rising clouds* of vapor that ascend from the surface of the planet and then gather to form those dark, ominous **clouds** that eventually dump their *rain* back on the earth. [12]

雫 雲

| 398 | thunder ^(N.) |

雷

The full rumble and roar and terror of **thunder** is best felt not with your head tucked under your pillow safe in bed, but out in an open *rice field* where you can get the real feel of the *weather*. [13]

| 399 | electricity |

電

Think of the legend of Benjamin Franklin out in the *rain* flying a kite with a key on the string. (If he had actually used a key, he would have run the danger of being electrocuted.) This character knows better, showing us only a pictograph of the kite. [13]

| 400 | frost ^(N.) |

霜

Think of **frost** as a venture in which the malevolent forces of *weather* cooperate with *one another*. See them sitting around a conference table and finally deciding to allow a small amount of moisture to fall just before a short and sudden freeze. [17]

| ❖ | ice |

冫

The condensation of the three drops we have been using to mean *water* into two drops signals the solidifying of *water* into **ice**. Note that when this primitive appears to the left, it is written like the first and the last strokes of the element for *water* to give us 冫 . However, when it appears under another primitive, it looks more like the first two strokes of the *water* primitive: 冫. [2]

| 401 | ice [N.] |

冰　This is the full character for **ice** from which we derived the primitive element in the previous frame. The presence of the primitive for *water* in its full form tells us that we have something to do with *water* here, and the primitive for *ice* tells us what kind of water. [6]

| 402 | winter |

冬　*Walking legs* slipping on the *ice* are a sure sign of **winter**. [5]

| 403 | heavens |

天　This character is meant to be a pictograph of a great man, said to represent the Lord of the **Heavens**. (You may, of course, use the elements *ceiling* and *St. Bernard dog* instead.) [4]

❖ The primitive can mean either the *heaven* of eternal bliss or the general term for sky, the *heavens*.

| 404 | die young |

夭　If you've ever wondered where the *St. Bernard dog* got its name, this character suggests a plausible answer. The first of these friendly Alpine canines, originally known simply as "Bernard dogs," **died young** in a sudden avalanche. Being blameless, she was wafted right up to her heavenly reward and fitted out with a halo one size too big for her hallowed head (the extended *drop* of the first stroke, written right to left). Centuries later she was "caninized" and came to be known as *St. Bernardette,* which later chauvinist theologians altered to *St. Bernard.* [4]

| 405 | pretend |

喬

To draw this character, you have only to take the "top hat" that the character for "tall" begins with and substitute it with the element for *die young*. To remember it, think of someone who **pretends** to be taller than he really is by wearing "elevator shoes" or a pompadour hairdo. When **pretending** turns into obsession, he may even be willing to undergo the gruesome leg-lengthening procedure known as the Ilizarov technique. The lengths people will go to just to **pretend** to be taller than nature intended them to be! Like most cosmetic surgery, the risk is that one will *die young* as a result of the self-deformation. [12]

❖ As a primitive meaning, this character will mean *angel* in memory of that angelic *St. Bernardette dog* who is now flying around the heavens serving brandy to those in need.

| 406 | bridge (N.) |

橋

The **bridge** shown here is made of *trees* in their natural form, except that the trunks have been carved into the forms of *angels*, a sort of "Ponte degli Angeli." [16]

木 橋

| 407 | attractive |

嬌

Associating a particularly **attractive** *woman* you know with an *angel* should be no problem. [15]

女 嬌

| 408 | standing up (ADJ.) |

立

The general posture of anything **standing up** is represented here by the pictograph of a vase **standing up**. [5]

丶 亠 立 立 立

❖ When used as a primitive, this character can also mean *vase*. When taking its character meaning, it is best to think of something *standing up* that is normally lying down, or something *standing* in an unusual way.

409

weep

泣

One **weeps** and **weeps** until one is *standing up* knee-deep in *water* (or until one has **wept** a large *vase*-full of *water*). [8]

氵　泣

410

station (N.)

站

Picture someone *telling fortunes* on a large Ming *vase* outside the **station** at which you most often catch your trains. [10]

立 ˈ 站

411

chapter

章

Imagine a large *sunflower* that grows miniature cloisonnée *vases* instead of seeds. The wee *vases* are just the right size for a keychain or bracelet. Your challenge is to associate this with the **chapter** of a book. [11]

立　章

412

compete

競

Two *teenagers* are shown here *standing up*—stretched to full height, face to scowling face—"*standing up*" to one other to **compete** for the attentions of the most popular girl in the school. [20]

立　竞　競

413

sovereign (N.)

帝

An uncommon, but not altogether unlikely picture of a reigning **sovereign** has him *standing up* in his *apron*, presumably at the behest of HIS **sovereign** (she who is to be obeyed), who needs help with washing the dishes.

Note how the last stroke of *standing up* doubles up as the first stroke of *apron*. [9]

414

童

juvenile (N.)

This frame shows up the image of a **juvenile** *standing* on top of a *computer,* or rather jumping up and down on it, because it refused to come up with the right answer. [12]

415

鐘

bell

This **bell** is made of cheap *metal,* and so badly made that when you ring it, it lets out a noise like the "**bell**owing" of *juveniles* who aren't getting their own way. [20]

金 鐘

416

商

salesman

See the peddler *standing* atop his motorcycle *helmet* as if it were a soapbox, hawking his wares to passersby. Make the *legs* and *mouth* represent the tools of the **salesman's** trade any way you can.

Note how the *legs* in the printed form in this frame look like *human legs,* while in the hand-drawn form below, they are clearly *animal legs*. There is no logical accounting for these variations—at least not yet. Once again, we recommend you imitate the hand-drawn form. [11]

商

antique

The primitive meaning **antique**, not itself a character, depicts a *vase* kept under a *glass cover* because it is *ancient.* As the character is drawn, the *vase* is out on display, but it will soon return to safer quarters. When you write it, think of the words *vase . . . glass cover . . . ancient*, and you won't have any trouble. [11]

417

適

suitable

Can you imagine anything less **suitable** to do with one's precious *antiques* than to display them in the middle of a crowded *road*? [14]

418

敵

enemy

Picture your most precious *antique* (it doesn't matter how old it really is, so long as it is the oldest thing YOU own) being knocked over by your most unlikable *taskmaster*, and you have a good picture of how people make themselves **enemies** for life. [15]

商 敵

419

匕

spoon (N.)

This character, a pictograph of a **spoon**, is easy enough to remember, provided you keep it distinct from that for *seven*, where the first stroke is written left to right (the opposite of here) and cuts noticeably across the second. [2]

ノ 匕

  As a primitive, this character can take on the additional meaning of *someone sitting on the ground*, of which it can also be considered a pictograph. In this case, the second stroke does not cut through the first at all, not even in the printed form, as we see in the following frames.

420

北

north

The cold air from the **north** is so strong that we see *two people sitting on the ground* back to back, their arms interlocked so they don't blow away. (Pay special attention to the drawing of the first three strokes.) [5]

丨　丬　北　北

421

背

back (N.)

The *part of the body* you turn to shield you from the cold wind from the *north* is your **back** [9]

北　背

422

比

compare

With *two spoons*, one in each hand, you **compare** your mother's cooking with your mother-in-law's.

Be careful here: the first stroke of the first *spoon* is drawn left to right, and the first stroke of the second *spoon*, from right to left. [4]

一　ト　比

423

昆

descendants

Like most proverbs, "There is nothing new under the *sun*" is not true all of the time. This character has us *comparing* family **descendants** under the *sun*. The resemblances are obvious, but it's also true that each generation brings something new to the family. [8]

日　昆

424

混

mix (V.)

Marriages that **mix** peoples and cultures traditionally kept apart from one another, this character suggests, *water* down the quality of one's *descendants*—the oldest racial nonsense in the world! [11]

氵　混

425 all

皆

Think of the housewives in those TV commercials *comparing* how *white* their laundry turned out. The clear winner is the one who used the popular detergent known as **All**. (If you don't know the brand, surely you've heard the phrases "**all**-purpose detergent" or "**all**-temperature detergent.") [9]

比　皆

426 this (literary)

此

To create an image of this most abstract of all the key words, picture a literary work whose opening sentence begins with the word **This**, the initial "T" of which is embellished in medieval style to fill up half the page. Look closely at the drawing and you will see the hundreds of little *footprints* and silver *spoons* that make it up. [6]

止　此

427 somewhat

些

The sense of the key word **somewhat** is that of "slightly" or "to some small degree." Then recall the minutely embellished "T" from the story for *this (literary)* and contrast it with the smaller and only **somewhat** fancy "T" that appeared in Volume *Two* of the work. [8]

此　些

428 it

它

In the children's game of tag, there is usually a designated place that renders one safe from being tagged and becoming "it." Here it is a little play*house* in the back yard, in which there is already *someone sitting on the ground.* [5]

宀　它

429　　　　　　　　　　　　　　　　　　　　　purpose

旨

Here we have a picture of a benevolent Fate giving **purpose** to those in her care, serving *spoon*ful after *spoon*ful of *sunshine* to them. [6]

匕　旨

430　　　　　　　　　　　　　　　　　　　　grease [N.]

脂

In the same way that one can think that the egg came first and that chickens are only the eggs' way of reproducing themselves, one might soon expect someone from the emerging academic discipline of Fat Studies to argue that **grease** or fat comes first, and that the *purpose* of the other *parts of the body* is only to serve as its carrier. [10]

月　脂

❖　　　　　　　　　　　　　　　　　　　　　reclining

尸

The picture is obvious: the first stroke represents the head, and the second the body of someone **reclining**. You may also use the synonyms *lying* or *lying down*. [2]

丿　尸

431　　　　　　　　　　　　　　　　　　　　　every

每

"Behind **every** successful person *lies* a woman…," who usually turns out to be one's *mother*! [7]

尸　每

432

梅

small plum

Behind *every* Jack Horner, there's a pie maker, and behind every pie maker, a *tree* full of **small plums** just the right size for little Jack's thumb. [11]

木　梅

433

海

sea

Behind *every* **sea**, the countless *drops of water* from which it originated. [10]

氵　海

434

乞

beg

See someone *lying down* in a public place with a *hook* in place of a hand and forced to **beg** a morsel of rice or a few pence. [3]

丿　乞

435

吃

eat

"**Eat** to live, not live to **eat**," goes the advice from *Poor Richard's Almanac.* Measured on that standard, those who have to *beg* for enough food to keep them alive are better off than those who stuff their *mouths,* every chance they get, with as much as they can **eat.** [6]

口　吃

436

乾

dry (ADJ.)

In times of drought everything is so **dry** that any relief at all is welcome. Here we see people *begging* for just a little *mist.* [11]

卓　乾

❖ double back

复

Let this primitive element take the connotation of turning around and heading back during one's travels. The character pictures a traveler who decides to interrupt his journey and **double back** to the nearest inn. Here we see him *lying down* after a full *day's* travels to rest a weary pair of *walking legs*. [9]

一 白 复

437 duplicate (v.)

複

Here we see a silk-screen mesh laid over a *cape* in order to **duplicate** a pattern—in this case, an advertisement for used cars being printed on the *cape* of an ageing superhero who has come on hard times. Picture yourself pressing the ink into the fabric with the squeegee, and then **doubling back** once again for good measure. [14]

衤 複

438 abdomen

腹

The secret to a picture-perfect **abdomen** is a little-known technique developed by circus acrobats. No need to fork out your hard-earned cash for some overpriced gym contraption. Just double the top half of your body forward till your nose touches your knees, then straighten up and **double back** until the back of your head hits your calfs. Forty times in a row and you've got **abs** to die for. [13]

月 腹

439 lack (v.)

欠

The pictograph hidden in this character is of someone yawning. The first stroke shows the head thrown back; the second, the arm bent at the elbow as the hand reaches up to cover the mouth; and the last two, the legs. Yawning is a sign that there is something you **lack**: psychologically, interest; physiologically, sleep. [4]

ノ ト 欠

❖ Used as a primitive, this character can mean either *yawn* or *lack*.

440

blow [v/]

吹

To **blow** is really no more than a deliberate effort to make one's *mouth lack* all the air that is in it. [7]

ロ 吹

441

song

歌

The **song** in this character is being sung by a chorus line of *can-can* girls. Why should the whole audience be *yawning* then?

Of course, you can always try the primitive for *older brother* on the audience instead of the *can-can* girls. [14]

哥 歌

442

soft

軟

If the cushions of one's *car* are too **soft**, one may begin to *yawn* at the wheel. [11]

車 軟

443

next

次

This key word connotes the "**next** in line" of a succession of people or things. Put yourself in a line of people who *lack ice* on the hottest day of summer, waiting impatiently for the distributor to call out "**Next**!" [6]

冫 次

❖ As a primitive, this character can either retain its key word meaning of *next* or the related meaning of *secondary*.

---

444   assets

資

The first *shells* (money) you earn, you use to pay your debts. The *next shells* you accumulate become your **assets**. [13]

次 資

---

445   looks (N.)

姿

This character depicts a *woman's* **looks** as a sort of *secondary self*. [9]

次 姿

---

446   consult with

諮

To seek the *words* of a *secondary mouth* is to **consult with** someone about something. [16]

言 訧 諮

LESSON 19

WE CONCLUDE our Plots by picking up most of the remaining primitives that can be built up from elements already at our disposal, and learning the characters that are based on them. When you have completed this section, you might want to run through all the frames from Lesson 13 on, jotting down notes at any point you think helpful. That way, even if you have not made any notations on your review cards, you will at least have some record of the images you used.

❖ muzzle

音

The element for **muzzle** shows a *vase* fixed over a *mouth*, perhaps with a rubber band running around the back of the head to keep it in place. [8]

立　音

---

447 compensate

賠

Picture a *clam* used as a *muzzle* to quiet the complaints of a fisherman's widow asking the Channel 7 weatherman to **compensate** her for the husband she lost at sea. [15]

貝　賠

---

448 cultivate

培

The barrel hoops used by some enterprising farmers to stretch clear plastic over rows of vegetables in a garden patch can be thought of as a way to *muzzle* the *soil*, creating a controlled environment that allows them to **cultivate** bigger and bigger vegetables. [11]

±　培

449 sound (N.)

音 The character for **sound** depicts something *standing* in the air over a *tongue wagging in a mouth*, much the same as a **sound** does for the briefest of moments before disappearing. [9]

立 音

❖ Used as a primitive, this character retains its meaning of a *sound*.

450 dark (ADJ.)

暗 Think of the **dark** emptiness of outer space, in which there is not only no *sun* but no *sound* either. [13]

日 暗

451 rhyme (N.)

韻 In this character **rhymes** are depicted as "*sound-employees*," as they indeed are for the poets who use them. [19]

音 韻

❖ kazoo

戠 This primitive's special usefulness lies not in its frequency but in its simplification of a few otherwise difficult characters. It pictures the *sound* of a *fiesta*, namely a **kazoo**. Note how the element for *sound* is written first, the fifth stroke extended so that it can be used in the element for *fiesta*. [12]

音 戠

452 knowledge

識 **Knowledge,** so the character tells us, is the ability to discriminate between mere *kazoo*-buzzing and *words* spoken intelligently. [19]

言　識

453	streamer

幟　Most **streamers** just flutter silently in the wind, but this one is a long, long *towel* with a *kazoo* attached to the end of it that buzzes as the **streamer** flutters in the breeze. [15]

巾　幟

454	unexpectedly

竟　This character gets its meaning from the following frame. It shows a queen *standing* in front of a mirror and asking who is the fairest of them all. **Unexpectedly,** the mirror sprouts a pair of *human legs* and begins to run around the room. A giant *tongue wagging in the mouth* appears on its surface, announcing that the mirror itself is fairer by far than the queen and all the maidens of the kingdom put together. [11]

音　竟

❖ The primitive meaning for this character will be a *mirror*.

455	mirror

鏡　After lakes but before glass, polished *metal* was used for **mirrors.** These *metal mirrors* are recalled in this character for a **mirror.** [19]

金　鏡

456	boundary

境　Imagine the **boundary** of a plot of *land* marked with gigantic *mirrors* enabling the landowner to keep trespassers in sight at all times. [14]

土　境

457 — deceased (ADJ.)

亡

A *top hat* hanging on a *hook* in the front hall, right where the **deceased** gentleman left it the day he died, reminds us of him and his courtly manner. [3]

丶　亠　亡

❖ In addition to *deceased*, the primitive meaning of *perish* will be used for this character.

458 — blind (ADJ.)

盲

If one's *eyes perish* before death, one remains **blind** for the rest of life. [8]

盲　盲

459 — absurd (ADJ.)

妄

It is **absurd** to waste time daydreaming about the "ideal *woman*," who can never be more than a delusion. Hence, *perish* the thought of her. [6]

亡　妄

460 — expect

望

As the *king* walks amid the remains of his fallen army, *perishing flesh* all around him, he **expects** the worst for his kingdom. [11]

亡　朢　望

461 — direction

方

Spinning a *dagger* about on its hilt on the top of a *top hat*— waiting to see in which **direction** it points when it comes to rest—one leaves to fate where one is going next. Take care in writing this character. [4]

亠　亠　方

❖ As a primitive, this character will take the sense of a *compass*, the instrument used to determine *direction*.

| 462 | hinder |

妨

Imagine a romantic *compass* that is disturbed every time a *woman* passes by: the mere smell of perfume **hinders** its ability to function, sending the needle spinning madly round and round. [7]

女　妨

| 463 | release (v.) |

放

The *taskmaster* **releases** an unruly servant into the wilderness, giving him no more than a quick glance at the *compass* and a boot from behind. [8]

方　放

| 464 | excite |

激

Some cosmic *taskmaster* hovering overhead **excites** the waves to make them dash violently against the shore. In the *white* foam that covers the *water* we see a broken *compass* floating, all that remains of a shipwreck. That ought to **excite** the unfortunate investors. [16]

氵　沪　潫　激

| 465 | (all-purpose preposition) |

於

The **all-purpose preposition**, set here in parentheses to indicate its grammatical function, is the Swiss Army knife of Chinese grammar. Its meanings include at, in, on, by, to, of, for, and from. In time, your grammatical *compass* will help you with the usage of this character, but for now kick your feet up under a beach *umbrella* and pour yourself a cold one on *ice*. [8]

方　於　於

466

side (N.)

旁

Think of the key word **side** in connection with the image of a **side**kick, an assistant or companion so named because he is always along**side** you. He, or she, is the one who carries the *compass,* the *crown,* and the *vase.* All you have to do is find a way to relate these three elements to the kinds of adventures the two of you are used to getting into. [10]

467

convert (V.)

兌

The key word should be understood in the sense of changing one thing into another, as when we **convert** currency. The character shows a *teenager* with a devil's *horns,* which most parents with adolescents will have no difficulty sympathizing with, as their *teenagers* systematically and continually **convert** their parents' hard-earned wages into feed for the vultures at the shopping mall. [7]

❖ The primitive meaning for this character will be *devil,* in line with the explanation above.

468

undress

脫

To **undress** is to expose the *flesh* and bring out the *devil* in one's onlookers. Ignore the moral if you want, but not the *devil.* [11]

月　脫

469

speak

説

"Sticks and stones may break my bones, but *words* will never hurt me." Yea, sure. Just think of all the ways that the *words one* **speaks** can bruise and wound and sting; they can be barbed and sharp, cruel and inflammatory. Let there be no doubt about it: there can be a *devil* in the *words* we **speak.** [14]

言　説

470 　formerly

曾

For the key word, think of individuals who **formerly** held office as administrators or heads of state. The character is composed of a pair of *horns* growing out of a *brain* impaled on the *horns* of a dilemma—with a *tongue wagging in the mouth* beneath. The dilemma of **formerly** prominent public figures is how to stay in the public eye even after retirement. The *wagging tongue* shows how so many of them do it, namely, by advertising their opinions on public policy. The *horns* growing out of the top show what a devilish nuisance they often make of themselves in the process. [12]

❖ The primitive meaning of this character, *increase*, comes from the next frame. Always think of something multiplying wildly as you watch.

471 　increase ^(v.)

増

In this character we see the *soil* **increase**, multiplying so fast that it literally buries everything in its path. [15]

土　増

472 　make a present of

贈

In today's world, there are fewer and fewer ways of **making a present of** something without seeing it as an investment awaiting its just return in time. And not only in today's world. How often unscrupulous colonizers in different parts of the world **made a present of** a handful of trinkets or *clams* (money) to unsuspecting locals as an investment that ended up *increasing* a million times over as they expropriated land, precious metals, and natural resources. Do not confuse this key word with the temporal word "present" (FRAME 251). [19]

貝　贈

We end this lesson by introducing a character that could have been introduced earlier, but which was saved until now in order to complete the following set of three characters.

473　　　　　　　　　　　　　　　　　　　　　east

東　As a "Western" language, English identifies the **east** as the direction from which the *sun* rises. In more fanciful terms, we see the *sun* piercing through a *tree* as it rises in the **east**. [8]

❖ Both the direction *east* and the part of the world called "the *East*" are primitive meanings of this character.

474　　　　　　　　　　　　　　　　　　　building

棟　This key word is used with a number as a classifier for counting **buildings**, not as a generic noun for structures. The elements suggests *trees* in the *East*—perhaps like the forests of innumerable **buildings** we find in Beijing or Tokyo. [12]

木　棟

475　　　　　　　　　　　　　　　　　　freeze (v.)

凍　The whole secret to breaking the *ice* with the *East* is to un-**freeze** those mysteriously "frozen smiles." [10]

冫　凍

Elements

WE COME NOW to the third major step in our study of the characters: the invention of plots from primitive elements. From now on, the ordering of the remaining characters according to their primitives will be taken care of, but the reader will be required to do most of the work. Particularly difficult characters will be supplied with supplementary hints, plots, or even whole stories.

You should now have a feel for the way details can be worked into a character story so as to create a more vivid ambience for the primitive elements to interact. What may be more difficult is experimenting with plots and discarding them until the simplest one is fixed on, and then embellished and nuanced. You may find it helpful occasionally to study some of the earlier stories that you found especially impressive, in order to discover precisely why they struck you, and then to imitate their vitality in the stories you will now be inventing. Equally helpful will be any attention you give to those characters whose stories you have found it difficult to remember, or have easily confused with those of other characters. As you progress through this final section, you may even wish to return and amend some of those earlier stories. But do it with the knowledge that once a story has been learned, it is generally better to review it and perhaps repair it slightly than to discard it entirely and start over.

LESSON 20

IF YOU HAVE found some of the characters in the last brief lesson difficult to work with, we can only assure you that it will get easier with time, beginning with this long lesson. Remember, however, that as it *does* get easier you should not skip over the stories too quickly, trusting only in the most superficial of images. If you spend up to five minutes on each character focusing the composition of the primitives into a tidy plot, and then filling out the details of a little story, you will not be wasting time, but saving yourself the time it takes to relearn it later.

476 也 · also

This character is a pictograph of the scorpion, the first two strokes representing its head and pincers, the last stroke its barbed tail, in which you may recognize the *fishhook*.

To associate this image with the key word, think of the two terms that the word "**also**" links in a sentence and place a scorpion there, its head biting on one word, its tail stinging the other. [3]

㇆　㐅　也

❖ The primitive meaning will remain *scorpion*, in line with the above explanation.

477 她 · she

Woman . . . scorpion. Note to male readers: to avoid any complications with the **she** in your life, you might want to adjust the second primitive to its character meaning, *also*. [6]

女　她

478 地 · ground (N.)

Soil and a *scorpion* (an "earth animal"). This is, of course, the full character from which the primitive for **ground** derives. [6]

土　地

479 池 · pond

Water . . . scorpion. It would be easy to slip into a "lazy image" in cases like this one, picturing, let us say, a *scorpion* near the *water*. But if you picture a *scorpion* letting its venom out *drop by drop* until it has made a whole **pond** of the stuff, the image is more likely to remain fixed. [6]

❖

虫 insect

Work with this primitive as you wish, to create the image of an insect. In fact, it will appear in characters for all sorts of worms and bugs and other creepy, crawling things. [6]

口　中　虫　虫

---

480 虫蟲 insects

Think here of a whole swarm of **insects**. [18]

口　中　虫　虫　蛊　蟲

---

481 蛇 serpent

Insect ... it. [11]

虫　蛇

---

482 蛋 egg

Zoo ... insect. [11]

疋　蛋

---

483 風 wind (N.)

Wind ... drops of ... insects. Hint: think of the last two primitives as representing a swarm of *gnats*, those tiny *drops of* pesky *insects*. This is the full character from which the primitive element of the same meaning derives. [9]

几　凡　風

---

484 諷 mock (V.)

Words ... swarm of gnats in the wind. [16]

言　諷

485   self

己

This character carries the abstract sense of the **self**, the deep-down inner structure of the human person that mythology has often depicted as a *snake*—of which it is a pictograph. Be sure to keep it distinct from the similar key word, *I (literary)* (FRAME 18) and *oneself* (FRAME 32).

ㄱ   ㄱ   己

❖ As a primitive element, this character will take the meaning of a *snake*, along with any of the various concrete symbolic meanings the *snake* has in myth and fable.

486   alter

改

Snake . . . taskmaster. To work the key word **alter** into the story, you might think of Ireland's most famous reformer, St. Patrick, who, legend has it, drove away the *snakes* from the land. [7]

己   改

487   remember

記

Words . . . snake. [10]

言   記

488   already

已

The *snake* with its mouth half closed (depicted in the slight extension of the final stroke) suggests that it is **already** dead and gone, ready to be stripped of its skin to become a belt or handbag. [3]

ㄱ   ㄱ   已

❖ When this character is used as a primitive, it changes shape to close the gap between the first and last strokes: 巳. Its meaning will be a *snakeskin*.

489		wrap (v.)
包	*Bind up . . . snakeskin.* [5]	

勹 包

490		bubbles
泡	*Water . . . wrap.* [8]	

氵 泡

491		begin
起	*Walk . . . snakeskin.* [10]	

走 起

❖		sow (N.)
豕	Let this primitive represent a fat **sow**. Easier than pulling it apart into smaller elements is remembering its shape as a highly stylized pictograph. Practice its seven strokes a few times before going on to examples of its use in the next few frames. [7]	

一 ⺈ 丁 丆 豸 豕 豕

492		house (N.)
家	This is the full character whose primitive form we learned already. To help a little, this character recalls the times when the "domestic" animals were, as the word itself suggests, really kept in the **house**. Hence: *house . . . sow.* [10]	

宀 家

❖		piggy bank
昜	This very helpful primitive element is worth the few moments it takes to learn it. To begin with, the primitive for *sow is* abbre-	

viated to the first five strokes, the third of which is pulled up toward the right. This turns the *sow* into a kind of "piggy." Above it is the character for *day*, to remind you each *day* to put a few pennies into the back of the **piggy bank** sitting on top of your dresser. [9]

日　旦　旦　号　号　易

493　　　　　　　　　　　　　　　　　　　　site

場　*Soil . . . piggy bank.* [12]

土　　場

494　　　　　　　　　　　　　　　　　　　soup

湯　*Water . . . piggy bank.* [12]

氵　　湯

495　　　　　　　　　　　　　　　　　　sheep

羊　This pictograph shows the animal *horns* at the top attached to the head (third stroke), the front and back legs (strokes four and five), and body (final stroke). [6]

丶　　丷　　丷　　半　　兰　　羊

❖ The primitive meaning remains *sheep*. As we saw with the *cow*, the "tail" is cut off when it is set immediately over another element: 羊. Note the change in stroke order, as exemplified in the following frame.

496　　　　　　　　　　　　　　　　beautiful

美　Try to think of what the Chinese were on to when they associated **beautiful** with a *large sheep*. [9]

丶　　丷　　丷　　半　　羊　　羊　　美

497   ocean

洋

Water . . . sheep. Be sure to keep the stories and key word of this character distinct from those for *sea*. (FRAME 433). [9]

氵   洋

---

498   fresh

鮮

Fish . . . sheep. [17]

魚   鮮

---

499   reach [v.]

達

On the *road* we find *soil* OVER *a sheep*. You may have to work with this character a while to associate these three elements to the key word. [12]

土   幸   達

---

500   appearance

樣

Tree . . . sheep . . . eternity. [15]

木   样   樣

❖   wool

羊

This rather uncommon primitive is made by pulling the tail of the *sheep* to one side to create a semi-enclosure. The meaning of **wool** is derived from the fact that the shearer is holding the *sheep* by the tail in order to trim its **wool**.

Note that in most printed fonts, the final vertical stroke looks as if it were broken into two, but it is best to follow the hand-drawn example below. [6]

兰   羊

501

fall short of

差

Wool ... I-beam. [9]

羊 差

❖

turkey

隹

This primitive is best remembered as an old **turkey**, complete with pipe and horn-rimmed glasses. Its writing is somewhat peculiar, so take note of the order of the strokes. Let the first four strokes stand for the *turkey's* head, neck, and drooping chin. The remainder can then be pictographic of the plumage. [8]

丿 亻 亻 亻 亻 亻 仹 隹

502

gather

集

Turkeys ... atop a tree. [12]

隹 集

503

advance (V.)

進

Turkey ... road. [11]

隹 進

504

standard (N.)

準

Think of a **standard** of measure or quality. *Water ... turkeys ... needle.* [13]

氵 淮 準

505

who?

誰

Words ... turkey. It might help if you think of the Cheshire Cat from the Disney production of "Alice in Wonderland" as a Cheshire *Turkey* asking passers-by "**W-h-o** aaaare you?" [15]

言 誰

506

售

vend

Let the key word suggest street peddlers who **vend** their wares. *Turkey . . . mouth.* [11]

佳 售

507

雖

although

A *mouth* full of *insects . . . turkey.* This is the first time you are on your own with a highly abstract word. Try to think of a phrase in which it is commonly used to make it more concrete. [17]

口 虽 雖

508

確

reliable

The *stone* on the left is clear enough, but take care with the unusual stroke order of the *turkey* on the right. It has the "chimney" on the *house* doubled up with the first stroke of the *turkey*. You might think of this as a *turkey house* (or *turkey pen*). [14]

石 矴 確

509

午

noon

With a bit of stretching, you might see a horse's head pointing leftward in this character. That gives the primary meaning of the Chinese zodiacal sign of the horse, which corresponds to the hour of **noon**. Note how this character differs from that for *cow* (FRAME 235). [4]

丿 ト 匕 午

❖ As a primitive, this character gets the meaning of a *stick horse.*

---

510   permit [(v.)]

許   *Words . . . stick horse.* [11]

言   許

---

511   feathers

羽   From the pictograph of two bird wings, we get **feathers**. [6]

]]] 羽

❖ The related image of *wings* can be added as a primitive
meaning. It can also take the form 羽 when used as a primitive, as we shall see in the following frame.

---

512   learn

習   *Feathers . . . white bird.* [11]

羽   習

---

513   soar

翔   *Sheep . . . feathers.* [12]

羊   翔

LESSON 21

THIS IS A GOOD TIME TO stop for a moment and have a look at how primitive elements get contracted and distorted by reason of their position within a character. Reference has been made to the fact here and there in passing, but now that you have attained greater fluency in writing, we may address the phenomenon more systematically.

1. At the left, a primitive will generally be squeezed in from the sides and slanted upwards. For instance, *gold* 金 comes to be written 釒 when it functions as the primitive for *metal*. Or again, *tree* has its character form 木 flattened into 朮 when it comes to the left.

2. Long strokes ending in a hook, which would normally flow out gracefully, are squeezed into angular form when made part of a primitive at the left. We see this in the way the character for *ray* 光 gets altered to 耂 in the character for *radiance* 輝. In like manner, the *spoon* that is spread out on the right side of *compare* 比 is compressed on the left. Certain characters are pressed down and widened when weighted down by other elements from above. Such is the case, for example, with *woman,* which is flattened into 女 when it appears in the lowest position of *banquet* 宴.

3. A long vertical stroke cutting through a series of horizontal lines is often cut off below the lowest horizontal line. We saw this in changing the *cow* 牛 to fit into *declare* 告, the *sheep* 羊 to fit into *beautiful* 美, and the *brush* 聿 that appeared in the character for *book* 書.

4. The long downward swooping stroke that we see in *fire* is an example of another group of distortions. Crowded in by something to its right, it is compressed into 灬. Hence *fire* 火 and *vexed* 煩.

5. Again, we have seen how horizontal lines can double up as the bottom of an upper primitive and the top of a lower primitive, for instance, when *stand* 立 comes in the character for *salesman* 商.

6. Finally, there are situations in which an entire character is changed to assume a considerably altered primitive form. *Water* 水, *fire* 火, and *heart* 心 can thus become 氵, 灬, and 忄 in other characters. Because the full forms are ALSO used as primitives, we have often altered the meaning or given distinctions in meaning in order to be sure that the story in each case dictates precisely how the character is to be written.

From this lesson on, the stroke order will not be given unless it is entirely new, departs from the procedures we have learned so far, or might otherwise cause confusion. All hand-drawn characters, you will remember, are indicated by frame number in Index I. Should you have any trouble with the writing of a particular primitive, you can refer to Index II, which will direct you to the page where that primitive was first introduced.

With that, we carry on with an enclosure, a roof, and a first group of characters using primitives associated with the "heart."

❖ 口	**pent in**
	This primitive depicts a corral or pen surrounding something, which is thus **pent in**. Note that this primitive is much larger than a mouth, in fact large enough to include a mouth inside of it in FRAME 520. [3] 丨 冂 口

514 困	**trapped**
	Pent in . . . trees. [7] 冂 冞 困

515 固	**solid**
	Pent in . . . ancient. Leave people out of your story to avoid complications later when we add the element for "person," which will also appear with the primitive for *pent in* (FRAME 736). [8]

516 國	**country**
	Pent in . . . or. [11]

517 圓	**round**
	Pent in . . . employee . [13]

518 因	**cause** (N.)
	Pent in . . . St. Bernard dog. [6]

519 園	park (N.) Pent in . . . Yuan. [13]

520 回	return (V.) The elements are *pent in* and *mouth*, but you may find it more helpful to forget the primitives and think of one circle revolving inside of another. [6]

冂　回　回

521 迴	revolve Return . . . road. [9]

522 圖	picture (N.) Pent in . . . mouth . . . top hat . . . return. [14]

❖ 广	cave This primitive combines the *cliff* (the last two strokes) with the first dot we use on the roof of the *house*. Together they make a "cliff house" or **cave**. It "encloses" other primitives beneath it and to the right. [3]

丶　亠　广

523 店	store (N.) Cave . . . tell fortunes. [8]

广　店

524 庫	warehouse Cave . . . car. [10]

525 褲	trousers Cloak / clothing . . . warehouse. [15]

526

廠

factory

Cave . . .spacious. [15]

广　廠

527

床

bed

Cave . . . tree. [7]

528

麻

hemp

Cave . . . woods. If it helps, this is the **hemp** marijuana comes from. [11]

529

心

heart

This character, a pictographic representation of the **heart**, is among the most widely used primitives we shall meet. [4]

丶　心　心　心

❖ As a primitive, it can take three forms, to which we shall assign three distinct meanings.

　In its character form, it appears BENEATH or to the RIGHT of its relative primitive and means the physical organ of the *heart*.

　To the LEFT, it is abbreviated to three strokes, ⺗, and means a wildly emotional *state of mind*.

　And finally, at the very BOTTOM, it can take the form ⺗, in which case we give it the meaning of a *valentine*. Examples will not appear until Book 2.

530

忘

forget

Perish . . . heart. [7]

亡　忘

531 忍	**endure**

Blade . . . heart. We give the drawing here to remind you that the third stroke is drawn somewhat differently than the printed form. [7]

刃　忍

532 認	**recognize**

Words . . . endure. [14]

533 志	**aspiration**

Soldier . . . heart. [7]

534 誌	**annals**

Words . . . aspiration. [14]

535 思	**consider**

Brains . . . heart. [9]

536 意	**idea**

Sound . . . heart. [13]

537 想	**think**

One another . . . heart. [13]

538 息	**breath**

Nose . . . heart. [10]

539 恐	**fear** (v.)

Work . . . ordinary . . . heart. [10]

540 感	**feel** (v.)

Everybody . . . heart. [13]

541

憾

regret [N.]

State of mind . . . feel. [16]

｜　丿　忄　㦓　憾

542

憂

worried

Ceiling . . . nose . . . crown . . . heart . . . walking legs. This character is going to be a challenge because it has no less than five distinct elements. Take your time and keep things as graphic as you can.

Note how the horizontal stroke of the *crown* doubles up as the final stroke of *nose*. [15]

一　百　直　憂　憂

543

怕

dread [V.]

State of mind . . . dove. [8]

544

忙

busy [ADJ.]

State of mind . . . perish. [6]

545

慣

accustomed to

State of mind . . . pierce. [14]

546

懷

cherish

State of mind . . . top hat and scarf . . . eyeball . . . snowflake. Unless you just had an easy time with *worried* (FRAME 542), you might appreciate a simple hint: the right side of the character is exactly the same as what we met in the character for *bad* (FRAME 380). [19]

忄　忤　悖　悖　悖　懷　懷　懷

547   certainly

 First note the stroke order of this character, which did not really evolve from the *heart* even though we take it that way. If one takes it as a pictograph "dividing" the *heart* in two, then one has arrived at a "certitude" about human anatomy: that each *heart* is **certainly** divided into two halves. [5]

丿　心　心　心　必

LESSON 22

IN THIS lengthy lesson we focus on elements having to do with hands and arms. As always, the one protection you have against confusing the elements is to form clear and distinct images the first time you meet them. If you make it through this lesson smoothly, the worst will be behind you, and you should have nothing more to fear the rest of the way.

548	hand
手	Any way you count them, there are either too many or too few fingers to see a good pictograph of a **hand** in this character. But that it is, and so you must. [4]

ノ　二　三　手

❖ Keep to the etymology when using this character as a primitive: a single *hand* all by itself.

549	look at
看	*Hand . . . eyes.* [9]

チ　看

550	hold (v.)
拿	*Fit . . . hand.* [10]

551	I
我	*Hand . . . fiesta.* Note how the second stroke of the *hand* is stretched across to double up as the first stroke of the tasseled arrow we use for *fiesta.* Be sure keep the meaning of this key word distinct from those in FRAMES 18, 32, and 485. [7]

ノ　二　于　手　扌　我　我

552 義	righteousness *Sheep ... I.* [13]

羊 義

553 議	deliberate (v.) The sense here is to discuss or exchange views on something. The primitives are: *words ... righteousness.* [20]

554 蟻	ant *Insect ... righteousness.* [19]

❖ 扌	fingers This alternate form of the primitive for *hand* we shall use to represent *finger* or *fingers*. It always appears at the left. [3]

一　丁　扌

555 抱	embrace (v.) *Fingers ... wrap.* [8]

扌 抱

556 抗	combat (v.) *Fingers ... whirlwind.* [7]

557 批	criticize *Finger ... compare.* [7]

558 招	beckon *Finger ... summon.* [8]

559 打	strike (v.) *Finger ... spike.* [5]

560 指	finger [N.] This is the full character for **finger**. Its elements: *Finger . . . purpose.* [9]
561 持	support [V.] *Fingers . . . Buddhist temple.* [9]
562 括	include *Fingers . . . tongue.* [9]
563 提	bring up The sense of this character is to mention or put forward, as when one **brings up** an idea, topic for discussion, and the like. Its elements: *fingers . . . be.* [12]
564 揮	brandish *Finger . . . army.* [12]
565 推	push *Fingers . . . turkey.* [11]
566 接	welcome [V.] *Fingers . . . vase . . . woman.* [11]
567 掛	hang *Fingers . . . bricks . . . magic wand.* [11]
568 按	press down on *Fingers . . . tranquil.* [9]
569 掉	drop [V.] *Fingers . . . eminent.* [11]

570 拉	pull
	Fingers . . . vase. [8]

571 啦	! !
	This character can be used at the end of a sentence to express exclamation, more or less the way an exclamation mark works. Its elements: *mouth . . . pull.* [11]

572 找	look for
	Fingers . . . fiesta. [7]

❖ 开	two hands
	Let this primitive represent a union of **two hands**, both of which are used at the same time. When this element appears at the bottom of another primitive, the drawing is not consistent. Sometimes it looks as if the first stroke is omitted (廾), and at other times, the second (丌). Since this is largely a function of font differences, there is no need to adjust the primitive meaning. [4]

一　二　干　开

573 研	grind away^(v.)
	Stone . . . two hands. As the key word suggests, this character means both to grind things to a fine powder and to study— when you **grind away** at the books. [9]

574 弄	play with
	King/ball . . . two hands. [9]

575 鼻	nose
	Let us share a rather grotesque image to help with this character. Imagine taking your *two hands* and reaching up into someone's *nostrils.* Once inside you grab hold of the *brain* and yank it out. At the end, you would have a picture something like that of this character, the full character for **nose**. [14]

自　畐　鼻

576

刑　　　　　　　　　　　　　　**punishment**

Two hands . . . saber. [6]

577

型　　　　　　　　　　　　　　**mold** (v.)

Punishment . . . soil. Once again, you might find it easier to
break the character up into its more basic elements, like this:
two hands . . . saber . . . soil. [9]

刑　型

578

才　　　　　　　　　　　　　　**genius**

Whatever one is particularly adept at—one's special "**genius**"—
one can do very easily, "with one finger" as the phrase goes. This
character is a pictograph of that one finger. Note how its distinctive form is created by writing the final stroke of the element for *fingers* backwards. [3]

一　十　才

❖ The primitive meaning, *genie*, derives from the roots of the
word *genius*. Use the *genie* out of the bottle when the primitive appears to the right of or below another primitive; in
that case it also keeps its same form. At the left, the form is
altered to 扌, and the meaning becomes a *genie in the bottle*.

579

財　　　　　　　　　　　　　　**riches**

Clams . . . genie. [10]

580

存　　　　　　　　　　　　　　**deposit** (v.)

Genie in the bottle . . . a child. The sense of the key word is to
place something somewhere for safekeeping. [6]

一　ナ　オ　存

581

在

at

The key word **at** is used to initiate an expression indicating location. Its elements: *genie in the bottle . . . soil.* [6]

582

乃

only then

This pictograph of a clenched fist is another of the "hand" primitives. Take note of its rather peculiar drawing. Begin by drawing a *fist* (the primitive meaning) and **only then** struggle to come up with a concrete connotation for this otherwise abstract key-word phrase. [2]

丿　乃

❖ The primitive meaning we will assign it is taken from the pictograph: a *fist*.

583

奶

milk (N.)

Woman . . . fist/only then. [5]

584

及

catch up with

The addition of a final stroke transforms this character from the primitive for a clenched *fist* into the character for **catch up with**. Observe how eliminating the hook in the second stroke and slanting it to the left gives the character a more elegant form.

Sometimes our emotions get ahead of us and it takes a little time for us to **catch up with** them. In this character, all it took was one "stroke" of kindness to turn a *fist* clenched in anger into a hand reaching out in reconciliation. [3]

乃　及

❖ As a primitive, this will stand for *outstretched hands.* Only take care not to confuse it with *beg* (FRAME 434).

585

吸

inhale

Mouth . . . outstretched hands. [6]

❖

丿乀

tucked under the arm

The picture of an arm dangling from the trunk of the body gives us the element for **tucked under the arm** (relative to the element below it). [2]

丿　乀

586

史

history

A mouth . . . tucked under the arm. [5]

口　史

587

更

even more

Ceiling . . . sun . . . tucked under the arm. [7]

一　曰　更

588

硬

hard

Stone . . . even more. [12]

589

又

again

You should have no trouble remembering this short two-stroke character, since you will meet it **again** and **again** in its primitive meaning. [2]

フ　又

❖ Etymologically, this character is said to be a pictograph of the right hand, hence its inclusion in this lesson. You can always take *right hand* as its primitive meaning, as we will see in just a few frames. More commonly, however, we will try to avoid confusing it with other primitives of similar meaning by assigning it the meaning of *crotch*, as in the *crotch* of an arm or a tree. Or whatever.

590 友	friend
	By one's side ... crotch. [4]

一 ナ 方 友

591 雙	pair
	Two turkeys ... crotch. [18]

592 隻	one of a pair
	Turkey ... crotch. [10]

❖ 蒦	bird of paradise

The two elements that make it up are *flowers* and *one of a pair*. But let's try something else.

The **bird of paradise** can refer either to the tropical African plant with brilliant orange, blue, and green flowers, or to the brightly colored bird found in New Guinea. Picture this **bird of paradise** as a combination of the two: a bird that has brilliant flowers for the plumage on its head and the body of a *turkey*. If you can imagine holding it in your *right hand* to feed it, you have all the elements covered.

This would be a good time to confirm the number of strokes. If you end up with one less than the assigned number, you might want to go back to page 99 and refresh your memory about the difference between the printed form of the element for *flowers* and the hand-drawn form. [14]

艹 萑 蒦

593 護	protect
	Words ... bird of paradise. [21]

594 獲	seize
	A pack of wild dogs ... bird of paradise. [17]

	stork
藋	Here we have a senile, old *turkey* that thinks it's a **stork**. The element for *chatterbox* refers to the incessant gobbling of the *turkey*, who is doing its best to keep its bundle in its stubby beak while he announces the new arrival to the entire neighborhood. The fragrant *flowers* have been added to improve the odor of the parcel. [18]

艹　　　前　　　藋

595	observe
觀	*Stork . . . see.* [25]

596	joyous
歡	*Stork . . . yawn.* [22]

	missile
殳	Although modern connotations are more suggestive, this primitive simply refers to something thrown as a weapon. Its elements: *wind . . . crotch.* [4]

几　　　殳

597	throw (v.)
投	*Fingers . . . missile.* [7]

598	not have
沒	*Water . . . missile.* [7]

599	establish (v.)
設	*Words . . . missile.* [11]

600	thigh
股	*Part of the body . . . missile.* [8]

601 支	offshoot

Needle . . . crotch/right hand. This key word is used to indicate a "branch" of an institution or organization, which helps us assign it a primitive meaning. [4]

十　支

❖ Used as a primitive this character will have the full range of meanings associated with the word *branch*.

602 技	skill

Fingers . . . branch. [7]

603 枝	branch

Tree . . . branch. [8]

604 叔	uncle

Above . . . small . . . right hand. [8]

上　朩　叔

605 督	superintend

Uncle . . . eye. [13]

606 寂	lonely

House . . . uncle. [11]

❖ 厂	drag (v.)

Although not a pictograph in the strict sense, this primitive depicts one stroke **dragging** another along behind it. Note that the drawing of the first stroke goes from right to left, which naturally helps its appearance to differ from that of *cliff*. In the printed form, however, this subtlety is lost in some fonts. [2]

一　厂

607 反	*Drag . . . crotch.* [4]	against

厂 反

608 板	*Tree . . . against.* [8]	plank

609 返	*Against . . . road.* [7]	go back

610 派	*Water . . . drag . . . bandana.* [9]	faction

氵 氵 沪 沂 泝 派

611 脈	*Flesh . . . drag . . . bandana.* [10]	blood vessels

612 爪 — claw (N.)

This character is a pictograph of a bird's **claw**, and from there comes to mean animal **claws** in general (including human fingernails). Since the first two strokes are the same as the element for *drag*, you can imagine a cat *dragging* its claws across a blackboard to get you started. [4]

丆 厂 爪 爪

❖ When this character is used as a primitive, we shall sometimes give it the graphic image of a *vulture*, a bird known for its powerful *claws*. It generally appears above another primitive, in which case it gets squeezed into the form ⺥.

613 抓	*Fingers . . . claws.* [7]	grab

614

pluck (v.)

采   *Vulture . . . tree.* [8]

ノ   ハ   ヘ   ᅲ   采

615

pick (v.)

採   This character is used to **pick** fruits from trees. Its elements: *fingers . . . pluck.* [11]

616

vegetable

菜   *Flowers . . . pluck* [12]

❖

birdhouse

爫   The *claw* and crown of the roof of a *house* (whose chimney is displaced by the *claw*) combine to give us a **birdhouse**. [6]

爫   爫

617

accept

受   *Birdhouse . . . crotch/right hand.* The sense here is "receive." [8]

618

confer

授   This key word has the sense of "bestow" and not "consult with," each of which has its own character (FRAMES 936 and 446) The elements: *fingers . . . accept.* [11]

619

love (N./v.)

愛   *Birdhouse . . . heart . . . walking legs.* [13]

爫   愛   愛

❖

elbow

厶   This pictograph of an arm bent at the **elbow** is obvious. Once again, there is some font variation in the way this character is written. [2]

ㄥ ㄙ

| 620 雄 | *By one's side . . . elbow . . . turkey.* [12] | grand |

ナ ナ 雄

621 台	*Elbow . . . mouth.* [5]	platform
622 治	*Water . . . platform.* [8]	govern
623 始	*Woman . . . platform.* [8]	commence
624 去	*Soil . . . elbow.* [5]	go
625 法	*Water . . . go.* [8]	method

| ❖ 亠 | The *elbow* hanging under a *ceiling* will become our element for a **wall**. [3] | wall |

一 亠

| 626 至 | *Wall . . . soil.* Be sure to give this key word a concrete image, perhaps in connection with a commonly used expression. [6] | until |

627	room
室	The key word **room** refers to a room in a house or building, not to the abstract sense of "space." Its elements: *house . . . until.* [9]

628	arrive
到	*Until . . . saber.* [8]

629	mutual
互	When you draw this character think of linking two *walls* together, one right side up and the other upside down. [4]

一　丆　歹　互

❖	infant
厶	Sudden **Infant** Death Syndrome (SIDS) has been responsible for the death of more babies under the age of one year than any other single cause. Here we see a kind of memorial to the fallen **infants** in the form of a great marble *wall* into which a small *drop* is carved with a name beneath it for each life cut short, creating the image of an ocean of innocents. When you use this primitive, however, think of a healthy toddler on all fours. [4]

丶　一　亡　厶

630	sufficient
充	*Infant . . . human legs.* [6]

631	education
育	The key word has to do with raising children to be strong both in mind and body. The elements are: *infant . . . flesh.* [8]

❖	baby Moses
㐬	This primitive is a combination of two elements, *infant* and the waters of a *flood*. We give it the meaning of **baby Moses** because of the image of Miriam placing her child in a basket and entrusting it to the swift waters of the Nile River. [7]

亠 㐬

632 流	*Water...baby Moses.* [10]	flow (v.)
633 梳	*Tree... baby Moses.* [11]	comb (N.)

LESSON 23

AFTER THAT LONG excursus into arm and hand primitives, we will take a breather with a much shorter lesson, beginning with two groups built up from the characters for *exit* and *enter*.

634	mountain
山	Note the clear outline of a triangular **mountain** here. [3]

丨　丄　山

635	exit [v.]
出	The character for **exit** pictures a range of mountain peaks coming out of the earth. Note how the drawing runs counter to what you might expect from the previous frame. [5]

乚　凵　屮　㞢　出

636	beat [v.]
擊	To the elements for *missile* and *hand*, try combining the elements for *car* and *mountain* into a jeep or similar *mountain-climbing vehicle* to get to your key word **beat**. [17]

車　軎　軎　毄　擊

637	secret [ADJ.]
密	Think of something that is **secret** to preserve the adjectival form of the key word. *House . . . certainly . . . mountain.* [11]

638	enter
入	Now that we know *exit*, we might as well learn the character for **enter**. This character is meant to be a picture of someone walking to the left, putting one leg forward in order to **enter** someplace. [2]

丿 入

639

内

internal

Glass cover . . . enter. [4]

冂 冃 内

640

呐

holler (v.)

Mouth . . . internal. [7]

641

分

part (N. / V.)

Here we combine the character for *eight* and the element for *dagger* to give the key word **part**. [4]

丿 八 分

642

貧

impoverished

Part . . . shells / clams. [11]

643

公

public (ADJ.)

Eight . . . elbows. Use the key word in its adjectival sense, not as a noun. [4]

644

松

pine tree

Tree . . . public. [8]

645

谷

valley

Look closely at the character in this frame and the one right above it and you will see the difference between the primitive element for *eight* and that for *animal legs*: the second stroke in *eight* bends gracefully outwards, while in *animal legs* it just kind of drops down.

But this doesn't tell you what *animal legs* are doing on top of an *umbrella*. The answer lies in the *mouth* of the **valley**, which is what you should think of when you see this key word. In order to stop the illegal immigration of all sorts of critters from the surrounding territories, a gigantic *umbrella*, obviously made of a material tough enough to resist the trampling of the *animal legs* trying to creep across the border, has been laid over the *mouth* of the **valley**. [7]

八　父　谷

646	bathe
浴	*Water . . . valley.* [10]
647	desire (v.)
欲	*Valley . . . yawn.* Be sure to keep the key word distinct from that of the following frame. [11]
648	lust (N.)
慾	*Desire . . . heart.* [11]
649	contain
容	This character depicts a *house* so large that it can **contain** an entire *valley*. [10]
650	dissolve
溶	*Water . . . contain.* [13]

LESSON 24

THE FOLLOWING GROUP of characters deals with primitive elements having to do with human beings. We shall have more to add to this set of primitives before we are through, but even the few we bring in here will enable us to learn quite a few new characters. We begin with another "roof" primitive.

❖ 尚	outhouse

The combination of the element for *small*, the basic "roof" structure here (in which the chimney is overwritten, as in the element for *birdhouse*), combined with the "window" (*mouth*) below, gives this element its meaning of **outhouse**. Although the window is not an essential part of an **outhouse**, we think you will agree that its inclusion is a boon to the imagination, greatly simplifying the learning of the characters in which it appears. [8]

丷　屮　尚

---

651 當	work as

The key word has to do with one's job or occupation, that is, what one **works as**. Its elements: *outhouse ... rice field*. [13]

---

652 檔	files (N.)

Tree ... work as. The **files** of this character are the kind you find in archives and offices. [17]

---

653 黨	political party

This key word refers to the actual group of people that make up a **political party**, not to the kind of gala affair they are famous for throwing. Its elements: *outhouse ... black*. [20]

---

654 常	often

Outhouse ... towel. [11]

655 堂	main room
	Outhouse . . . soil. [11]

656 皮	covering ^(N.)

656 皮 — covering ^(N.)

The simplest way to remember this character is to see it as built up from the primitive element for *branch*. Besides the "barb" at the end of the first stroke, the only other change is the second stroke, which can stand for something "hanging" down from the *branch*, namely its bark or **covering**. Merely concentrating on this as you write the following small cluster of characters should be enough to fix the form in your mind. [5]

⼁　⼚　⼴　⽪　⽪

657 波 — waves

Water's . . . covering. [8]

658 婆 — old woman

Waves . . . woman. [11]

659 破 — break ^(V.)

Stone . . . covering. [10]

660 被 — quilt ^(N.)

Cloak . . . covering. [10]

661 歹 — malicious

This character is meant to be a pictograph of a bone attached to a piece of flesh (or vice versa). The key-word meaning, **malicious**, should not be far behind. Note how the first stroke serves to keep this character distinct from that for *evening* (FRAME 108), which has a similar form. [4]

⼀　歹

❖ When this character is used as a primitive, its meaning will
be *bones*.

---

662   line up

列   *Bones ... saber.* [6]

---

663   intense

烈   *Line up ... cooking fire.* [10]

---

664   death

死   *Bones ... spoon.* Note how the first stroke is extended to the
right, forming a sort of "roof" overhead. [6]

---

665   inter [v.]

葬   *Flowers ... death ... two hands.* Compare the similar key word
bury (FRAME 171). [13]

艹　　苑　　葬

---

666   ear

耳   To the newcomer to Chinese characters, the pictograph for **ear**
might look like that for *eye*, but you are far enough along now
that the differences stand out dramatically. [6]

一　　厂　　丌　　丌　　丌　　耳

---

667   take

取   *Ear ... right hand.* [8]

---

668   interest

趣   The sense of the key word **interest** is one of curiosity or concern; it has nothing to do with finance. Its elements: *walk ...
take.* [15]

669 最	**most** Sun . . . take. Note how the top stroke of the *ear* stretches out to give the *sun* something to rest on. [12]

670 職	**job** The key word refers to one's occupation or employment. In contrast to the verb *work as* (FRAME 651), this character functions as a noun. Its elements: *ear . . . kazoo*. [18]

671 聖	**holy** *Ear . . . submit*. [13]

672 敢	**brave** (ADJ.) *Spike . . . ear . . . taskmaster*. [12]

673 嚴	**strict** *Chatterbox . . . cliff . . . brave*. [20]

674 曼	**drawn out** *Sun . . . net . . . crotch*. The sense of the key word is not restricted to time, as the English expression suggests, but can also refer to space. [11]

曰　　晶　　曼

❖ Used as a primitive, this character will change its meaning to a brightly colored *mandala*. As always, the key-word meaning can also be used as a primitive meaning.

675 慢	**slow** (ADJ.) *State of mind . . . mandala*. [14]

676 漫	**overflow** (V.) *Water . . . mandala*. [14]

677

ring (N.)

環 Jewel . . . net . . . ceiling . . . mouth . . . scarf. The number of elements is large here, so take care. Learn it in conjunction with the next frame, since these are the only two cases in this book where the combination of elements to the right appears. [17]

678

give back

還 Net . . . ceiling . . . mouth . . . scarf . . . road. [16]

679

husband

夫 The character for a **husband** or "head of the family" is based on the character for *large* and an extra line near the top for the "head." Recall the character for *heavens* already learned back in FRAME 403, and be sure to keep your story for this character different. [4]

一　二　夫　夫

680

regulations

規 Husband . . . see. [11]

681

replace

替 Two husbands . . . day. [12]

682

lose

失 "To **lose**" here takes the sense of "misplace," not the sense of *defeated*, whose character we learned in FRAME 61. It pictures a *husband* with a *drop of* something falling from his side as he is walking along, something he **loses**. [5]

ノ　失

683

feudal official

臣 This character is actually a pictograph for an eye, distorted to make it appear that the pupil is protruding towards the right.

This may not be an easy form to remember, but try this: Draw it once rather large, and notice how removing the two vertical lines gives you the pictograph of the eye in its natural form.

As for what this has to do with the meaning, the "pop-eye" image belongs to a **feudal official** standing in awe before his Emperor. [6]

一　丁　丂　互　臣　臣

❖ When this character is used as a primitive, the meaning becomes *underling*.

---

684 臨	**be about to**
	Underling . . . reclining . . . goods. [17]

❖ 臥 Scrooge

The primitive element to which we are assigning the meaning of **Scrooge** offers a perfect description of the penny-pinching protagonist of "A Christmas Carol." Happily, the two pieces that make it up, *underling* and *again*, reflect what happens in the story: a young boy (the *underling*) who grew up without family love, ends up exploiting the poor and lacking all feeling for them. In the end, the spirit of Christmas catches up with him and he is able to relive his past, recover his sympathy for others, and relinquish his superiority to become an *underling again*— this time deliberately and with love.

We have only two examples of this primitive in this lesson, but it will prove useful later on as well. [8]

---

685 賢	**worthy**
	Scrooge . . . clams. [15]

---

686 堅	**firm** (ADJ.)
	Scrooge . . . soil. [11]

687

力

power

With a little imagination, one can see a muscle in this simple, two-stroke character meaning **power**. [2]

フ　力

❖ When used as a primitive, this character can mean either *muscle* (not to be confused, of course, with the character of the same meaning in FRAME 60) or *power*.

688

另

another

Mouth ... muscle. [5]

689

別

don't

Another ... sword. [7]

另　別

690

拐

turn (V.)

Fingers ... another. [8]

691

男

male (N.)

Rice fields ... power. This character is reserved for humans. [7]

692

功

achievement

Work / I-beam ... power. [5]

693

奴

slave (N.)

Woman ... crotch. [5]

694

努

toil (V.)

Slave ... muscle. [7]

695 加	*Muscles . . . mouth.* [5]	add
696 賀	*Add . . . shells.* [12]	congratulate
697 架	*Add . . . trees.* [9]	shelf (N.)
698 協	*Needle . . . muscles* (three of which give us "triceps," or *muscles* on top of *muscles*). [8]	cooperate

699 行 — line of business

The key word refers to the work or **line of business** one is engaged in, but to make it easy to remember think of queues of people lining up to buy whatever your **line of business** has to sell them. First look at the left side of the character. Let the first two short lines represent the first two people in line, followed by a long line of others (the third stroke). As always, there are those who try to cut in line, as you can see from the next two strokes. More often than not, this starts a precedent as others try to creep in after them (the final stroke). [6]

丿 彳 彳 彳 行 行

❖ As a primitive, this character has two forms. Reduced to the left side only, 彳 it can take the meaning of a *queue,* from the above explanation. When the middle is opened up to make room for other elements, it becomes a *boulevard.*

700 律	*Queue . . . brush.* [9]	law
701 復	*Queue . . . double back.* [12]	recover

702 得	must ^(AUX. V.)

702 得 — must ^(AUX. V.)

Queue . . . daybreak . . . glue. [11]

703 待 — treat ^(v.)

This key word has to do with how one deals with others or **treats** them. The elements: *queue . . . Buddhist temple.* [9]

704 往 — toward

Queue . . . candlestick. This character has the special sense of moving or journeying in the direction of or **toward** (or **towards**, if you come from the British Isles) something. [8]

❖ 悳 — 10 commandments

Think of Moses coming down the mountain with the tablets of the **10 commandments** in hand and fire in his eyes. Now look closely at the tablets and you will notice that there is a small safety *net* attached to the bottom. This is just in case Moses gets it into his head to smash them a second time. The people's gaze is fixed on the tablets and once again they are of *one heart.* [12]

十 · 甴 · 甴 · 悳

705 德 — morality

Queue . . . 10 commandments. [15]

706 聽 — listen

Ear . . . king . . . 10 commandments. [22]

707 廳 — hall

Cave . . . listen. [25]

708 微 — tiny

Queue . . . mountain . . . ceiling . . . wind . . . taskmaster. [13]

709

街   *Boulevard . . . bricks.* [12]

street

LESSON 25

WE RETURN ONCE again to the world of plants and growing things, not yet to complete our collection of those primitives, but to focus on three elements that are among the most commonly found throughout the Chinese writing system.

Now and again, you will no doubt have observed, cross-reference is made to other characters with similar key words. This can help avoid confusion if you check your earlier story and the connotation of its respective key word before proceeding with the character at hand. While it is impossible to know in advance which key words will cause confusion for which readers, we will continue to point out some of the likely problem cases.

710 禾	standing grain

This character depicts stalks of **grain** that have not yet been harvested but are **standing** at attention in the field awaiting the farmer's sickle. [5]

丿 二 千 千 禾

❖ When this character is used as a primitive element, its meaning will change to *wild rice*.

711 程	journey (N.)

Wild rice ... submit. [12]

712 和	harmony

This key word has to do with peaceful co-existence and, by extension, with all sorts of **harmony**. Its elements: *wild rice ... mouth.* [8]

713 移	shift (V.)

Wild rice ... many. [11]

714 秋	autumn *Wild rice ... fire.* [9]
715 愁	gloomy *Autumn ... heart.* [13]
716 利	profit (N.) *Wild rice ... saber.* [7]
717 香	perfume (N.) *Wild rice ... sun.* [9]
718 季	seasons *Wild rice ... child.* [8]
719 委	committee *Wild rice ... woman.* [8]
720 秀	elegant *Wild rice ... fist.* [7]
721 透	penetrate *Elegant ... road.* [10]
722 誘	entice *Words ... elegant.* [14]
723 歷	experience (N./V.) *Cliff ... two wild rices ... footprints.* [16]
724 米	rice This character has a pictographic resemblance to a number of grains of **rice** lying on a plate in the shape of a star. [6]

丶 丷 丷 半 半 米

| 725 迷 | *Rice . . . road.* [9] | lost |

| 726 謎 | *Words . . . lost.* [16] | riddle |

| 727 類 | *Rice . . . pooch . . . head.* [18] | kind (N.) |

728 竹 — bamboo

Bamboo grows upwards, like a straight *nail*, and at each stage of its growth (which legend associates with the arrival of the new moon) a new joint forms (the first stroke). Two such **bamboo** stalks are pictured here. [6]

丿 ㇒ 𠂉 ㇒ 𥫗 竹

❖ When this character is used as a primitive, the meaning remains the same, but the vertical lines are severely abbreviated so that they can take their place at the top where, like *flowers*, they are always to be found.

| 729 笑 | *Bamboo . . . die young.* [10] | laugh (V.) |

| 730 箱 | *Bamboo . . . one another.* [15] | box (N.) |

| 731 筆 | *Bamboo . . . brush.* [12] | pen |

732 等	etc. *Bamboo . . . Buddhist temple.* [12]
733 算	calculate If you have ever used an abacus to **calculate**, you should have no trouble with this character. The *bamboo* sticks provide the frame, and in place of beads you have *eyeballs*. Now all you need to do is add your *two hands* to do your gruesome calculations. [14]
734 答	answer [v.] *Bamboo . . . fit.* [12]
735 策	strategy *Bamboo . . . thorn.* [12]

LESSON 26

THIS LESSON WILL take us beyond the halfway mark. From there on, it will all be downhill. The final uphill push will involve what appears to be the simplest of primitive elements. It was withheld until now because of the difficulty it would have caused earlier on.

736	person

人   The character for *enter* (FRAME 638) showed someone walking to the left. The one for **person**, shown here, represents someone walking to the right. [2]

$$ ノ \quad 人 $$

❖ Used as a primitive, this character keeps its character form except when it appears to the left (its normal position), where it is made to stand up in the form 亻.

The primitive meaning is another matter. The general idea of *person* is already implied in many of the characters in which the primitive appears. But so many of the previous stories have also included people in them that simply to use *person* as a primitive meaning would be risky. We need to be more specific, to focus on one particular *person*. Try to choose someone who has not figured in the stories so far, perhaps a colorful member of the family or a friend whom you have known for a long time. That individual will appear again and again, so be sure to choose someone who excites your imagination.

737	prisoner

囚   *Pent in . . . person.* [5]

738	portion

份   *Person . . . part.* [6]

LESSON 26 | 241

---

739   **occupy**

占 The meaning of this key word is to "take possession of" a place.
Its elements: *person . . . telling fortunes.* [7]

---

740   **furniture**

傢 *Person . . . house.* [12]

---

741   **you**

你 *Person . . . reclining . . . small.* You will have to do something
about the "hook" at the end of *reclining* (for example, imagine
lying face down, with the hook representing your feet). [7]

---

742   **you (respectful)**

您 *You . . . heart.* [11]

---

743   **what?**

什 *Person . . . needle.* [4]

---

744   **strip** (N.)

條 *Person . . . walking stick . . . taskmaster . . . tree.* [11]

---

745   **value** (N.)

值 *Person . . . straight.* [10]

---

746   **make**

做 *Person . . . deliberately.* [11]

---

747   **however**

但 *Person . . . daybreak.* [7]

748	dwell
住	*Person ... candlestick.* [7]

イ   住

749	position (N.)
位	*Person ... vase.* [7]

750	piece
件	*Person ... cow.* The key word here refers to things like an "article" of clothing or an "item" of furniture. [6]

751	still (ADV.)
仍	*Person ... fist.* [4]

752	he
他	*Person ... scorpion.* [5]

753	rest (V.)
休	*Person ... tree.* [6]

754	faith
信	*Person ... words.* [9]

755	depend on
依	*Person ... clothing.* [8]

756	example
例	*Person ... line up.* [8]

757	individual
個	*Person ... solid.* Grammatically, this character is a "classifier" or "measure word," in fact the most common of all. [10]

| 758 健 | Person ... build. [11] | healthy |

亻　律　健

| 759 停 | Person ... pavilion. [11] | halt [v.] |

| 760 倒 | Person ... arrive. [10] | upside down |

| 761 仁 | Confucius used this character to refer to the fullness of humanity that can only be achieved in a relationship between *two persons* that is characterized by **benevolence**. [4] | benevolence |

| 762 優 | Person .. worried. [17] | excellent |

| 763 傷 | Person ... reclining ... piggy bank. [13] | wound [n.] |

| 764 保 | Person ... dim-witted. [9] | safeguard [v.] |

| 765 堡 | Safeguard ... soil. [12] | fort |

| 766 付 | Person ... glue. [5] | pay [v.] |

| 767 府 | Cave ... pay. [8] | government office |

768 俯	bow one's head Person . . . government office. [10]
769 代	substitute for Person . . . arrow. [5]
770 袋	bag (N.) Substitute for . . . clothing. [11]
771 化	transform Person . . . spoon. [4]
772 花	flower (N.) Flower . . . transform. This is the full character from which we derived the primitive element of the same meaning. [8]
773 貨	commodities Transform . . . shells. [11]
774 何	whatwhichwhowherewhy? This character is an all-purpose, all-weather interrogative made up of the primitives person and can. [7]
775 便	convenient Person . . even more. [9]
776 丈	100 Chinese inches We already met the Chinese inch (FRAME 153). To remember how to write the character for a hundred of them, draw the three strokes in the order shown below, saying as you go "10 times 10." If you think it helps, you can use the element for tucked under the arm that appears in the final two strokes. [3] ノ 𠂇 丈

| 777 | use ^(v.) |

使 *Person ... 100 Chinese inches ... mouth.* [8]

| 778 | long time |

久 This character uses the diagonal sweep of the second stroke to double up for *bound up* and a *person*. Think of a mummy, and the key word will not be far behind. [3]

ノ　ク　久

| 779 | Chinese acre |

畝 The **Chinese acre**, whose size can differ from region to region, is written *top hat ... rice field ... long time.* [10]

| 780 | third |

丙 Those no-frills flights the airlines offer with only **third**-class seating to attract customers should help create an image from *ceiling ... person ... belt.* [5]

| 781 | handle ^(N.) |

柄 *Tree ... third.* [9]

| 782 | meat |

肉 Here see why the character for *moon* was also assigned the primitive meaning of *flesh* and *part of the body*: over time the character for **meat** shown here often converged with that for *moon* (月) when it appeared as a part of other characters. The only difference in drawing the character in this frame is that the two horizontal strokes are replaced with two *persons*, one atop the other. [6]

冂　内　肉

| 783 | rotten |

腐 *Government office ... meat.* [14]

assembly line

從

The duplication of the character for *person* gives us this primitive for **assembly line**. You will be tempted to think of the *persons* as working on the **assembly line**, but why not imagine clones of your chosen *person* rolling off an assembly line in a factory? [4]

---

784 multitude

眾

Net . . . person . . . assembly line. To begin with, remember what we said way back in Lesson 2 about the triplication of a primitive indicating "everywhere" or "heaps of." Next, note how the middle element on the bottom is actually the primitive for *person* as it normally shows up on the left. To account for the rather dramatic distortion of the *person* in the middle, think of the last time you found yourself crushed in a crowd. [11]

罒　罕　罞　眾

---

785 sit

坐

Assembly line . . . soil. [7]

从　丛　坐　坐

---

786 seat [N.]

座

Sit . . . soil. [10]

---

debate

兟

The image here is a *meeting* of two *persons* engaged in heated **debate**. They are pictured as standing on opposing podiums shouting at one another; hence the *mouths* wide open and leaving little room for their heads. [13]

787 檢	examine
Tree . . . debate. [17]	

788 臉	face (N.)
Moon . . . debate. [17]	

789 來	come
A *tree* with an *assembly line* in it. [8]	

790 麥	wheat
Come. . . walking legs. [11]	

❖
曷

siesta

Conjure up the classic portrait of a Latin **siesta:** a muchacho (your *person*) propped up against something or other, *bound up* from neck to ankles in a sarape fastened with a *fishhook*, one of those great, broad-rimmed mariachi hats pulled down over his face, and the noonday *sun* beating down overhead. [9]

日　号　昜　曷

791 喝	drink (v.)
Mouth . . . siesta. [12]	

792 渴	thirsty
Water . . siesta. [12]	

LESSON 27

IN THIS LESSON we pick up a *small* group of unconnected characters and elements that have fallen between the cracks of the previous lessons, mainly because of the rarity of the characters themselves, of their primitive elements, or of the way in which they are written. Later, in Lesson 50, we will do this once again.

❖ **porter**

壬 Let the extended dot at the top represent the load that the *soldier* is carrying as part of the secondary role he has been asked to take on: the drill sergeant's **porter**. [4]

ノ 二 千 壬

---

793 **appoint**

任 *Person ... porter.* [6]

---

794 **royal court**

廷 *Porter ... stretch.* [7]

---

795 **court of law**

庭 *Cave ... royal court.* [10]

❖ **plow**

⺁ Take this as a pictograph of a **plow**. Note how the completed hand-drawn form looks as if it were drawn with one stroke. In fact, aside from the characters in the next two frames, it is. [1/2]

丿 レ

---

796 **by means of**

以 Picture a *person* dragging a *plow* behind, and the *drop of* sweat which falls from his brow as he does his work. Think of him (or her, for that matter) making a living "**by means of** the sweat of his/her brow." [5]

丷　丿　以

797　　　　　　　　　　　　　　　　　　　**similar**

似　Keep this key word distinct from *be like* (FRAME 98) and *likeness* (FRAME 1414). Its elements: *person . . . by means of.* [7]

❖　　　　　　　　　　　　　　　　　　　**puzzle**

开　Think of this element as a jigsaw **puzzle** in which the pieces interlock. Its elements: *horns . . . two hands.* [6]

丷　开

798　　　　　　　　　　　　　　　　　　**combine**(v.)

併　The sense of the key word is to **combine** distinct things together. Its elements: *person . . . puzzle.* [8]

799　　　　　　　　　　　　　　　　　**piece together**

拼　*Fingers . . . puzzle.* [9]

800　　　　　　　　　　　　　　　　　　**spine**

呂　This character is a clear pictograph of a **spine** with two vertebrae on it. [7]

801　　　　　　　　　　　　　　　　　**associate**(N.)

侶　The sense of this key word is that of a colleague or co-worker. *Person . . . spine.* [9]

❖　　　　　　　　　　　　　　　　　　**firehouse**

炎　The primitive element for a **firehouse** shows—what else?—a *house* with two blazing torches of *fire* at either end of the roof instead of a chimney. [10]

炊　燚

802　　　　　　　　　　　　　　　　　　　　　　glory^(N.)

榮　*Firehouse . . . tree.* [14]

炊　燚　榮

803　　　　　　　　　　　　　　　　　　　　　　labor^(N.)

勞　*Firehouse . . . power.* [12]

804　　　　　　　　　　　　　　　　　　　　　　camp^(N.)

營　*Firehouse . . . spine.* [17]

805　　　　　　　　　　　　　　　　　　　　　　virtuous

善　*Sheep . . . horns . . . mouth.* Pay special attention to the writing of
this character. [12]

羊　羊　羊　羞　善

806　　　　　　　　　　　　　　　　　　　　　　year

年　In an odd fashion, the character for **year** joins together the element for *stick horse,* on the top, and half of what looks to be a
pair of glasses—or as we shall call it, a *monocle.* [6]

丿　ヒ　ヒ　ヒ　⻗　年

807　　　　　　　　　　　　　　　　　　　　　　night

夜　First of all, be sure not to confuse the connotations of **night**
with those of *evening* (FRAME 108), *nighttime* (FRAME 185), and
daybreak (FRAME 29). Its elements: *top hat . . person . . .walking
legs . . . drop.* Take care in drawing the last two strokes. [8]

亠　宀　疒　疒　疒　夜

808	liquid
液	*Water . . . night.* [11]

❖	sled dogs
奐	The *four St. Bernard dogs* with the brandy kegs around their necks and *bound up* to make a team of **sled dogs** wouldn't give Alaskan huskies much of a run for their money, but they could always blame it on being driven under the influence.

The final stroke of *four* doubles up with the first stroke of *St. Bernard dog.* Observe that in the hand-drawn sample below, the "human legs" in the primitive for *four* are stylized to look like a "person." Feel free to use either way of drawing this middle element, but stick to it in the frames that follow. [9]

ク 勹 勼 奐

809	call out ^(v.)
喚	*Mouth . . . sled dogs.* [12]

810	exchange ^(v.)
換	*Fingers . . . sled dogs.* [12]

LESSON 28

WE COME NOW TO a rather simple group of primitives, built up from the three elements that represent *banners, knots,* and *flags.*

❖	banner

扩

Here we have a unique enclosure made up of two elements: *compass* and *reclining*. Think of the **banner** as a standard for rallying around. When the **banner** is upright and fluttering in the breeze, it serves as a *compass* to give direction to soldiers following it. In defeat, however, it is retired and made to *lie down* as a symbol of surrender. [6]

方　方

---

811   travel ^(v.)

旅   *Banner . . . bandana.* [10]

方　扩　扩　扩　旅

---

812   execute

施   *Banner . . . scorpion.* The key word has nothing to do with capital punishment. It means rather "to carry out." [9]

---

813   go swimming

游   *Water . . . banner . . . child.* [12]

---

814   tour ^(v.)

遊   *Banner . . . child . . . road.* [12]

---

815   not

勿

Go back to page 195 and recall how we created the little "piggy" in the primitive for *piggy bank*. Hack off the first stroke of the piggy (the body), and all you have left is the tail with the little "knot" at the end—a homonym that, by way of exception, we will use to remember the abstract key word, **not**. [4]

丿 勹 勹 勿

❖ As a primitive element, this shape will mean a *knot*.

---

816   **suddenly**

忽   *Knot . . . heart.* [8]

---

817   **thing**

物   *Cow . . . knot.* [8]

---

818   **easy**

易   *Sun . . . knot.* [8]

---

819   **grant** (v.)

賜   *Shells . . . easy.* [15]

❖   **flag**

尸

The pictographic representation of this element is obvious. Depending on the character in which this primitive appears, you might want to adjust the national **flag** you use in composing your story. [3]

コ コ 尸

---

820   **corpse**

屍   *Flag . . . death.* [9]

---

821   **nun**

尼   *Flag . . . spoon.* [5]

---

822   **woolen cloth**

呢   *Mouth . . . nun.* [8]

823 泥	mud
Water ... nun. [8]	

824 屋	habitation
Flag ... until. The key word **habitation** is meant to cover a wide range of meanings, from a house and a room to a roof over your head. [9]	

825 握	grip [(v.)]
Fingers ... habitation. [12]	

826 居	reside
Flag ... ancient. Do not confuse with *dwell* (FRAME 748). [8]	

827 鋸	saw [(N.)]
Metal ... reside. [16]	

828 層	story
The **story** referred to here is a floor of a building. Its elements: *flag ... increase.* [15]	

829 局	bureau
Flag ... sentence. Note how the *flag's* long stroke doubles up with (and elongates) the first stroke of *sentence.* [7]	

830 戶	door
A drop of ... flag. [4] Note that in the printed form of the font used here, and in the following three frames, the first stroke looks more like an *eyedropper* (a long *drop of*) and slants downward from right to left, whereas in the hand-drawn form it is shorter and slants left to right. ˋ 户	

831 房	domicile
Door . . . compass. [8]	

832 雇	hire (v.)
Door . . . turkey. Be sure to keep distinct from *employee* (FRAME 54). [12]	

833 顧	look back
Hire . . . head. [21]	

LESSON 29

IN THIS LESSON WE pick up a series of primitives related pictographically to one another and based on the image of a seed. But first we include a stray element that does not really fit into any of our other categories but is very useful in forming some common and elementary characters: the *altar*.

834	show [v.]
示	Although the elements *two* and *small* are available for the using, it may be easier to remember this character as a picture of an altar. Something is placed on the altar to **show** it to those gathered around or to the deity above in whose honor it is placed there. [5]

❖ As a primitive, this character means *altar*. The abbreviated form this element takes when it stands at the left is almost identical to that for *cloak* (衤), except that it lacks the short stroke: 礻.

835	society
社	Altar . . . soil. [7]

丶 フ ラ 礻 礻 社

836	inspect
視	Altar . . . see. [11]

837	happiness
福	Altar . . . wealth. [13]

838	prohibit
禁	Woods . . . altar. [13]

| 839 襟 | **front of a garment** |
| | *Cloak . . . prohibit.* [18] |

| 840 宗 | **religion** |
| | *House . . . altar.* [8] |

| 841 崇 | **worship** (v.) |
| | *Mountain . . . religion.* [11] |

| 842 祭 | **offer sacrifice** |
| | *Flesh . . . crotch/right hand . . . altar.* Note how both the top elements get distorted in order to fit into the space available. [11] |

| 843 察 | **scrutinize** |
| | *House . . . offer sacrifice.* [14] |

| 844 擦 | **scrub** |
| | *Fingers . . . scrutinize.* [17] |

| 845 由 | **wherefore** (N.) |

Think of the phrase "whys and **wherefores**" to capture the key word's sense of the reason for something. The character does this graphically by depicting a seed in a *rice field* sending up a single sprout, which is the whole why and **wherefore** of the seed's existence. (When the *flower* appears, you will recall from FRAME 221, we have a full *seedling*.) [5]

丨 冂 冃 由 由

❖ Used as a primitive, in conformity to the explanation above, this character will be taken to mean a *shoot* or a *sprout*.

| 846 抽 | **take out** |

Fingers . . . sprout. The sense of the key word is "draw out." It has nothing to do with dating. [8]

847	oil
油	Water ... sprout. [8]

848	first
甲	This character reverses the element for *sprout*, giving the image of roots being sent down into the earth by a seed planted in the *rice field*. To connect this to the key word, remember that the **first** root in many plants is the taproot from which other roots spread out. This the **first** of the series for which we have already learned *second, third,* and *fourth* (FRAMES 91, 780, and 86). [5]

\ 冂 冂 日 甲

❖ Keeping with the image of roots in the story above, we shall assign this primitive the meaning of *radish* (which has the same "root" as the obsolete word "radix").

849	pawn (v.)
押	Fingers ... radish. Compare and contrast with *take out* (FRAME 846). [8]

850	express (v.)
申	The sense of this key word is to **express** in words as opposed to gestures, actions, or art. Its primitives are a *tongue wagging in the mouth* ... with a *walking stick* rammed through it and coming out at both ends. [5]

日 申

❖ While this character has obvious affinities to the "seed" group, it also happens to be the zodiacal sign of the *monkey*, which we will take as its primitive meaning.

851	extend
伸	Person ... monkey. [7]

852

gods

神　Altar . . . monkey. [9]

853

fruit

果　The final stage of the seed is reached when the plant has reached its full growth (the *tree*) and comes to fruition, producing **fruit** full of new seeds that can return to the earth and start the process all over again. The main thing to notice here is the element for *brains* at the top, which might prove more helpful than *rice field* for creating an image. [8]

丶　冂　冂　曰　旦　甲　果　果

854

lesson

課　Words . . . fruit. [15]

855

granule

顆　Fruit . . . head. [17]

LESSON 30

BY NOW YOU WILL have learned to handle a great number of very difficult characters with perfect ease and without fear of forgetting. Some others, of course, will take review. But let us focus on the ones you are most confident about and can write most fluently, in order to add a remark about what role the stories, plots, and primitives should continue to play even after you have learned a character to your own satisfaction.

This course has been designed to move in steps from the full-bodied story to the skeletal plot to the heap of bones we call primitive elements. This also happens to be roughly the way memory works. At first the full story is necessary (as a rule, for every character, no matter how simple it appears), in that it enables you to focus your attention and your interest on the vivid images of the primitives, which in turn dictate how you write the character. Once the image has strutted through the full light of imagination, it will pass on, leaving its footprints on the interstices of the brain in some mysterious way. And those footprints are often enough of a clue about the nature of the beast to enable you to reconstruct the plot in broad outlines. Should you need to, you can nearly always follow the tracks back to their source and recall your whole story, but that is generally unnecessary. The third stage occurs when even the plot is unnecessary, and the key word by itself suggests the meaning of the primitives; or conversely, when seeing a character at once conjures up a specific key word. Here again, the plot is still within reach if needed, but not worth bothering with once it has fulfilled its task of providing the proper primitive elements.

There is yet a fourth stage to be reached, as you have probably realized by now, but one you ought not trust until you have completed the full list of the characters given here. In this stage, the primitive elements flow naturally one into the other, without any need to associate them with their meanings. Quite early on, you will recall, we insisted that visual memory of the character as a whole is to be discarded in favor of imaginative memory of its component parts. It may now be clear just why that is so. But it should also be becoming clear that visual memory of the whole will take over as a matter of course once recall of the parts has become automatic. This is a process not to be rushed, however appealing its rewards in terms of writing fluency.

Insofar as you have experienced these things in your own study, fears about the inadequacy of the key words should be greatly allayed. For in much the same way that the character slowly finds its way into the fabric of memory and muscular habits, the key word will gradually give way to a key concept distinct from the particular English word used to express it. Hence the substitution of a Chinese word—or even a number of words—will prove no stumbling block. Quite the contrary, it will help avoid confusion between key words with family resemblances.

In short, the number of steps required to learn the Chinese writing system has not been increased by what we have been doing. The steps have simply become more pronounced here than in traditional methods of drawing and redrawing the characters hundreds of times until they are learned, and in that way the whole process has become much more efficient. Pausing to think about just what your mind has been doing through this book should make the ideas mentioned in the Introduction much more plausible now than they must have seemed way back then.

But we must be on our way again, this time down a road marked "tools."

| 856 | catty (N.) |

斤

A **catty** is exactly one-half kilogram (or a little more than a pound). This character is a picture of a small ax of exactly that weight, a **catty**—the two vertical lines being the handle and the horizontal strokes, the blade. Note the writing order carefully: it begins like the primitive element for *drag*. [4]

゛ 厂 斥 斤

❖ As a primitive, this character will mean a *tomahawk*.

| 857 | place (N.) |

所

Door . . . tomahawk. Two lessons ago, we saw how the first stroke for *door* was drawn differently from the printed form. Here, however, to keep the balance of the character, the hand-drawn form resembles the printed form. [8]

戶 所

| 858 | near |

近

Tomahawk . . . road. [7]

| 859 斬 | hew |
| Car . . . tomahawk. [11] | |

| 860 暫 | temporary |
| Hew . . . days. [15] | |

| 861 漸 | gradually |
| Water . . . hew. [14] | |

| 862 質 | quality (N.) |
| Two tomahawks . . . shells. [15] | |

| 863 斥 | reprimand (v.) |
| Tomahawk . . . a drop of. [5] | |

| 864 訴 | accuse |
| Words . . . reprimand. [12] | |

| 865 乍 | for the first time |
| This character is a picture of a saw. We leave it to you to make an association to the key word: **for the first time**. [5] | |

丿　𠂉　　个　乍

❖ In line with the above explanation, the primitive meaning of this character will be a *saw*. Keep this element distinct from the character of the same meaning (FRAME 827).

| 866 怎 | how? |
| Saw . . . heart. [9] | |

| 867 昨 | yesterday |
| Day . . . saw. [9] | |

868	do
作	*Person . . . saw.* [7]

	broom
彐	The pictographic representation here is of the bristles on the head of a **broom**. [3]

丿　彐　彐

869	snow (N.)
雪	*Rain* that undergoes a change so that it can be swept aside with a *broom* is **snow**. [11]

870	anxious
急	*Bound up . . . broom . . . heart.* [9]

871	seek
尋	*Broom . . . I-beam . . . mouth . . . glue.* [12]

872	married woman
婦	*Woman . . . broom . . . apron.* [11]

873	sweep
掃	*Fingers . . . broom . . . apron.* [11]

	snowman
彔	The *snowflakes* at the bottom of this primitive are here piled up to form a **snowman**, and the three strokes at the top (彑) are meant to represent a *whisk broom* he is holding in his hand. If you take the second, horizontal stroke of *broom*, bend it, and draw it first, the rest will follow naturally. Take a moment to trace it out in the order shown below, since we will not be introducing it formally as a primitive element. [8]

ㄥ　ㄅ　彑　彔

| 874 錄 | Metal . . . snowman. [16] | record (v.) |

| 875 碌 | Stone . . . snowman. [13] | commonplace (ADJ.) |

| ❖ 尹 | A single vertical stroke transforms *broom* into a **rake**. When an element comes BELOW the **rake**, the vertical stroke is shortened, as we have seen before with other similar primitives such as *sheep* and *cow*. Moreover, when something comes ABOVE the **rake** and joins to it at the top, the vertical stroke begins at the top horizontal stroke, as in the following two frames. [4]

フ　ユ　ヨ　尹 | rake |

| 876 爭 | Vulture . . . rake. [6] | contend |

| 877 淨 | Water . . . contend. [9] | clean (ADJ.) |

| 878 事 | This key word here refers to abstract **matters**. The elements are: *one . . . mouth . . . rake*. Note how the *rake* handle reaches out the top and bottom of the character. [8] | matter |

| 879 唐 | The key word here refers, of course, to the **Tang** Dynasty in China (and not to the name of the drink astronauts take with them into outer space, though this could be useful for the next frame). Its elements: *cave . . . rake . . . mouth*. [10] | Tang |

| 880 糖 | Rice . . . Tang. [16] | sugar |

881	hale (ADJ.)
康	This key word—which means "in good health"—is half of the "**hale** and hearty" duo (not to be confused with Laurel and Hardy). Its elements: *cave . . . rake . . . snowflakes.* [11]

882	overseer
尹	The only thing distinguishing this character from a *rake* is the bent handle that does not cut through the top horizontal stroke. It depicts the swish-swash motion of a mop, as demonstrated here by the **overseer** of a group of sanitary engineers. [4]

$$ ⺕ \quad 尹 $$

883	Queen Elizabeth
伊	This character is used now chiefly for its phonetic value in proper names like Iraq, Iguaçu, Illinois, and **Queen Elizabeth** (whose predecessor reportedly was not amused). Its primitives: *person . . . overseer.* [6]

884	monarch
君	The **monarch** referred to in the last frame may come in handy for this frame and the next two after it. *Overseer . . . mouth.* [7]

885	skirt (N.)
裙	*Clothing . . . monarch.* [12]

886	crowd (N.)
群	*Monarch . . . sheep.* [13]

887	and
而	The character for **and** is a pictograph of a comb. If you have trouble remembering how many "teeth" are in this comb, think of a questionnaire or form that uses vertical lines to insure that each letter is separated from the others around it. As it turns out, if you look at the character you will see that there are just enough spaces to spell out the word **a-n-d**. [6]

一 一 广 广 丙 丙 而

❖ The primitive meaning of this character is a *comb*, to be kept distinct from the character of the same meaning (FRAME 633).

888

need [v.]

需

The sense of the key word **need** is best captured by thinking of the economics of supplying what consumers demand. The primitives: *rain . . . comb*. [14]

889

Confucian

儒

Person . . . need. [16]

❖

prospector

嵩

The primitives suggest an image of someone who is *combing* the *mountains*—in this case, an old **prospector** roaming the hills with his gear strapped to the back of his faithful donkey. He is looking for gold not by panning for it but by literally *combing* the *mountains* with a giant *comb*. [9]

山 嵩

890

auspicious

瑞

Ball . . . prospector. [13]

891

upright

端

Vase . . . prospector. [14]

892

bent

曲

Picture yourself grabbing hold of the two strokes poking out the top of the character and wrenching them apart, thus giving the sense of **bent**. If you think of them as deriving from the element for *brains* beneath (of course, the middle stroke has been reduplicated and pulled out to where it can be grabbed hold of), you can associate the key word with someone's mind that has been **bent** to your point of view. [6]

丶　冂　日　由　曲　曲

893

斗

Big Dipper

The **Big Dipper** here is, of course, the constellation of Ursa Major, of which this character is a sort of pictographic representation. The primitive elements (*ice* and a kind of distorted *ten*) are there if you need them. [4]

丶　冫　三　斗

❖ Since we already have a primitive element for a "dipper"— namely, the *ladle*—we shall let this one stand for a *measuring cup*. By the way, it would make a rather large one, since the character is also used for a measure of about a decaliter!

894

料

material (N.)

Rice . . . measuring cup. [10]

895

科

academic discipline

Think of the faculty or **academic discipline** you chose at your university using the elements: *wild rice . . . measuring cup.* [9]

896

用

utilize

Flesh . . . walking stick. Be sure to keep this key word distinct from that for *use* (FRAME 777). The stroke order is exactly as you would expect it from the order of the primitive elements as given. [5]

丿　冂　月　月　用

❖ When this character is used as a primitive element, we shall substitute the image of a *screwdriver*, perhaps the most "utilized" of all tools around the house. An example will follow in the next lesson.

LESSON 31

IN THIS LESSON WE pick up a few primitives of quantity to complement those we learned in Lesson 7, as well as some others related closely to elements learned earlier.

❖
卋

salad

The printed form of the element for *flowers* joins with the long horizontal stroke beneath it to create the picture of a bowl of **salad**. [4]

一　卜　卅　卋

897
昔

times past

Salad . . . days. This is the character for the **times** that we refer to as **past**. [8]

898
借

borrow

Person . . . times past. [10]

899
錯

mistaken

Metal . . . times past. [16]

900
散

scattered

Salad . . . flesh . . taskmaster. [15]

901
撒

scatter

Fingers . . . scattered. Be sure to keep this and the previous frame apart by attaching different connotations to the key words. [12]

902
備

prepare

Person . . . salad . . . cliff . . . screwdriver. Note: In cases like this you can jumble up the primitives into any order that seems best for the composition of a story, provided you feel confident about the relative position that those primitives take to one another in the completed character. Also note the exception in the second stroke of *cliff*, as remarked back in FRAME 114. [13]

903	twenty

廿

The two *tens* joined at the bottom by a short line actually make up the old character for **twenty**, which we might as well learn since we need its primitive form. It is written the same as *salad*, except for the shorter final stroke. [4]

一 十 卄 廿

❖	caverns

庐

The primitive for **caverns** differs from that for *cave* by the presence of the primitive for *twenty*, suggesting a maze of underground *caves*. [7]

广 庐

904	mat

席

Caverns . . . towel. [10]

905	degrees

度

This key word refers to a gradation of measurement, not to academic diplomas. Its primitives: *caverns . . . crotch.* [9]

906	ferry (N./V.)

渡

Water . . . degrees. [12]

907	half (N./ADJ.)

半

The two **halves** of this character are mirror images of one another, the last stroke dividing it in **half** right down the middle. It is easier to draw it with this in mind than to try working directly with the primitives (*horns*, *two*, and *walking stick*).

When this character appears to the left as a primitive, the final stroke is gently bent toward the left, as we will see presently in FRAME 910. [5]

丶　丷　丷　䒑　半

908

伴　*Person . . . half.* [7]

partner

909

胖　*Flesh . . . half.* [9]

fat (ADJ.)

910

判

judge (V.)

Half . . . saber. You might recall the famous scene in which King Solomon is called on to **judge** between two harlots claiming to be the mother of a newborn boy. The King offers to slice the baby in two with a *saber* to give *half* to each of the disputing women, when the true mother reveals herself by relinquishing her claim in order to save the life of the child. In his wisdom, the King **judges** her to be the mother and gives her the child. [7]

❖

关

quarter

This character simply splits the vertical stroke of a *half* in half once again, to get a **quarter**. In so doing, it spreads the split stroke out to form a sort of enclosure under which other primitives will be placed. [6]

丶　丷　丷　䒑　䒑　关

911

眷

dependents

Any of you who have ever had to fill out tax forms know what this key word refers to. For those of you yet to experience that thrill, it refers to family **dependents**. *Quarter . . . eyeball.* [11]

912

拳　*Quarter . . . hand.* [10]

boxing (N.)

913

勝　*Moon . . . quarter . . . muscle.* [12]

victory

914	slice (N.)
片	This character is based on the pictograph of a tree split unevenly down the middle. The right side, shown here, is really no more than a thin **slice**. Note the stroke order. [4]

) ノ' ㇒ 片

915	printing plate
版	Although this character also carries the sense of an "edition" of a publication, the elements, *slice* and *against*, more readily suggest its other meaning of a **printing plate**, or the thin *slice of metal* which is covered with ink and pressed *against* the surface to be printed on. [8]

❖	bunk beds
爿	This character shows the left side of the tree that was unevenly split down the middle in FRAME 914. If you stare at it for a few seconds, you will see the **bunk beds** in no time. The stroke order of this character may surprise you, even though it follows the rules. [4]

ㄴ 丬 爿 爿

916	put on makeup
妆	*Bunk beds . . . woman.* [7]

917	robust
壮	*Bunk beds . . . soldier.* [7]

918	hamlet
莊	*Flowers . . . robust.* [11]

919	attire (N.)
裝	*Robust . . . clothing.* [13]

920 將 **General**

The **General** of this character is a military officer. The elements that go into making it up are: *bunk beds ... flesh ... glue.* [11]

921 之 **of**

As abstract as this key word sounds, remembering it is simplicity itself. All you need do is think of the famous "sign of Zorro," which is etched exactly like the bottom part of this character, just below the *drop*, of. [3]

` ㇌ 之

❖ Used as a primitive element, this character will takes its meaning from the explanation above: *sign of Zorro.*

922 乏 **weary**

Eyedropper ... sign of Zorro. [4]

923 眨 **blink** (v.)

Eyeball ... weary. [9]

924 不 **no**

Play with the primitives of this character as you wish (*ceiling ... person ... a drop of*), but you will probably find that its simplicity, and its frequency, make it easy to remember just as it is. [4]

一 �71 不 不

❖ As a primitive element, this character will mean the internationally recognized NO *symbol:* ⊘.

925 否 **negate**

NO *symbol ... mouth.* [7]

926 杯 **cup**

Tree ... NO symbol. [8]

LESSON 32

WE TURN NOW TO the weapons that remain to be examined. To the *saber*, the *dagger*, and the *arrow*, we add two more primitives in the course of this lesson to the list: the *spear* and the *snare*.

927 矢	dart (N.)
	When shot high into the *heavens*, the **dart** gets so small it looks like a mere *drop*. Although this character could as well mean "arrow," it has no connection with the primitive of that meaning. Hence the new key word. [5]

928 族	tribe
	Banner . . . dart. [11]

929 知	know
	Dart . . . mouth. [8]

930 智	wisdom
	Know . . . sun. [12]

931 矛	spear (N.)
	The **spear** shown here is from a **spear**-gun, which accounts for the barbs and hooks, and also for the line you use to reel in your catch (the final stroke). [5]
	⁻ マ ⁊ 予 矛

932 柔	gentle
	Spear . . . tree. [9]

933 揉	knead
	Fingers . . . gentle. [12]

934 務	tasks
	Spear . . . taskmaster . . . muscle. [11]

935 霧	fog
	Weather/rain . . . tasks. [19]

936 予	bestow
	This character differs from the *spear* shot from a spear-gun (FRAME 931) by the absence of the final stroke, the line for reeling in one's catch. Imagine an initiation ritual in which a tribal chief **bestows** on a young man a long "ceremonial spear" as a symbol of his coming of age. It is "given" without strings attached. [4]
	❖ As a primitive element this character will keep the meaning of a *ceremonial spear* from the story above.

937 序	preface (N.)
	Cave . . . ceremonial spear. [7]

938 預	beforehand
	Ceremonial spear . . . head. [13]

939 野	wild (ADJ.)
	This character refers to **wild**life or **wild** things. Its elements: *computer . . . ceremonial spear.* [11]

940 班	class (N.)
	The key word refers to a group of students gathered in the same **class**room or studying the same subject matter. Its elements: *saber . . . two balls/kings.* [10]

941 弓	bow (N.)
	This character pictures the bent wooden **bow**. In Book 2 we will learn how to make the *bowstring* that goes with it. If you stretch this character out and see the indentation on the left as its handle, the pictography should be clearer. [3]

ㄱ ㄱ 弓

| 942 | draw ^(v.) |

弓丨 In addition to the association with *bows* and arrows, this character is also used to **draw** water from a well or **draw** attention or opinions out of people. The elements: *bow . . . walking stick.* [4]

| 943 | strong |

強 *Bow . . . elbow . . . insect.* Note how the *elbow* is elevated to make room for the *insect* beneath. [11]

| 944 | weak |

弱 Two *bows* . . with *ice* on them. [10]

| 945 | bullet |

彈 *Bow . . . list.* [15]

| ❖ | dollar sign |

弗 Composed of two *walking sticks* running through a *bow*, this character is infrequent as a primitive, and yet easy to remember for what it looks like: the dollar sign, $. When it is written under another element, the first vertical stroke is abbreviated to a short "tail" as the final stroke, and the second vertical stroke is cut off at the top: 弗. Examples follow. [5]

弓 弗 弗

| 946 | Buddha |

佛 *Person . . . dollar sign.* [7]

| 947 | expense |

費 *Dollar sign . . . clams.* [12]

948 弟	younger brother
	Horns . . . dollar sign. [7]

949 第	No.
	The key word **No.** is the abbreviation for "number." Its elements: *bamboo . . . dollar sign.* [11]

❖ 丂	snare
	The **snare** of this primitive is drawn something like the last two strokes of a *bow.* [2] 一　丂

950 巧	adroit
	I-beam . . . snare. [5]

LESSON 33

ALTHOUGH WE still have a number of primitives left relating to human activities, we may at this point pick up what remains of those having to do specifically with people and parts of the human body, and a few others.

951

身

somebody

The key word **somebody** was chosen to convey the double meaning of this character: person and body (though it could also be a chassis or a fuselage). Its composition is based on the *nose* (which, you will recall, is also the character for *oneself*). The extension of the bottom and far right strokes of that element, together with the unusual diagonal stroke, forms the pictograph of **somebody** with a prominent paunch. [7]

｀　ｆ　ｆ　ｆ　自　身　身

952

射

shoot (v.)

Since this character is used to **shoot** guns and bows, we can call to mind the famous verse: "I shot an arrow into the air, It fell to earth I know not where." (Poor Henry Wadsworth must have lost a lot of arrows.) This character, however, tells us where it DID land: *glued to . . . somebody.* [10]

953

謝

thank

Words . . . shoot. [17]

954

老

old man

In the character for an **old man** the element for *soil* is drawn first to indicate that one has come close to the age when "dust to dust" begins to take on a personal meaning; the diagonal *walking stick* is added to help the **old man** get around, and the *spoon* for those times when he needs to be *spoon*-fed. [6]

一　十　土　耂　耂　老

❖ When this character is used as a primitive and its shape adjusted to 耂, the meaning is changed to *Santa Claus*. If the long white beard is not enough, think of this: by some accounts he is already well over 1,700 years old.

❖

与

slingshot

We could not introduce this element in the last lesson, where it rightly belongs, because only now do we have enough pieces to make a character with it. The **slingshot** is like a *bow*, except for the handle that you pull the sling back with. [2]

一　与

955

考

take an exam

Santa Claus . . . slingshot. Note how the top of the *slingshot* gets absorbed into the final stroke of *Santa Claus.* [6]

956

烤

roast (v.)

Fire . . . take an exam. [10]

957

孝

filial piety

Santa Claus . . . child. [7]

958

教

teach

Filial piety . . . taskmaster. [11]

959

者

someone

Santa Claus . . . tongue wagging in the mouth. Think of "that special **someone**" in your life to avoid confusing this key word with *somebody* (FRAME 951). [8]

❖ As a primitive it means a *puppet*-on-a-string—or if it helps, a *Santa Claus puppet.*

960	-ing
著	*Flowers . . . puppet.* The key word is used to indicate ongo-**ing** action. [11]

961	pig
豬	*Sow . . . puppet.* [15]

❖	maestro
自	To remember with this primitive meaning, you might picture a tuxedo-clad **maestro** waving his baton about wildly. The baton is, of course, the little *drop* at the top. And the two boxes attached to the long vertical stroke may represent his tuxedo tails, if you wish. [6]
	′ 丨 丿 𠂤 𠂤 自

962	chase
追	*Maestro . . . road.* [9]

963	commander
帥	*Maestro . . . towel.* [9]

964	teacher
師	The only thing that distinguishes a **teacher** from a *commander* is the element for *ceiling*. The *commander's* battlefield is outdoors and the **teacher's** indoors. [10]

965	lion
獅	*Pack of wild dogs . . . teacher.* [13]

966	bureaucrat
官	By replacing the *maestro's* baton (the *drop*) with the roof of a *house*, we have his equivalent in the institutional world of big government: the **bureaucrat**. [8]

967 管 — pipe

The key word here should be thought of in the sense of a conduit or tubing. Its elements: *bamboo . . . bureaucrat*. [14]

968 父 — father

The kindness and hard work of the ideal **father** are seen in this abbreviation of the *taskmaster* that leaves off his rod or whip and replaces it with the sweat of the **father's** brow (the two *drops* at the top). [4]

ノ ハ グ 父

969 交 — mingle

Top hat . . . father. [6]

970 效 — effect (N.)

Mingle . . . taskmaster. [10]

971 較 — relatively

Cars . . . mingle. [13]

972 校 — school (N.)

Tree . . . mingle. [10]

973 足 — lower leg

This character depicts the lower leg, that is, the part from the kneecap (the *mouth*) to the foot (the part that leaves the *trail of footprints*). [7]

❖ As a primitive on the left, it is amended to 𧾷. Its meaning remains *lower leg*, but should be thought of as a *wooden leg* in order to avoid confusion with other similar elements, namely *human legs, animal legs,* and *walking legs*.

974 跑 — run (V.)

Wooden leg . . . wrap. [12]

| 975 跳 | jump [v.] |
| Wooden leg . . . portent. [13] | |

| 976 路 | path |
| Wooden leg . . . each. [13] | |

| 977 露 | dew |
| Rain . . . path. [21] | |

| 978 骨 | skeleton |

This character and primitive refer to the *part of the body* composed of the bones and their joints. The top part of the character, terminating in the element for *crown*, is a pictograph of a bone joint. We leave it to you to put the pieces together, so to speak. [10]

丶　�冂　冎　冎　冎　咼　骨

| 979 滑 | slippery |
| Water . . . skeleton. [13] | |

| ❖ 咼 | jawbone |

The meaning of this primitive is taken from the combination of "the joint" above and the *mouth* in the monk's *cowl* below. [9]

冂　円　咼

| 980 過 | cross [v.] |
| Jawbone . . . road. [12] | |

LESSON 34

THE NEXT GROUP OF primitives we shall consider has to do mainly with topography and exhausts the list of primitives remaining in that category.

❖

阝

pinnacle

This primitive meaning has been chosen because of its connotation of "the highest point," thereby suggesting the image of the highest point in a village, that is, a hill or mountain on which sacred or festive events take place. If you have a clear image of the Athenian acropolis, you might use it to express this element for a **pinnacle**. Note that this primitive appears only on the left. On the right, as we shall see later, the same form takes a different meaning. [3]

⁊　ʒ　阝

981

阿

Apollo

Transcribing the word **Apollo** into Chinese requires three characters, of which the character in this frame is the first. Since this character is used primarily for its sound value, the choice of a key word has nothing to do with the meaning of the character, as was the case earlier with *Queen Elizabeth*. Its elements are: *pinnacle . . . can.* [8]

982

啊

aah!

Mouth . . . Apollo. Like the English "oohs and aahs," this character is a particle which is used for expressing admiration, among other things. [11]

983

際

occasion

Pinnacle . . . offer sacrifice. [14]

984 險	perilous
Pinnacle . . . debate. [16]	

985 隨	as you wish
Pinnacle . . ͵ left . . . moon . . . road. [15]	

986 陽	Yang
Pinnacle . . . piggy bank. Here we meet the second of the Yin-Yang couple. Yin will show up later (FRAME 1189). [12]	

987 陳	exhibit [v.]
Pinnacle . . . east. [11]	

988 防	ward off
Pinnacle . . . compass. [7]	

989 附	attach
Pinnacle . . . pay. [8]	

990 院	Inst.
This key word, the abbreviation for **Institution**, represents the use of that word as a suffix affixed to certain buildings and organizations. Its primitive elements: *pinnacle . . . finish.* [10]	

991 陣	battle formation
Pinnacle . . . car. [10]	

992 隊	team
Pinnacle . . . animal horns . . . sow. [12]	

993 降	descend
Pinnacle . . . walking legs . . . monocle. Note that the drawing for *monocle* in the character for *year*, where it was first introduced (FRAME 806) was somewhat irregular because it doubled	

up with other strokes. From now on *monocle* will be written as shown below. [9]

阝 阞 阞 降 降

994 stairs

階 *Pinnacle ... all.* [12]

995 hole

穴 *House ... eight.* [5]

宀 宀 穴

❖ As a primitive, this character uses an alternate form: the *eight* at the bottom is replaced with the primitive element for *human legs.*

996 research

究 *Hole ... baseball.* [7]

宀 宀 宂 究

997 abruptly

突 *Hole ... chihuahua* [9]

998 empty

空 *Hole ... I-beam.* [8]

999 control (v.)

控 *Fingers ... empty.* [11]

1000 border

邊 *Nostrils ... hole ... compass ... road.* [18]

自 鼻 鼻 邊

❖	paper punch
宀儿	This primitive simply discards the first stroke of the character for *hole* to become a **paper punch**. When found at the top of another primitive, it undergoes the same change, the *eight* becoming *human legs* (see FRAME 995). [4]

1001	deep
深	*Water . . . paper punch . . . tree.* [11]

| 1002 | spy ^(N.) |

1002	spy [N.]
探	*Fingers . . . paper punch . . . tree.* [11]

1003	hill
丘	Since this supposedly pictographic representation of a **hill** looks like anything but, picture a row of *tomahawks* driven into the ground up to their heads, and see if that doesn't present you with a more memorable image of **hill**—at least a riskier one for sliding down! [5]

1004	troops
兵	*Hill . . . animal legs.* [7]

Lesson 35

THE PRIMITIVE FOR *thread* is one of the most common in all the characters. This means that you are likely to be putting it where it doesn't belong and forgetting to include it where it does—all the more reason to give it a vivid image each time. Fortunately, nearly all the thread-related characters to be covered in this book will appear in this lesson, so you can learn them all at once.

❖

                                      thread

Remember when your granny used to ask you to bend your arms at the *elbows* and hold them out so that she could use them like a rack to hold a skein of yarn (here **thread**) while she rolled it up into a ball? Can you see at the top the two *elbows* (with the second stroke overwriting the end of the first *elbow*), and the element for *small* below? [6]

1005   **silk**

絲 Silk *thread* is so fine that it needs to be twined together ("doubled") to be used in sewing. Note that in the hand-drawn example below the bottom half of *thread*, as it appears on the left, is a little different from the printed form. It is abbreviated, with the *small* being written as a series of uphill dots drawn in sequence. [12]

絲 絲

1006   line [N.]

線 *Thread . . . spring.* [15]

1007	maintain

維 *Thread . . . turkey.* We give the hand-drawn character here to remind you that the third stroke of *turkey* differs from that of the printed form. [14]

糸　維

1008	silk gauze

羅 Although commonly used as a family name, the character has its own meaning: **silk gauze.** Its primitives: *net . . . maintain.* [19]

1009	continue

續 *Thread . . . sell.* [21]

1010	overall

統 *Thread . . . sufficient.* [12]

1011	give

給 *Thread . . . fit.* [12]

1012	tie (v.)

結 *Thread . . . aerosol can.* [12]

1013	end (n.)

終 *Thread . . . winter.* [11]

1014	rank (n.)

級 *Threads . . . outstretched hands.* [9]

1015	epoch

紀 *Thread . . . snake.* [9]

1016	red

紅 *Thread . . . I-beam.* [9]

1017 約	**make an appointment** *Thread ... ladle.* [9]
1018 細	**fine** (ADJ.) *Thread ... brains.* The key word **fine** covers the sense of small and delicate as well as the sense of superb quality. [11]
1019 緊	**tight** *Scrooge ... thread.* [14] 臤　　緊
1020 織	**weave** (V.) *Thread ... kazoo.* [18] 糹　　織
1021 網	**net** (N.) This is actually the full character for **net**, whose abbreviation (the *eye* lying on its side, 罒) we have been using as a primitive with that meaning. Its component elements are: *thread ... glass cover ... animal horns ... perish.* [14]
1022 綠	**green** *Thread ... snowman.* [14]
❖ 繡	**needlepoint** Note the unusual writing: the *words* are drawn first and both *threads* are drawn in their abbreviated form. [19] 言　　結　　繡
1023 彎	**curved** (ADJ.) *Needlepoint ... bow.* [23]

1024	bay (N.)
灣	Water ... curved. [23]

1025	be enamored of
戀	Needlepoint ... heart. [23]

1026	change (V.)
變	Needlepoint ... taskmaster. [23]

❖	spool
巠	The *stream* hanging from the *ceiling* here is not made of water but hundreds of different colored strings, each of them reaching down to a **spool** (the *I-beam*) on one of the hundreds of sewing machines lined up in a sweatshop. [7]

一　　巠　　巠

1027	scripture
經	Thread ... spool. [13]

1028	lightweight (ADJ.)
輕	Car ... spool. [14]

❖	cocoon
幺	The two triangular shapes here and their final stroke are intended as a pictograph of a **cocoon**, spun in circles and tied up at the end. It is like the character for *thread*, except that the silkworm's actual product has not yet emerged clearly at the bottom. [3]

乚　　幺　　幺

1029	behind
後	Queue ... cocoon ... walking legs. [9]

1030

幾

Two cocoons . . . person . . . fiesta. [12]

how many?

幺　幺幺　丝　丝　幾

❖ As a primitive, this character will mean an *abacus*, the bead-instrument used in the Orient to calculate *how many*. Be sure you don't confuse this *abacus* with the one that appeared in the story for *calculate* in FRAME 733.

1031

機

Tree . . . abacus. [16]

machine

1032

斷

Fishhook . . . two cocoons "divided by" (the horizontal line) two cocoons . . . tomahawk. [18]

sever

丝　丝　丝丝　斷　斷

1033

繼

The sense of this key word is "to continue," but be careful to keep its association distinct from the character we already learned with that meaning (FRAME 1009). *Thread . . . two cocoons "divided by" (the horizontal line) two cocoons . . . fishhook.* [20]

carry on

1034

顯

Sun . . . two cocoons . . . cooking fire . . . head. [23]

obvious

1035

樂

Dove between two cocoons. . . tree. [15]

music

白　帛　樂　樂

1036

藥

Flowers . . . music. [19]

medicine

1037 雞	chicken

Vulture . . . cocoon . . . St. Bernard dog . . . turkey. [18]

1038 麼	(suffix)

As was the case back in FRAME 465, this key word is set in parentheses to indicate the grammatical function of this character, which has no identifiable meaning as such. Its elements: *hemp . . . cocoon.* [14]

1039 系	lineage

The single stroke added to the beginning of the primitive for *thread* gives the image of threads woven into a single cord. Hence the meaning, **lineage**. [7]

❖ As a primitive, this character will take the meaning of *yarn*, as the uniting of many *threads* into *one* (slightly warped) strand is most obvious with *yarn*.

1040 係	relate to

Person . . . lineage / yarn. [9]

1041 孫	grandchild

Person . . . lineage / yarn. [10]

LESSON 36

EARLIER WE CREATED an image for *seal* (FRAME 154). Here we come to a set of primitives based on seals and stamps.

❖ 卩	stamp (N.)

This character is a kind of pictograph of a **stamp** that may best be imagined as a postage **stamp** to distinguish it from other stamp-like things to come up later. [2]

ㄱ　卩

1042 卻	withdraw

The sense of this key word is to step back from something; it has nothing to do with taking money out of the bank. Its primitives: *valley . . . stamp.* [9]

1043 腳	foot

Part of the body . . . withdraw. [13]

1044 服	apparel

Flesh . . . stamp . . . crotch. The *stamp* is stretched out here. [8]

1045 命	fate

This character connotes life in general, but also the particular **fate** meted out to one by virtue of the distinctive character with which one is born. Its elements: *fit . . . stamp.* The bottom portion of *fit* is nudged to the left to make room for the *stamp.* [8]

❖ 卯	letter opener

In its full form, this primitive looks like a *stamp* and its mirror image on the left: 卯. This is the form it takes when there is nothing below it. When there is, it is condensed to the shape shown in this frame. Let us take advantage of the fact that the right side becomes a *dagger* and assign this primitive the meaning of a *letter opener.*

If you take care to draw the strokes of this condensed form in the order shown below, the drawing of the full form will follow automatically. [5]

丿　⺈　⺈　切

1046　　　　　　　　　　　　　　　　　　　　stay (v.)

留　*Letter opener ... rice field.* [10]

1047　　　　　　　　　　　　　　　　　　　　slide (v.)

溜　*Water ... stay.* [13]

1048　　　　　　　　　　　　　　　　　　　　chat (v.)

聊　*Ear ... letter opener.* [11]

1049　　　　　　　　　　　　　　　　　　　　willow

柳　*Tree ... letter opener.* [9]

❖　　　　　　　　　　　　　　　　　　　　chop

卩　The **chop** is the engraved piece of wood or stone used in the Orient to certify documents, generally using red ink. Unlike the *stamp*, the top stroke here reaches a good distance to the left of its vertical stroke. Note that in printed characters, this primitive is sometimes abbreviated to ⺄. In hand-drawn characters, this is almost always the case. Compare the printed form in FRAMES 1051–1053 with their hand-drawn forms in Index I. [2]

フ　マ

1050　　　　　　　　　　　　　　　　　　　orders (N.)

令　*Meeting ... chop.* [5]

人　仒　令

1051 冷 *Ice ... orders.* [7]	cold
1052 零 *Rain ... orders.* [13]	zero
1053 領 *Orders ... page.* [14]	collar (N.)
❖ 甬 Western *chops* and seals often *utilize* **sealing wax** rather than red ink to leave their impression. [7] ᑦ 甬	sealing wax
1054 通 *Sealing wax ... road.* [10]	communicate
1055 勇 *Sealing wax ... muscle.* [9]	courageous
❖ 巳 The primitive for **fingerprint** is like that for *stamp* except that the second stroke bends back towards the right, like an arm. [2] ᒋ 巳	fingerprint
1056 犯 *Wild dogs ... fingerprint.* [5]	criminal (N.)
1057 危 *Bound up ... on a cliff ... fingerprint.* [6]	danger

1058	fragile
脆	*Flesh . . . . danger.* [10]

❖	staples
上	This primitive represents a number of small **staples**, like the kind commonly used in an office and at school. Note that the second stroke is sometimes extended, especially in the printed form.

When there are two sets of facing staples with something between them, we will take the related meaning of a *zipper* (which is much more convenient for closing your trousers than stapling them). An example will follow below. [4]

ˊ 𠂆 𠂉 𠂊

1059	print (N. / V.)
印	*Staples . . . stamp.* [6]

1060	excitement
興	*Zipper . . . same . . . tool.* [16]

𠂉   𦥑   𦥯   舉   興

LESSON 37

THIS NEXT cluster of characters has to do with primitives related to the activities of eating and drinking.

❖ 酉	**whiskey bottle** This primitive will mean *whiskey bottle*. In its pictograph, you can see the loosely corked lid, the bottle, and the contents (about one-third full). You might also think of the Spanish *porrón*, a decanter shaped like a long-necked bird. [7] 一 厂 冂 丙 西 酉 酉
1061 酒	**liquor** *Water . . . whiskey bottle.* [10]
1062 配	**distribute** *Whisky bottle . . . snake.* [10]
1063 酋	**chieftain** *Animal horns . . . whisky bottle.* [9] ソ ソ 片 酋 酋
1064 尊	**venerate** [v.] *Chieftain . . . glue.* [12]
1065 遵	**abide by** *Venerate . . . road.* [15]
1066 豆	**beans** This character is supposed to depict a pot of **beans**, but in its present form, it looks a lot more like a table on which you might place the pot. [7]

一　口　尸　豆　豆

❖ Used as a primitive, this character will also take the meaning of a *table*. Be sure to avoid confusing this image with the one you have for the primitive meaning *small table* (see page 40).

| 1067 頭 | head (N.) |

Here we meet at last the full character on which the primitive for **head** is based. The elements: *table . . . head*. [16]

| 1068 短 | short |

Dart . . . table. [12]

| 1069 禮 | ceremony |

Altar . . . bent . . . table. [17]

| 1070 體 | body |

Skeleton . . . bent . . . table. [23]

| ❖ 壴 | drum |

The element for **drum** shows a *soldier* over a *table*. The top stroke of the *table* appears to be missing, but actually it has doubled up with the final stroke of the element for *soldier*. [9]

| 1071 鼓 | drum |

The full character for the *drum* adds a *branch*, apparently to serve as a **drum**stick, to the primitive for *drum*. [13]

| 1072 喜 | joyful |

Drum . . . mouth. [12]

| 1073 廚 | kitchen |

Cave . . . drum . . . glue. [15]

1074

樹 — **timber**

This character really has the same meaning as the pictograph for *tree* that we learned in FRAME 191. Since this character is more elaborate, we choose a more sophisticated key word to represent it. The elements: *trees ... drum ... glue.* [16]

❖

皿 — **dish**

The primitive for **dish** is, clearly, the pictograph of a painted or carved bowl, seen from the side. [5]

丶 冂 冖 冊 皿

1075

血 — **blood**

The *drop* in the *dish* is **blood**. It is similar to the *drop* we saw earlier on the *dagger* in the character for *blade* (FRAME 80). [6]

1076

盡 — **exhausted**

A *brush* with one clump of bristles (the fourth stroke) burned off by the *cooking fire ... dish.* [14]

ヨ 肀 圭 肃 盡

1077

儘 — **to the utmost**

Person ... exhausted. [16]

1078

蓋 — **lid**

Flowers ... gone ... dish. [14]

1079

溫 — **temperature**

Water ... prisoner ... dish. [13]

1080

監 — **supervise**

Underlings ... reclining ... drop ... dish. Consult the handwritten form in Index I, where you will see why we have chosen to name the third primitive *drop* rather than *floor.* [14]

❖ The primitive meaning changes to *hidden camera*. Keep this in mind when creating your story for the key word.

1081 籃	basket
Bamboo ... hidden camera. [20]	

1082 藍	blue
Flowers ... hidden camera. [18]	

❖ 艮 **silver**

We give this element the meaning of **silver** from the character in the following frame. The primitive elements that make it up are more trouble to hunt out than they are worth. It is best simply to learn it as is. In doing so, take careful note of the stroke order, and also the fact that when this element appears on the left, the penultimate stroke is omitted, giving us simply 艮. [6]

フ　ヨ　ヨ　尸　尸　艮

1083 銀	silver
Metal ... silver. [14]	

1084 跟	heel [N./V.]
Wooden leg ... silver. Although this character is used as a noun for **heel**, it can also take the verbal meaning of "follow" (close on another's **heels**). [13]	

1085 很	very
Queue ... silver. [9]	

1086 根	root [N.]
Tree ... silver. [10]	

1087 即	immediately
Silver ... stamp. [7]	

1088 節	Bamboo ... immediately. [13]	holiday
1089 退	Silver ... road. [9]	retreat (v.)
1090 腿	Flesh ... retreat. [13]	leg
1091 限	Pinnacle ... silver. [9]	limit (N./v.)
1092 眼	Eye ... silver. [11]	eyelet
1093 良	Drop of ... silver. [7]	high-quality (ADJ.)

` 良

❖ When using this character as a primitive, take the image of a saint's *halo*. As with *silver*, when this element is drawn on the left, the penultimate stroke is omitted, giving us 皀.

1094 浪	Water ... halo. These are waves that crest or break into foam, not electrical **breakers** or people who do "break dancing." [10]	breakers
1095 娘	Woman ... halo. [10]	mom
1096 食	If *umbrella* and *halo* aren't enough, break the *halo* down into *drop* and *silver*—or "silverware," an additional primitive. [9]	food

❖ As a primitive this character keeps its meaning of *food*, but, as with *silver* and *high-quality*, on the left the final two strokes are combined into one: 飠.

1097

meal

飯   *Food ... against.* [12]

1098

dine

餐   *Magic wand ... evening ... right hand/crotch ... food.* [16]

1099

Bldg.

館   The abbreviation of **Building** suggests that this character is used in proper names, as indeed it often is. Keep your connotation distinct from *Inst.* (FRAME 990) when working with the elements: *food ... bureaucrat.* [16]

1100

raise (v.)

養   *Sheep ... food.* The key word is used in connection with **raising** animals, family, flowers, and so forth. [15]

❖

waitress

旡   If you can doodle with the first two strokes on your own, the addition of the *human legs* will give you this primitive's meaning of **waitress**. [4]

一   匸   尹   旡

1101

since

既   *Silver ... waitress.* The key word **since** should not be used as a preposition or adverb to indicated "from a point in the past," but as a conjunction meaning "now that." [9]

1102

approximate (ADJ.)

概   *Root ... waitress.* It is also possible to divide the character up into *tree* and *since*. [13]

Lesson 38

A NUMBER OF primitives relating to plant life remain to be considered, and we shall devote the next few pages to doing so. If it seems that new primitives with only limited use are piling up, remember that they will be needed when you move on to Book 2.

1103   **even** (ADJ.)

平 This character is easiest remembered as a pictograph of a water lily floating on the surface of the water, which gives it its meaning of **even**. The fourth stroke represents the calm, smooth surface of a pond, and the final stroke the long stem of the plant reaching underwater. [5]

一   丆   丆   亚   平

❖ As a primitive, this character can keep its pictographic meaning of a *water lily*.

1104   **evaluate**

評 *Words . . . water lily.* [12]

1105   **level ground**

坪 *Ground . . . even / water lily.* [8]

1106   **ooh!**

乎 This character is an "exclamatory particle" and it is written as a *water lily* except for its stylishly tilted hat at the top and chic hook at the bottom. **Ooh!** la la. [5]

1107   **shout** (V.)

呼 *Mouth . . . Ooh!* [8]

❖ **sheaf**

乂

These two strokes are a crude drawing of a bundle of stalks bound together into a **sheaf**. [2]

ノ 乂

1108 **hope** (v.)

希 *Sheaf . . . cloth.* [7]

1109 **scarce**

稀 *Wild rice . . . hope.* [12]

❖ **Carmen Miranda hat**

臼

Like the elements that make up this primitive (*zipper,* two *sheaves,* and *crown*) the **Carmen Miranda hat**—named after the famous Brazilian entertainer—is an outlandish fruit basket of a headpiece that can be several times the size of one's head. [13]

ﾚ ﾚ 臼 臼 臼

1110 **study** (v.)

學 *Carmen Miranda hat . . . child.* [16]

臼 學

1111 **senses** (N.)

覺 *Carmen Miranda hat . . . see.* [20]

1112 **stir** (v.)

攪 *Fingers . . . senses.* [23]

❖ **pit**

凵

The primitive element for **pit**, a perfect pictograph, refers to a trap hole made to catch animals. Do not confuse your image with that for the character learned in FRAME 295. [2]

㇄ ㄩ

1113

匈   *Sheaf ... pit.* [4]

sinister

乂 凶

1114

兇   *Sinister ... human legs.* [6]

cruel

1115

胸   *Part of the body ... bound up ... sinister.* [10]

bosom

❖

离

Fagan

The *top hat* and *cruel* by themselves suggest the villainous figure of Charles Dickens' **Fagan**, the unscrupulous archthug who uses Oliver Twist and his companions as pickpockets. Now all you have to do is work in the *belt* and *elbow*. [10]

亠   卥   峇   离

1116

離

leave [v.]

Fagan ... turkey. This is potentially one of the most difficult characters to remember. Tackle it positively and let the image "sink in" by carrying it around with you today and calling it up in your spare moments. [18]

1117

禽   *Umbrella ... Fagan.* [12]

fowl

1118

辛

peppery

The character in this frame pictures food whose taste is so hot and **peppery** that it makes the hairs on your body *stand up* as straight as *needles*. [7]

立 辛

❖ When this character is used as a primitive, it can take the additional meaning of a *chili pepper*, except when two extra strokes are added to the bottom, giving it the form of a *pepper plant*: 亲. Not your ordinary *pepper plant*, mind you, but one where little bottles of *chili peppers* grow ready for the market.

1119   **manage**

辦   Two *chili peppers . . . muscle.* [16]

辛 勃 辦

1120   **dispute** (V.)

辯   Two *chili peppers . . . words.* [21]

❖   **hot sauce**

辟 One way American children learn to cope with food they are forced to eat against their will is to smother it with **hot sauce**. We see this depicted in the *mouth* with the *flag* over it (in this case, the Stars and Stripes), set beside the element for *peppery*. [13]

尸 启 辟

1121   **partition** (N.)

壁   *Hot sauce . . . ground.* [16]

1122   **evade**

避   *Hot sauce . . . road.* [16]

1123   **new**

新 *Pepper plant . . . tomahawk.* Note that in some printed fonts (as is the case here), the final two strokes of *pepper plant* are attached to the *tree*. In drawing, however, it is better to be guided by the handwritten example that follows. [13]

亲　新

1124	fuel
薪	*Flowers . . . new.* [17]

1125	relatives
親	*Pepper plant . . . see.* [16]

1126	inner garments
襯	*Clothing . . . relatives.* [17]

1127	good fortune
幸	Simply by turning the dot at the top of the primitive for *peppery* into a cross shape, we move from things bitter and *peppery* to **good fortune**. [8]

1128	clench (v.)
執	*Good fortune . . . bottle of pills* [11]

1129	newspaper
報	*Good fortune . . . stamp . . . crotch.* For the right side of this character, compare FRAME 1044. [12]

❖	cornucopia
凵	Considering the lack of circular lines in the Chinese writing system, this character is not a bad pictograph of a **cornucopia**. Despite the appearance of the printed form, what looks like the first two strokes is actually written as one. [2]

ㄴ　凵

1130	call (v.)
叫	*Mouth . . . cornucopia.* [5]

1131 收	receive
	Cornucopia . . . taskmaster. [6]

❖ 先	rice seedling
	To distinguish this primitive element from the character for *seedling* (FRAME 221) and the primitive for *sprout* (page 257), think of a whole handful of **rice seedlings** being stuck in the muddy soil of a paddy field. The component pieces are *soil* and *human legs.* [5]

土　先

1132 陸	land ^(N.)
	The sense of **land** carried by this character is distinct from *soil* (FRAME 147) and *ground* (FRAME 478) in that it is meant to represent **land** seen from a distance, that is, *land* as opposed to "water." Its elements: *pinnacle . . . rice seedlings . . . ground.* [11]

❖ 執	rice stalk
	The story behind the element is the little-known tale of "Jackie and the **Rice Stalk**." After fertilizing the *ground* around his little *rice seedling* with a *bottle of* steroid *pills*, little Jackie Chan awakens the following morning to find that it has grown into a mammoth **rice stalk**, at the top of which dwells a ferocious giant. After conquering the beast, as we all know, Jackie goes on to earn international fame as a movie star. [11]

1133 勢	force ^(N.)
	Rice-stalk . . . muscle. Think here of things like the **force** of habit or the negative **forces** influencing events. [13]

1134 熱	heat ^(N./V.)
	Rice stalk . . . cooking fire. [15]

1135 藝	technique
	Flowers . . . rice stalk . . . rising cloud. [19]

1136	sign of the hog

亥 This character is the 12th sign of the Chinese zodiac: the **sign of the hog.** It is best learned by thinking of an acorn-eating **hog** in connection with the primitive meaning given below. [6]

❖ The *top hat* represents the external shape of the *acorn,* and the unusual but easily written complex of strokes beneath it (which you might also see as distortions of an *elbow* and *person*) stands for the mysterious secret whereby the *acorn* contains the oak tree in a nutshell.

1137	nucleus

核 *Tree . . . acorn.* [10]

1138	tot

孩 *Child . . . acorn.* [9]

1139	carve

刻 *Acorn . . . saber.* [8]

1140	should

該 *Words . . . acorn.* [13]

	resin

术 This *drop* added to the primitive for *tree* is a *drop of* **resin.** As mentioned in FRAME 191, the *tree* becomes a *pole* (that is, a *tree* with its branches not touching) occasionally. To account for this difference, in the following two frames think of the *resin* from the *tree* as sap dripping down gently on the trunk; and the *resin* on the *pole* as a tree leaking *resin* profusely—the result of a naive but greedy gardener anxious to siphon off as much of the stuff as he can, as quickly as possible. [5]

1141 述	narrate
	Resin . . . road. [8]

1142 術	art
	Boulevard . . . resin. [11]

1143 殺	kill
	Sheaf . . . resin . . . missile. [11]

❖ 圭 | **wire mesh**

This primitive for **wire mesh** looks very close to that for *salad*, except that an extra horizontal line has been included. [5]

一　二　圭　井　圭

1144 襄	aid [v.]

Top hat and scarf . . . chatterbox . . . wire mesh. To put this all together, think of a flock of well-educated, upper-class carrier pigeons (hence the *top hats and scarves)* who are employed to **aid** you in sending messages. Instead of transporting little notes tied to their legs, they communicate verbally. Here we see them in their *wire mesh* cage, gabbing away at each other as they await their next assignment, *chatterboxes* that they are.

As is so often the case—too often to mention each time—this character is commonly used as a family name. [17]

❖ As a primitive, this character will take the meaning of a *pigeon coop*, from the explanation above.

亠　品　窠　襄

1145 讓	yield
	Words . . . pigeon coop. [24]

1146 壤	territory
	Ground . . . pigeon coop. [20]

❖	hamster cage
寏	The image of a **hamster cage** should be easy to compose from the elements: *house . . . wire mesh . . . animal legs.* [10]

宀　宭　寏

1147	frigid
寒	*Hamster cage . . . ice.* [12]

1148	competition
賽	*Hamster cage . . . oysters.* [17]

LESSON 39

THE REMAINDER OF plant-related primitives are built up from combinations of vertical and horizontal lines, representing respectively plants and the earth from which they spring. Accordingly, it would be a good idea to study the remaining elements of this section at a single sitting, or at least to review them before passing on to the next grouping.

❖ 主	**grow up**

As the plant **grows up** it sprouts leaves and a stalk, depicted as a single horizontal stroke added to the element for *soil*. Think of something (its accompanying primitive) **growing up** in a flash to many times its normal size, much like little Alice in Wonderland, who **grew up** so fast she was soon larger than the room in which she was sitting. [4]

一　二　キ　主

1149

毒　**poison**^(N.)

Grow up . . . mother. [9]

1150

素　**vegetarian diet**

Grow up . . . thread. [10]

1151

青　**blue or green**

This character can be used for either **blue or green**. The primitives suggest a 300-foot telescope on your roof, all *grown up* (stretched out as far as it will go) and fixed on the *moon*, that orb of **green** cheese in the evening sky. Once in a **blue** *moon,* you might actually see the cheesemaker! [8]

❖ When used as a primitive element, this character will take the meaning of a *telescope*.

1152 精	refined
	Rice . . . telescope. [14]

1153 請	invite
	Words . . . telescope. [15]

1154 情	feelings
	State of mind . . . telescope. [11]

1155 睛	eyeball
	Eye . . . telescope. By this time there shouldn't be any confusion between this key word and the primitive meaning earlier associated with *eye* (page 24). [13]

1156 清	pure
	Water . . . telescope. [11]

1157 靜	quiet
	Telescope . . . contend. [16]

1158 責	responsibility
	Grow up . . . clams. Since this character will be used as an element in several others (two examples follow immediately), it would be good to give it as concrete an image as possible. Perhaps you can think back to the first heavy **responsibility** you had in your first summer job when you were *growing up* and where you earned your first *clams.* [11]

1159 績	accomplishments
	Thread . . . responsibility. [17]

1160 積	accumulate
	Wild rice . . . responsibility. [16]

1161 表	surface (N.)
	Grow up . . . scarf. [8]

1162 錶	watch (N.)
	Metal . . . surface. [16]

1163 生	life
	Think of the microscopic *cell*, that miraculous *drop* of **life**, that *grew up* to become you. [5]

ノ 生

❖ The primitive meaning will remain *cell.*

1164 星	star (N.)
	Sun . . . cell. [9]

1165 姓	surname
	Woman . . . cell. [8]

1166 性	sex
	State of mind . . . cell. [8]

1167 害	harm (N./V.)
	House . . . grow up . . . mouth. [10]

1168 割	cut off (V.)
	Harm . . . saber. [12]

❖ 丰	bushes
	The element for **bushes** differs from that for *grow up* only in the extension of the single vertical stroke beneath the final horizontal stroke and in the order of writing. [4]

三 丰

1169 慧	intelligent
	Two *bushes* ... *broom* ... *heart*. [15]

1170 豐	plentiful
	Two *bushes* ... *mountain* ... *beans*. It might help to think of a "hill of beans." [18]

丨　丰丨　丰丰　豐丰丨　豐

❖ 夫	bonsai

The element for *bushes* has an extra stroke added to give the image of the crutches Japanese gardeners use to hold up a tree that is being bent into shape. From there it is but a short leap to the art of cultivating miniature **bonsai** plants, which began in China and was further developed in Japan.

Note the discrepancy between the printed form and the hand-drawn form below in the writing of the final stroke. These are largely font variations but, as before, we suggest you follow the latter. [5]

三　丰　夫

1171 春	springtime
	Bonsai ... *sun*. [9]

1172 泰	tranquil
	Bonsai ... *snowflakes*. [10]

❖ 丰	cornstalk

The element for *bushes* extended the vertical stroke beneath the final horizontal stroke; the **cornstalk** omits that final stroke altogether, leaving only the **stalk** and the leaves bursting forth on all sides. [3]

二　丰

1173	proffer [v.]
奉	The sense of the key word **proffer** is to "offer respectfully." *Bonsai . . . cornstalk.* Use a ritualistic, religious meaning. [8]

1174	cudgel [N.]
棒	*Tree . . . proffer.* [12]

❖	spinach
堇	You no doubt recognized the top primitive of this element as *twenty*. We could use it, of course, but prefer to look at it as the element for *salad*, in this case a healthy **spinach** *salad*. The reason the last stroke is shorter than normal is that it is being shoved down a little boy's *mouth* from above, the excuse being that it will help him *grow up* healthy and strong. [11]

艹　苫　堇

1175	diligent
勤	*Spinach . . . muscle.* [13]

1176	careful
謹	*Words . . . spinach.* [18]

1177	merely
僅	*Person . . . spinach.* [13]

❖	Popeye
菓	By twisting the final two strokes of the primitive for *spinach* into a pair of legs, we get the ideal *husband* that little boys who eat their *spinach* will grow up to be like—**Popeye.** [11]

艹　苫　菓

1178 漢	Han

Water . . . Popeye. The key word refers to the **Han** people who gave the name "hanzi" to Chinese characters. [14]

1179 難	difficult

Popeye . . . turkey. [19]

1180 攤	vendor's stand

Fingers . . . difficult. [22]

❖ 丰	silage

The drawing of this element is difficult to do smoothly, and should be practiced carefully. It is a pictograph of all sorts of plants and grasses thrown together to make **silage**. The vertical stroke will always double up with another primitive element's vertical stroke. [6]

一 二 干 开 丰 丰

1181 華	splendor

Flower . . . silage . . . needle. [11]

丶 亠 艹 艹 芒 苧 芒 苎 苧 莗 華

1182 嘩	clamor (N.)

Mouth . . . splendor. [14]

1183 垂	droop

Porter . . . silage. Note how both the third stroke and the final two strokes of this character double up for the two primitives. This is clearer in the hand-drawn form. [8]

一 二 三 千 垂 垂 垂 垂

1184	hammer [N.]
錘	*Metal . . . droop.* [16]

1185	sleep [V.]
睡	*Eyes . . . droop.* [13]

LESSON 40

THIS LESSON will cover the final few characters relating to time and direction to be treated in Book 1. Only a few will remain, and they will be taken up in Book 2.

1186	now
今	The final stroke of this character is a rare shape, which we have not met before and will only meet in this character and others that include it as a primitive. We are more accustomed to seeing it straightened out as part of other shapes—for instance, as the second stroke of *mouth*. If you need any help at all with this stroke, you may picture it as two hands of a clock pointing to what time it is **now**. The element above it, *meeting*, should easily relate to that image. [4]

人　今

❖ We shall use *clock* as the primitive meaning of this character, in line with the above explanation.

1187	harbor (v.)
含	*Clock . . . mouth.* The key word is used for **harboring** things like grudges and resentment. [7]

1188	miss (v.)
念	Not "miss a train," but **miss** one's friends. *Clock . . . heart.* [8]

1189	Yin
陰	This is the **Yin** of the famous **Yin**-Yang (dark-light) couple, and refers to the "shady side of the slope." Its elements: *pinnacle . . . clock . . . rising cloud.* [11]

1190	shady
蔭	**Shady** as opposed to "sunny." The primitives: *flowers. . . Yin.* [15]

1191	west

西

In our way of naming off the directions, the **west** always comes fourth. So it is convenient to find the character for *four* in this character. But since we want only *one* of the *four* directions, the **west** adds the *one* at the top and sucks the *human legs* a bit out of their *mouth* in the process. [6]

一　厂　厂　丙　丙　西

❖ When this character is used as a primitive, the meaning of *west* can be expanded to refer to the *Old West* of cowboy-movie fame, just as the meaning of the character for *east* was expanded into "the *East*." Note, however, that in its primitive form the *legs* are straightened out and reach down to the bottom of the *mouth*. Hence, we get the shape 襾.

1192	want (v.)

要

Old West . . . woman. [9]

1193	waist

腰

Part of the body . . . want. [13]

1194	ticket

票

Old West . . . altar. [11]

1195	drift (v.)

漂

Water . . . ticket. [14]

1196	mark (N.)

標

Tree . . . ticket. This character figures in a variety of compounds for everything from road signs to trade**marks**. [15]

1197	merchant

賈

Old West . . . oysters. [13]

1198 價	Person . . . merchant. [15]	price
1199 煙	Fireplace . . . Old West . . . ground. [13]	smoke [N.]
1200 南	Belt . . . good fortune. Note how the *belt* runs through the middle of *good fortune*, which affects the stroke order. [9]	south

十　内　南

LESSON 41

This next collection of characters is based on the primitive for *gate*. From there we shall go on to consider other elements related to entrances and barriers in general.

1201	gate

門 The pictograph of two swinging doors to represent a **gate** is so clear in this character that only its stroke order needs to be memorized. In case you should have any trouble, though, you might doodle with the shapes on a piece of paper, taking care to note the difference in the stroke order of the two facing doors. The two doors of the **gate** usually serve as an enclosure, and are written BEFORE whatever it is they enclose. [8]

｜　｢　｢　｢　｢＇　門　門　門

❖ As a primitive, we shall continue to give it the meaning of *gate*, but recommend the image of swinging doors (like the kind once common at entrances to saloons) to distinguish it from the primitive for *door*.

1202	(plural)

們 *Person . . . gate.* Here again, the parentheses around the key word indicate this character's grammatical function rather than its meaning. [10]

1203	leisure

閒 *Gate . . . moon.* [12]

1204	ask

問 *Gate . . . mouth.* [11]

1205 閒	interval

Gate ... sun/day. This **interval** applies to time and space alike, but the latter is better for creating an image. [12]

1206 簡	simple

Bamboo ... interval. [18]

1207 開	open (v.)

Gate ... two hands. [12]

1208 聞	hear

Gate ... ear. Compare the connotation you associated with the character meaning *listen* (FRAME 706). [14]

1209 倉	storehouse

The single swinging door under the element for *meeting* is meant to represent not one *gate*, but many of them. Add *mouth* (as an entrance here) and the *meeting of gates* becomes a **storehouse**. [10]

人 𠆢 倉

1210 槍	gun

Tree ... storehouse. [14]

1211 創	initiate

Storehouse ... saber. [12]

1212 非	non-

This key word, a negating prefix, is a doodle of a heavy iron pole with bars extending in both directions, to create the picture of a jail cell. From there to "**non-**" is but a short step. [8]

丨 ㇆ ㇕ ㇕ 非 非 非 非

❖ When this character serves as a primitive, we shall draw on the explanation above for the meaning of *jail cell.*

1213 排	row (N.)
Fingers . . . jail cell. [11]	

1214 罪	guilt
Eye/net . . . jail cell. [13]	

1215 靠	lean on
Declare . . . jail cell. [15]	

❖ ㄗ	key

This element gets its name and meaning from the pictographic representation of a key. The shape should be familiar: the third and fourth strokes of the character for *five.* [2]

ㄱ　ㄗ

1216 侯	marquis

Person . . . key . . . dart. Hint: the pun suggested by the pronunciation of the key word and the primitive for *key* may come in helpful. [9]

1217 候	wait (V.)

Marquis . . . walking stick. Note where the *walking stick* is positioned in this character. [10]

❖ 夬	guillotine

This element depicts a large, sharpened *key* coming down on the head of a criminal *St. Bernard dog.* [4]

ㄱ　ㄗ　ㄅ　夬

1218	decide
決	The etymology of **decide** (de-cidere = cut off) will help here; the elements are: *water . . . guillotine*. [7]

1219	fast^(ADJ.)
快	*State of mind . . . guillotine*. [7]

1220	chopsticks
筷	*Bamboo . . . fast*. [13]

1221	tanned hide
韋	The vertical stroke added here (the third stroke) turns the primitive element for a *key* into a kind of "locket." Below that, we find a square container (the *mouth*) and a *monocle*. Now all you have to do is fix the locket to a long strip of **tanned hide** and figure out something interesting to use it for. Note that the final vertical stroke of the *monocle* reaches all the way through to touch the *mouth*. This is another of those characters commonly used in family names and transliterations. [9]

⁻   芍   吾   壴   垚   韋

❖ When using this character as a primitive, we will stay with the meaning of a *locket*.

1222	surround
圍	*Pent in . . . locket*. [12]

1223	great
偉	*Person . . . locket*. [11]

1224	defend
衛	*Boulevard . . . locket*. Do not confuse with *ward off* (FRAME 988), *guard* (FRAME 181), or *safeguard* (FRAME 764). [15]

Lesson 42

THE NEXT FEW primitives are only loosely connected in the sense that they all build up on the form introduced in the character of the opening frame. The final five characters, although unrelated to the rest of the lesson, form a useful learning unit.

1225 干	**offend** (v.) Let the key word suggest the phrase that people use right before they launch a major insult: "I don't mean to **offend** you, but…" Since the character already looks like your neighbor's revolving circular clothesline (viewed from the side), give it a spin to the dingy sheets on the other side and complete the sentence. [3] 一 二 干 ❖ The primitive meaning is *clothesline*.
1226 岸	**shore** *Mountain … cliff … clothesline.* [8]
1227 幹	**trunk** *Mist … umbrella … clothesline.* The key word refers to the main stem of a tree. [13]
1228 旱	**drought** *Sun … clothesline.* [7]
1229 趕	**hurry** (v.) *Walk … drought.* [14]
1230 于	**Yu** Note how this character, a surname, differs from *offend* by virtue of the small hook at the end of the third stroke. Playing

on the *clothesline* primitive, think of this character's shape as a *clothing conveyor*, the kind you see when you walk into a dry-cleaning shop. The little "hook" at the bottom represents the hooks used for attaching the cleaned and plastic-covered clothes to the revolving *conveyor*. The celebrated **Yu Qian**, who led the rout against the Mongolian invaders in the mid-fifteenth century and saved the city of Beijing from being overrun, later opened his own string of dry-cleaning establishments named You Soil—**Yu Clean**. [3]

❖ From the above explanation, the primitive meaning of this character will change to *clothing conveyor*.

1231		eaves
宇	*House . . . clothing conveyor.* [6]	

1232		*moi*
余	This character is now used chiefly as a surname, but it was used in the past by sovereigns to refer to themselves—the way you might, placing your hand against your breast and elevating your nose slightly in the air, declare, "As for **moi**...." Its elements: *umbrella . . . clothing conveyor . . . small*. The last stroke of *clothing conveyor* and the first of *small* overlap here. [7]	

❖ Since the key word is too abstract, we shall take the image of a *scale* whose indicator spins round and round on the dial because *moi* has been overeating.

1233		excess
餘	*Food . . . scale.* [15]	

1234		eliminate
除	*Pinnacle . . . scale.* [10]	

1235		route [N.]
途	*Scale . . . road.* [10]	

1236   bundle up

束   *Tree . . . mouth.* When people **bundle up** in cold weather, the only thing they have to leave exposed is their face. Since *trees* don't have eyes and noses, when you **bundle up** your favorite *tree* in scarf, overcoat, leggings, and mittens, the only thing you have to be sure to leave exposed is that little *tree mouth* that the squirrels run in and out of. [7]

     一　曰　冎　吏　束

❖ When used as a primitive, this character will add the meaning of a *bundle*.

1237   quick

速   *Bundle . . . road.* [10]

1238   spicy hot

辣   *Chili pepper . . . bundle.* [14]

1239   entire

整   *Bundle . . . taskmaster . . . correct.* [16]

❖   horned toad

柬   The primitive to which we assign the meaning of **horned toad** is just what its name, and its appearance, suggest: a *bundle* of *animal horns*. [9]

    一　厂　冂　冂　帀　回　東　東　柬

1240   practice (v.)

練   *Thread . . . horned toad.* [15]

1241   opt for

揀   *Fingers . . . horned toad.* [12]

1242	heavy
重	*Thousand ... li.* Note how the long vertical stroke doubles up to serve both elements. [9]

ノ 一 育 盲 重 重

1243	understand
懂	*State of mind ... flowers ... heavy.* [16]

1244	move (v.)
動	*Heavy ... muscle.* [11]

1245	species
種	*Wild rice ... heavy.* [14]

1246	collide
衝	*Boulevard ... heavy.* [15]

Lesson 43

We may now pick up the remainder of the enclosure primitives to be treated in Book 1, leaving only a few related to animals, which we will take up toward the end of the book, in Lessons 53 and 54. This lesson should give you a chance to review the general principles governing enclosures.

❖ 疒	**sickness** The enclosure shown in this frame is composed of a *cave* with *ice* outside of it. It is used for a number of characters related to **sickness**. If you want to picture a *cave*man nursing a hangover with an *ice*-pack, that should provide enough help to remember the shape of this element and its meaning. [5] 广　疒　疒
1247 病 *Sickness . . . third.* [10]	**illness**
1248 痛 *Sickness . . . sealing wax.* [12]	**ache** [v.]
1249 瘋 *Sickness . . . wind.* [14]	**insane**
❖ 匚	**box** This enclosure, open at the right, represents a **box** lying on its side. When it is not used as an enclosure, its form is cramped to look like this: ㄈ. You may distinguish its meaning by picturing it then as a very small **box**. [2] 一　匚

1250	match ^(v.)

匹 The sense of this key word is "to be equal to." The primitives are: *box . . . human legs.* [4]

一 兀 匹

1251	region

區 *Box . . . goods.* [11]

1252	hub

樞 This key word refers to a center of activity or commerce, not to the center of a wheel. Its primitives: *tree . . . region.* [15]

1253	Europe

歐 *Region . . . yawn.* This character is an abbreviation of the name of the continent of **Europe.** [15]

1254	physician

醫 *Box . . . dart . . . missile . . . whiskey bottle.* [18]

❖	stamp collection

卩 The combination of a *box* and *stamps* gives us a **stamp collection.** Take care not to confuse this primitive with that for *letter opener* (page 292).[4]

龴 卩

1255	look up to

仰 *Person . . . stamp collection.* [6]

1256	greet

迎 *Stamp collection . . . road.* [7]

❖	teepee

ㄗㄟ The dots at the top of this tent are the wooden poles protruding outside the canvas walls of a **teepee**. [5]

丁　丆　丆ʼ　丆ʼˣ　ㄗㄟ

1257	ascend

登 Let the key word suggest someone **ascending** a ladder. In this case, it's a stepladder resting precariously on a *table* inside a *teepee*. Little Hiawatha placed it there so he could **ascend** and change a light bulb at the top. This should help to keep the key word distinct from *rise up* (FRAME 40). [12]

❖ This character will be useful as a primitive, when it will take the meaning of a *stepladder* from the explanation above.

1258	lamp

燈 *Fire . . . stepladder.* [16]

1259	evidence

證 *Words. . . stepladder.* [19]

1260	send out

發 Let the key word suggest someone that you **send out** to deliver a message or a parcel. The image suggested by the elements is a guided *missile* being shot from a *bow* through the hole at the top of a *teepee*. Since the intentions are completely pacific, the *missile* does not have explosives inside, but a courier who will deliver the parcel in person. [12]

❖ Though we have only one instance of this character serving as a primitive in Book 1, it will be helpful to assign it the meaning of a *courier* in connection with the above explanation. It will reappear in Book 2.

1261	discard (v.)

廢 *Cave . . . courier.* [15]

LESSON 44

We come now to a class of elements loosely associated with shape and form. To these we may append the remaining elements in Book 1 having to do with color.

❖ 彡	**rooster tail** The three simple strokes of this element depict a **rooster tail**. [3]
1262 形	**shape** (N.) *Two hands . . . rooster tail.* [7]
1263 影	**shadow** (N.) *Scenery . . . rooster tail.* [15]
1264 彩	**hue** *Pluck . . . rooster tail.* [11]
1265 須	**have to** *Rooster tail . . . head.* This is the only time that the *rooster tail* is placed to the left of its relative element, the *head.* [12]
❖ 参	**cocktail** The little *umbrella* used as a garnish in tropical drinks combines with a *rooster tail* to give us a perfect way to remember the primitive for a **cocktail**. [5]
1266 珍	**rare** *Jewel . . . cocktail.* [9]
1267 參	**participate** The three elbows at the top represent a row of lushes leaning on a bar and throwing back *cocktails* one after another. They are

all there to **participate** in a weekly encounter of AF (Alcoholics Forever). [11]

❖ When this character is used as a primitive, we will take it to mean *drunks at a bar* from the explanation above.

1268 **wretched**

 State of mind . . . drunks at a bar. [14]

1269 **repair** (v.)

修 *Person . . . walking stick . . . taskmaster . . . rooster tail.* [10]

1270 **literature**

文 When you think of your first classes in **literature**, your mind no doubt goes back to similes, metaphors, synecdoches, litotes, and all those other figures of speech and highfalutin' language patterns that you had to memorize, with the result that you all but lost your taste for the subject. The *top hat* indicates a connoisseur of fine **literature** who keeps under his hat that whole tangle of patterns (the "criss-cross" strokes—not really a *sheaf*, but close). [4]

❖ To make the criss-cross pattern mentioned above easier to remember, think of the Scottish plaid on a tam-o'-shanter (the *top hat*) and kilt. From there, we get the primitive meaning of this character: a *Highlander*.

1271 **mosquito**

蚊 *Insect . . . Highlander.* [10]

❖ **bungi-jumper**

This element shows a **bunji-jumper** standing on the edge of a *cliff* and hesitating about whether to cast off or not. He is none other than our *Highlander* in his tam-o'-shanter and kilt, wondering whether he is properly dressed for the occasion. [6]

1272 彥	*Bungi-jumper . . . rooster tail.* [9]	erudite
1273 顏	*Erudite . . . head.* [18]	countenance (N.)
1274 產	*Bungi-jumper . . . cell.* [11]	products
❖ ㄚ ㄑ	The four strokes here, which usually come two on each side of another primitive to tell you what it is that is sparkling, can appear as drops (ㄚ ㄑ), as straight lines (ニ ニ), or as shown in this frame, which is a lot closer to what *sparklers* look like. You can always follow the hand-drawn sample below, but you are bound to run into the other two alternatives from time to time. Take care to keep this distinct from the two primitive forms we learned for *snowflake* (氺 and ⺍). [4] `` ` 丷 丷 丷 ``	sparkler
1275 率	As in a "tax **rate**." *Top hat . . . cocoon-sparkler . . . needle.* [11]	rate (N.)
1276 摔	*Fingers . . . rate.* [14]	tumble (V.)
1277 央	The elements depict a *St. Bernard* with its head and paws keeping their stick-like form, but with the middle or **center** of its body filled out in a box-like shape. [5]	center

丶　冂　冋　央　央

1278 英	England

Flowers . . . center. This is another abbreviation used to identify a country by the pronunciation of the character. [9]

1279 巴	crust

This character—whose principal use is for its phonetic value in transliterations—is shaped roughly like the *snake*, but pay attention to the difference when writing it. Think of the indentations your grandma made with her thumb on the outer rim of a pie **crust** to beautify it, though it can also refer to the kind of **crust** that sticks to pots and skillets during cooking. [4]

乛　冖　刀　巴

❖ Even though the key word is graphic and useful on its own, the added primitive meaning of a *mosaic* or piece of a *mosaic* can also come in handy.

1280 把	grasp (v.)

Fingers . . . mosaic. [7]

1281 爸	papa

Father . . . mosaic. [8]

1282 吧	bar (N.)

Mouth. . . mosaic. The key word refers to the kind of **bar** at which drinks are served. [7]

1283 色	color (N.)

Bound up . . . mosaic. [6]

1284 絶	discontinue

Thread . . . color. [12]

Lesson 45

A NUMBER OF containers of various sorts can be brought together in this lesson. here. The classification is somewhat arbitrary since we are getting hard pressed to organize the leftover primitives into tidy categories. In addition, from this lesson on, most references to key words learned earlier in the book that might have similar connotations will be omitted. Try to think of them yourself as you are going through these characters

---

1285	sweet

甘   This character is a pictograph of a small wicker basket. (The extra short stroke in the middle helps keep it distinct from the character for *twenty*.) All one needs to add is the image of something **sweet** carried in the basket, and the union of picture and meaning is complete. [5]

一 十 廿 廿 甘

❖ Used as a primitive, this character takes the pictograph's meaning of a *wicker basket*, the small kind you take on a picnic.

1286	such and such (ADJ.)

某   The key word here refers to an undetermined or unspecified person or thing. Its elements: *wicker basket . . . tree.* [9]

1287	his-hers-its-theirs

其   This container, which is a bit larger than the *wicker basket* and has two *legs* at the bottom, is a clothes hamper filled with towels marked **his, hers, its** (for the cat), and **theirs.** [8]

一 十 廿 廿 甘 甘 其

❖ When used as a primitive, this character will retain the meaning of a *hamper*.

1288 期	**period of time** *Hamper . . . month.* As the *month* indicates, this has to do with **periods of time.** [12]

| 1289 基 | **base** ^(N.)
This refers to the foundation of something, not to a chemical substance or the "base" of baseball. Its primitives are: *hamper . . . soil.* [11] |

| 1290 斯 | **Sphinx**
This character is used in family names, but also appears as the first and last character of the Chinese word for the mythical **Sphinx.** Its elements: *hamper . . . tomahawk.* [12] |

| 1291 甚 | **tremendously**
Hamper . . . match. Note how the *animal legs* are overwritten by the *human legs* in the lower half of the character. [9] |

| ❖ 虫 | **purse**
By adding a single stroke at the bottom of the character for *middle*, we get a sort of pictograph of a **purse.** [5]

口　中　虫 |

| 1292 貴 | **expensive**
Purse . . . shells. [12] |

| 1293 遺 | **bequeath**
Expensive . . . road. [15] |

| 1294 舞 | **dance** ^(N./V.)
The top two strokes show someone *reclining*, and the next six are a pictograph of an *oaken tub* ribbed with metal strips, like the kind once used for bathing. At the bottom, *evening* and *monocle* round off the character. |

This character can be used as a noun or a verb. [14]

ᄼ　ᄼᄼ　仨　仨　乒　乒　無

舞　舞

1295　　　　　　　　　　　　　　　　　　　　　　**nothing**

無　This character is the Japanese character for the supreme phil-
/ \\\　osophical principle of much Oriental thought: **nothing**ness.
Make use of the *oaken tub* from the previous frame, and add to
that the *cooking fire* at the bottom. [12]

1296　　　　　　　　　　　　　　　　　　　　　　**comfort**[v.]

撫　*Fingers . . . nothing.* [15]
/ \\\

1297　　　　　　　　　　　　　　　　　　　　　　**moreover**

且　The pictographic representation in the primitive shown here is
a small stand with horizontal shelves. (It differs from the character and primitive for an *eye* only in its final stroke, which
extends beyond the two vertical strokes at both ends.) Think of
the shelves as filled up with knickknacks, so that you can only
put **more** "**over**" it on the top, where they risk falling off. [5]

月　且

❖ This character's meaning as a primitive element will remain
shelf.

1298　　　　　　　　　　　　　　　　　　　　　　**older sister**

姐　*Woman . . . shelf.* [8]

1299　　　　　　　　　　　　　　　　　　　　　　**group**[n.]

組　*Thread . . . shelf.* [11]

1300　　　　　　　　　　　　　　　　　　　　　　**ancestor**

祖　*Altar . . . shelf.* [9]

1301 assist [v.]

助 *Shelf . . . power.* The reason the *shelf* appears on the left here is that the right side is the normal position for *power*, the stronger primitive. [7]

LESSON 46

THIS, THE shortest lesson in Book 1, is built up from two basic characters, both of which have to do with a positional relationship. You will want to take special care with the first of them, which undergoes a change in shape and meaning.

1302	side by side

並 This character is a slightly stylized duplication of all three vertical strokes in the character for *stand up*. By lengthening the sixth and seventh strokes, you will see how this is done. [8]

丷　丷　丫　亣　亣　並　並

❖ The primitive meaning remains the same as that of the character, but special attention has to be given to the change in shape this element undergoes when the first three strokes are moved to the last three, giving us: ⧗. We will incorporate this modification by changing its meaning to *side by side and upside down*.

1303	universal

普 *Side by side . . . sun.* [12]

1304	profession

業 *Side by side and upside down . . . not yet.* [13]

业　业

1305	that's right

對 This character's key word indicates a judgment that what someone has said is accurate. *Side by side and upside down . . . soil . . . glue.* [14]

1306	together
共	*Salad . . . animal legs.* We leave it to your culinary imagination to decide what kind of *animal legs* best go **together** with your favorite *salad.* [6]

1307	supply [N./V.]
供	*Person . . . together.* [8]

1308	different
異	*Brains . . . together.* [11]

1309	lane
巷	*Together . . . snakeskin.* [9]

1310	port [N.]
港	*Water . . . lane.* [12]

1311	choose
選	Two *snakeskins . . . together . . . road.* [15]

LESSON 47

THIS NEXT LESSON IS composed of characters whose primitives are grouped according to shape rather than meaning. Each of them makes use, in one way or another, of squares and crossing lines. While this might have brought confusion earlier, we know enough primitives at this stage to introduce them together without risking any confusion.

1312	well (N.)

井 Recalling that there are no circular strokes, and that the shape of the square and the square within a square (FRAME 520) have already been used, it should be relatively easy to see how this character can be consider a pictograph of a **well**. [4]

一 二 丰 井

1313	Asia

亜 Think of the character for **Asia** as representing the entire work-force of the most populous part of the world standing on an *I-beam*, with the result that it splits and bends outwards under the weight.

If you learned the writing correctly for *convex* (FRAME 31), you should have a "feel" for the unusual writing order of this character. [8]

一 丆 丆 丆 丐 丣 亜 亜

1314	evil (N./ADJ.)

惡 *Asia ... heart.* [12]

1315	angle

角 *Bound up ... glass cover ... soil.* [7]

勹 角 角

❖ When this character is used as a primitive, it might be helpful to think of a *carpenter's square,* a meaning suggested directly by the key word.

1316	untie
解	*Carpenter's square . . . dagger . . . cow.* [13]

1317	orifice
嘴	This character really has the same meaning as the simple pictograph for *mouth* that we learned in the very first lesson. Since it is far more elaborate, we choose a more elegant key word to represent it. The elements: *mouth . . . this (literary) . . . carpenter's square.* [16]

1318	once more
再	*Ceiling . . . glass cover . . . soil.* Note how the final stroke of *soil* extends outside of the *glass cover,* unlike the character for *angle* that we just learned. [6]

$$一 \quad 冂 \quad 再$$

1319	weigh
稱	The top stroke of *once more* is replaced with a *vulture.* That, together with *wild rice* gives us **weigh**. [14]

❖	sieve
冓	Think of the **sieve** you use for sifting small amounts of flour. Squeezing on the handle moves the flour over the *wire mesh* to separate out coarser elements *once more*—just to be safe. Note how the final stroke of *wire mesh* and the first stroke of *once more* double up. [10]

$$丰 \quad 冓$$

1320	lecture [v.]
講	*Words . . . sieve.* [17]

1321 構	frame^(v.)

1321 構 **frame** (v.)

Tree . . . sieve. The key word **frame** covers a range of meanings: to compose, construct, falsely incriminate, and so forth. [14]

❖ 冊 **tome**

If you rip off the cover of a thick **tome**, on the spine you will see stitching and binding that looks pretty much like this character. Caution: this is sure to get you into serious trouble with the librarian. [5]

冂　冃　冃　冊

1322 扁 **flat** (ADJ.)

The *book cover* that you just ripped off the *tome* in the last frame, the "*door*" to the *tome*, is lying **flat** on the floor, right where you let it fall, and where you will soon join it when the librarian comes in to punch your lights out. [9]

戶　扁

❖ When this character is used as a primitive, it takes on the meaning of *book cover* from the explanation above.

1323 篇 **piece of writing**

Bamboo . . . book cover. [15]

1324 編 **compile**

Thread . . . book cover. [15]

❖ 侖 **library**

The primitive for a **library** is drawn as a *meeting* of *tomes*. [8]

亼　侖

1325	theory
論	Think of a **theory** as something you construct with *words* in a *library* and a story should not be far behind. [15]

1326	wheel
輪	*Car . . . library.* [15]

1327	canon
典	We introduce the character for a **canon** (a collection of scriptural or authoritative books) here because of its connection to the characters treated immediately above. It is based on the character for *bent* (FRAME 892), whose last stroke is lengthened to coincide with the first stroke of the element for *tool*. [8]

LESSON 48

A FEW PRIMITIVES having to do with groupings and classifications of people remain to be learned, and we may bring them all together here in this lesson.

1328 氏	**family name** Pay close attention to the stroke order of the elements when learning to write this character. The elements: *eyedropper* . . . *plow* . . . a *one* . . . *fishhook*. [4]
	⼀ 厂 ⻘ 氏
1329 紙	**paper** *Thread . . . family name.* [10]
1330 昏	**dusk** *Family name . . . sun.* [8]
1331 婚	**marriage** *Woman . . . family name . . . day.* You could, of course, use *dusk* in place of the final two primitives, but this is one of those cases in which breaking a compound primitive up into its original parts is helpful in composing a story. [11]
❖ 氐	**calling card** *Family name . . . floor.* The primitive meaning refers to the **calling cards** used by professionals to identify their name and position. [5]
1332 低	**low** *Person . . . calling card.* [7]

1333 底	**bottom** *Cave . . . calling card.* [8]
1334 民	**people** In place of the *drop* at the start of the character for *family name*, we have a *mouth*, which makes you think of the "vox populi." [5] ㇇ ㇕ 尸 民 民
1335 眠	**slumber**(N.) *Eyes . . . people.* [10]
1336 甫	**Fu** This key word is a surname. In case there is no one named **Fu** in your circle of immediate acquaintances, you might take the evil genius with the trademark moustache, Dr. **Fu** Manchu, as a hitching post for the primitives in this character: *needle . . . screwdriver . . . drop.* [7] 一 厂 𠃌 冂 冃 甫 甫 ❖ Since the key word refers to a surname, when the character serves as a primitive, you can think of it as a "dog tag," either the kind you actually hang around the neck of Rover or an identification tag handed out to soldiers.
1337 補	**patch**(v.) *Cloak . . . dog tag.* [12]
❖ 尃	**gummed label** The elements for *dog tag* and *glue* should be easy enough to associate with the primitive meaning, **gummed label**. [10] 甫 尃

| 1338 博 | *Needle . . . gummed label.* [12] | knowledgeable |

| 1339 搏 | *Fingers . . . gummed label.* [13] | wrestle |

| ❖ 阝 | On the left, and rather more pressed in its form, this element means the high spot of a village, or its *pinnacle*. On the right side, in the form shown here, it means the lowest part of the city, around which its walls rise up as a protection against invaders. Hence we nickname this element: **city walls**. [3] | city walls |

| 1340 都 | *Puppet . . . city walls.* [11] | metropolis |

| 1341 部 | *Muzzle . . . city walls.* [11] | department |

| 1342 郎 | *Halo . . . city walls.* [9] | young man |

| ❖ 纟 | The elongated final stroke of this primitive gives us an image of nature's own dental **floss** unwinding from within a *cocoon*. It is particularly popular among young spiders and other creepers and crawlers that get things caught in their teeth where normal brushing doesn't reach. [3] | floss |

| 1343 鄉 | *Floss . . . young man.* [12] | countryside |

| 1344 響 | *Countryside . . . sound.* [21] | echo (N.) |

LESSON 49

In this short lesson of thirteen characters we introduce three new primitives. They could have been left for the next lesson, but we put them here to give you a breather before you head down the home stretch.

1345 段	section (N.) The character for **section** shows us a new element on the left: the familiar primitive for *staples* with an additional stroke cutting through the vertical stroke. It is easiest in these cases to make a primitive related to what we already know. Hence, we call it a *staple gun*. To the right, *missile*. [9] ﾃ　ﾃ　段
1346 鍛	forge (v.) Not the illegal copying of documents, but the tempering of metal or, by extension, one's physique. *Metal . . . section.* [17]
❖ ﾌ	clothes hanger The primitive for **clothes hanger** looks like its name. [1]
1347 幻	unreal *Cocoon . . . clothes hanger.* [4]
1348 司	take charge of *Clothes hanger . . . one . . . mouth.* [5]
1349 詞	word (N.) Here we meet the proper name for all the various images of "words" we used to make the character for *say* more concrete when used as a primitive. Its elements suggest that when you *say* things you are *taking charge of* the **words** that a language puts at your disposal. [12]

1350	boat
舟	After *drop* and *glass cover*, we come to a combination of three strokes that we met only once before, in the character for *mother* (FRAME 99). The pictographic meaning we gave it there has no etymological relationship to this character, but use it if it helps. [6]

′ 丿 刀 刀 舟 舟

❖	belch
凸	A **belch** is a little more complicated than *wind* in the *mouth*, but the effect is the same. In addition to the example in the following frame, we will meet others in Book 2. [5]

几 凸

1351	ship (N.)
船	*Boat . . . belch.* [11]

1352	sort (N.)
般	*Boat . . . missile.* [10]

1353	tray
盤	*Sort . . . dish.* [15]

1354	relocate
搬	*Fingers . . . sort.* [13]

1355	melon
瓜	The only thing that distinguishes this from the *claw* is the *elbow*, made by doubling up the third stroke and adding a fourth. [5]

′ 厂 瓜 瓜 瓜

1356	orphan
孤	*Child . . . melon.* [8]

Lesson 50

As we said we would do back in Lesson 27, we now leave the beaten path to gather up those characters left aside, either because they form exceptions to the rules and patterns we have been learning, or simply because they fell between the cracks along the way. The list is not large and has a number of repeating patterns; fortunately, because this is probably the most difficult lesson thus far.

1357	benefit [N.]
益	The bottom part of this character is clearly a *dish*. The top part, however, can be taken in several ways: (1) a *snowflake* lying on its side, (2) a *sparkler* with a *one* in the middle, or (3) *horns* and *animal legs*. [10]

❖	braces [N.]
段	The primitive for **braces** begins with the *mouth* full of *staples* that you actually pay someone to inflict on you. And as if this weren't enough, the right side of the primitive shows another **brace**, reaching from your *mouth* all the way around your head and back *again*, in order to keep your jaw from growing while your teeth are growing straight. [9]
	ˀ 尸 尸 段

1358	vacation [N.]
假	*Person . . . braces.* [11]

1359	shrimp
蝦	*Insect . . . braces.* [15]

1360	air [N.]
氣	This character refers to the changeable moods and **airs** of one's personality as well as to the **air** that we breathe. It is also used for that mysterious yet very real vital energy or life force that

the Chinese call *qi*. Its elements are: *reclining . . . floor . . . fish-hook . . . rice*. [10]

1361   **vapor**

汽   Think of this character as a sibling of that for *air*. Simply replace *rice* with drops of *water* on the left in order to get *vapor*. [7]

1362   **fly** (v.)

飛   The two large *hooks* have little propellers (the two *drops* on each *hook*) attached to help them **fly**. Beneath is the *liter* which serves as the fuel tank for this **flying** contraption.

    The stroke order of this character (on which, incidentally, there is a total lack of uniformity) will cause some problems, so take care with it. [9]

1363   **face-to-face**

面   The shape of this character aside, there are really only two elements that make it up: *hundred* and *eyeball*. Look at the first four strokes in the drawing sample below and you will see that they are the start of the character for *hundred*, only drawn more broadly to leave room for the *eyeball*.

    Let the key word **face-to-face** suggests two people "facing" each other, but here we see a *hundred* of them, fifty on a side, staring each other down, right up close, *eyeball* to *eyeball*. [9]

1364   **noodles**

麵   *Wheat . . . face-to-face.* [20]

1365	leather [N.]

革 After the *twenty* at the top, we have a *mouth* and a *needle*. Think of a tanner preparing a fine piece of **leather** to make a belt, with the *twenty mouths* being the holes, and the *needle* a strange replacement for the buckle. [9]

艹　苫　苴　革

1366	shoes

鞋 *Leather . . . bricks.* [15]

❖	civil war

声殳 Think of any **civil war** you want for this primitive element. The basic ingredients are always the same: *soldiers,* a *flag* split down the middle (the extra vertical line), and *missiles* being cast by countrymen against each other. [11]

士　吉　吉　吉　声　殳

1367	fragrant

馨 *Civil war . . . perfume.* [11]

1368	voice [N.]

聲 *Civil war . . . ear.* [17]

1369	Wu

吳 Surely you have heard the song routinely voted the best rock song of all time, Led Zeppelin's "Stairway to *Heaven*." The lyrics are perfect for remembering how to write the character in this frame, used chiefly for a family name: "Ooh (**Wu**), it makes me wonder... To be a rock and not to roll...." The square rock at the top is clearly resting on the first step (the bent line that would otherwise be the first stroke of *heaven*) on the *stairway to heaven*, solid and non-rolling. [7]

口　吕　吳

❖ In line with the explanation above, the primitive meaning will remain *stairway to heaven*.

1370　　　　　　　　　　　　　　　　　　　　　**amusement**

娛

What this *woman* is doing for **amusement** is, as the lyrics remind us, "buying the *stairway to heaven*" [10]

女　娛

1371　　　　　　　　　　　　　　　　　　　　　　**error**

誤

"'Cause you know, sometimes *words* have two meanings…" on the *stairway to heaven*. One of them is right and the other one an **error**. [14]

1372　　　　　　　　　　　　　　　　　　　　**undertake**

承

The key word suggests a new venture or challenge that one **undertakes**. The elements overlap each other and require care in writing correctly: the second stroke of *-ed* and the first of *water* overlap; and the element for *three* is tucked in the middle of the whole character.

To weave this all together, think of yourself swimming in a 200-meter race. You have just *-ed* (suffer-*ed* or enjoy-*ed*, at any rate complet-*ed*) *three* laps in the *water* and the only thing left to **undertake** is that difficult final lap. The problem is, you have never swum more than *three* laps in your life. Exhausted, but determined to finish, you grab hold of the lane rope and drag yourself along, gasping for breath, into last place—and a cellophane ribbon. [8]

了　手　手　承　承

1373　　　　　　　　　　　　　　　　　　　　**steam** (v.)

蒸

The *flower* at the top and the *floor* with the *cooking fire* beneath are familiar. The problem lies in between: the character for *-ed,* that doubles up with the first stroke of *water*. [13]

艹　芋　芽　茏　蒸　蒸

LESSON 51

THE FINAL grouping of characters revolves about elements related to animals. It is a rather large group, and will take us all of four lessons to complete. We begin with a few recurring elements related to parts of animal bodies.

1374	tooth

牙　If you play with this primitive's form with pencil and paper, you will see that it begins with a *box*-like shape, and ends with the final two strokes of the *spear*, a convenient combination for the **tooth** protruding from the mouth of an animal. [4]

一 　 匚 　 午 　 牙

❖ The primitive meaning of this character will be changed to the more colorful image of a *tusk*.

1375	pass through

穿　Take advantage of the elements *hole* and *tusk* to remember this key word in the very concrete sense of one object being made to **pass through** another. [9]

1376	wow!

呀　*Mouth . . . tusk.* This character is used as a particle to express surprise. [7]

❖	droppings

釆　Having already met the primitive for human *footprints*, we now introduce the one for the **droppings** that count as animal tracks. Its elements are simply: *drops of . . . rice.* [7]

1377	explain

釋　*Droppings . . . net . . . good fortune.* [20]

1378

番

try ^(N.)

Droppings . . . rice field. This key word carries the sense of taking the time and effort to do something—to have a **try** at something. There are many ways of saying this: as in to have a go, take a whack, a crack, a stab, or a shot at something. [12]

❖ When this character is used as a primitive element, we choose the image of *fertilizer*, from the combination of elements that make it up.

1379

翻

turn over

Fertilizer . . . feathers. [18]

番　翻

1380

播

broadcast ^(V.)

Fingers . . . fertilizer. [15]

1381

毛

fur

This character simply reverses and elongates the final stroke of *hand* to produce **fur**. If you reverse your *hand* and put it palm down, you will have the side on which **fur** grows. [4]

⸗　毛

1382

尾

tail

Flag . . . fur. [7]

❖

乇

fur ball

This element is clearly derived from that for *fur*. By leaving out the second stroke, we get a **fur ball**, one of those clumps of animal hair you find around a house with cats or dogs. [3]

1383

宅

dwelling ^(N.)

House . . . fur ball. [6]

| 1384 | entrust |
| 託 | *Words . . . fur ball.* [10] |

| ❖ | dove tail |
| 兩 | So as not to confuse this primitive element with the character for *feathers*, think of the neatly arranged feathers of the *dove tail*. Although it has primitive elements (*coat hanger* and *cooking fire*), it may be easier to remember it pictographically. [5] |

ㄱ　兩

| 1385 | act (v.) |

為 The sense of the key word here is "to do"; it has nothing to do with dramatic acting. Although the *dove tail* is visible here, the character as a whole falls outside the normal patterns of composition. Still, with a little concentration, you should be able to learn it quickly.

Think of the first two strokes as *animal horns*. The second of them is drawn l-o-n-g because it will serve as a foundation for the next stage. Your next step is to draw the "enclosure" stroke of the *dove tail* not one but three times, like steps beginning under the first of the *horns* and going downwards.

If you draw the character once with the above explanation in mind and "feel" the progression of the three steps, you should find that it falls off the pen naturally and gracefully. [9]

丶　ノ　尹　尹　為　為

| 1386 | bogus |
| 偽 | *Person . . . act.* [11] |

| ❖ | barrette |
| 爻 | Here we have a quasi-pictograph of the colorful and decorated **barrette**, that clip used to bind up long hair. Note its similarity to the *scarf*, which differs only in the way the first stroke is drawn. As we will see, the first stroke of **barrette** frequently doubles up with the final stroke of the primitive above it. [4] |

一　厂　戶　伏

1387 長 — long

In line with the story of the preceding frame, the *hair* that needs the *barrette* is **long**—a real "mane," in fact, that needs a pretty **long** *barrette* to keep it in tow. The single vertical stroke followed by three horizontal lines depicts someone walking left, against the wind, their **long** hair blowing behind them. [8]

一　厂　F　F　E　E　E　長

❖ Used as a primitive this character has two more shapes in addition to that of the character itself. Above or below another primitive, it is abbreviated to the form 長. When abbreviated to 彐, it will mean the *mane* of a horse. Note also that when accompanied by the *rooster tail* on the right (髟), it will mean *hair*.

1388 張 — stretch (v.)

Bow ... long. [11]

1389 漲 — swell (v.)

Water ... stretch. [14]

1390 套 — cover (n.)

St. Bernard dog ... long. [10]

1391 髮 — hair of the head

This is the full character from which we take the primitive element for *hair*. Note the *chihuahua* below, with the extra stroke that seems to be falling off of it like a long *drop*. It may help if you imagine the relatively "hairless" little puppy losing the final **hair of its head**, like the last leaf of autumn falling from a tree. Note the stroke order of the bottom half. [15]

髟　髟　髮　髮　髮

1392	unfold

展 *Flag . . . salad . . . barrette.* Note that the final stroke of *salad* and the first stroke of *barrette* double up here. [10]

1393	funeral

喪 *Soil . . . chatterbox . . . barrette.* Note that the final stroke of *soil* and the first stroke of *barrette* double up, and that the *chatterbox* is drawn before the final stroke of *soil.* [12]

十　㞢　㦯　喪

LESSON 52

WE TURN NOW to the animals themselves, beginning with a few of our feathered friends. Some of the primitives introduced here and in the remainder of Book 1 come with few examples, but they will prove useful when you get to Book 2.

❖ 隹	The combination of the elements for *person* and *turkey* give us a new superhero—**birdman**. [10]	**birdman**
1394 雁	*Cliff . . . birdman.* [12]	**wild goose**
1395 應	*Cave . . . birdman . . . heart.* [17] 广　雁　應	**ought to**
1396 鳥	*Dove . . . one . . . dove tail.* This is, of course, the character from which we derived the primitive meaning of *dove*. Note the lengthening of the second stroke. [11] ノ　ｒ　ｒ　ｒ　ｐ　白　鳥　鳥	**bird**
1397 鷹	*Cave . . . birdman . . . bird.* [24]	**hawk**
1398 鴨	*First . . . bird.* [16]	**duck** [N.]

1399	island
島	The *bird's tail* is tucked under here, because it has come to stop on a *mountain* to rest from its journey across the waters. Thus the character comes to mean an **island**. [10]

❖	Talking Cricket
禺	We may combine the *insect* with a *brain* (observe the writing) and a *belt* to create the **Talking Cricket** who served as Pinocchio's conscience. (The *belt* is there because he pulls it off to give the unrepentant little marionette a bit of "strap" now and again.) [9]

日　　号　　禺　　禺　　禺

1400	encounter [v.]
遇	*Talking Cricket . . . road.* [12]

1401	ten thousand
萬	*Flowers . . . Talking Cricket.* [13]

❖ As a primitive element, this character will take the meaning of the *Great Wall of China*, from the fact that Chinese writes it as a wall of *10,000 li*.

1402	stride [v.]
邁	*Great Wall of China . . . road.* [16]

❖	mountain goat
屵	What could be simpler than a pair of *animal horns* on a *mountain* to signify a **mountain goat**? [6]

ㄨ　　屵

1403	ridge of a hill
岡	*Glass cover . . . mountain goat.* [8]

1404

剛

just now

Ridge of a hill ... saber. This character is used to refer to things that have just happened. [10]

❖

缶

tin can

Although the primitive meaning has no reference to animals, one of the parts does: a *stick horse* on a *mountain*. (The primitive meaning of **tin can** is a fanciful modernization of a now infrequent character that originally meant "clay vessel.") [6]

午　缶

1405

缺

deficient

Tin can ... guillotine. [10]

1406

寶

treasure (N.)

House ... jewel ... tin can ... shells. [20]

❖

䍃

canned meat

Think of a familiar tin of **canned meat** for this primitive element's meaning. It is composed of *flesh* and a *tin can*. [10]

1407

遙

remote (ADJ.)

Canned meat ... road. [13]

1408

搖

shake (V.)

Fingers... canned meat. [13]

1409

兔

rabbit

This character is supposed to be a pictograph of a **rabbit**, but like most such characters it is easier to recognize it as such than to reproduce it. So we revert to playing with the component primitives: *bound up ... mouth ... human legs ... a drop.* Note how the first of the two *human legs* runs through the *mouth*.

As the final stroke suggests, this is one of those cute little backyard bunny **rabbits** that we associate with Easter. [8]

ク 凸 疒 免 兔

1410 flee

逸 *Rabbit ... road.* [11]

1411 avoid

免 The rabbit becomes a *hare* by taking away the fluffy cotton tail, a trick that nature has devised to help them **avoid** being so visible to hunters and other critters that prey on them. [7]

> ❖ The primitive meaning will remain *hare*.

1412 nightfall

晚 *Sun ... hare.* [11]

1413 elephant

象 A *rabbit's* head with the body of a *sow* represents an **elephant**. Little wonder that the character also means "phenomenon"! [12]

⼧ 凸 ⼧ 凸 象 象 象

1414 likeness

像 This key word refers to the kind of **likeness** that a portrait or effigy captures. Its elements: *person ... elephant.* [14]

LESSON 53

NOW THAT WE have come as far as the elephant, we may continue on with more of the larger animals. Fortunately, this group will cause us much less of a headache than the preceding series, since there are fewer new primitives and their use is more frequent.

1415	horse
馬	Let the extra vertical stroke in the *mane* combine with the first vertical stroke to give an image of the **horse's** long neck. The odd thing is the *dove tail* at the end, but these "**horsefeathers**" should present a good image to remember the character by. The fact that the last stroke of *mane* and the first of *dove tail* coincide should no longer surprise you. [10]

一　厂　厂　厃　厍　馬　馬

1416	mama
媽	Woman . . . horse. [13]

1417	scold (v.)
罵	Net . . . horse. [15]

1418	yes or no
嗎	This character is a particle added to the end of a sentence to turn it into a question that anticipates a **yes or no** answer. Its elements: *mouth . . . horse.* [13]

1419	check (v.)
驗	Horse . . . debate. [23]

1420	ride (v.)
騎	Horse . . . strange. [18]

1421	startled
驚	*Revere . . . horse.* [23]

1422	tiger
虎	The character in this frame recalls the famous Bengali fable about the group of magicians (the *magic wand*) who decided to make a **tiger**. It seems that each of them knew how to make one part of the beast, so they pooled their talents and brought all the pieces (*diced* into pieces) together, at which point the fabricated **tiger** promptly ate its makers up (the bodiless *human legs*). Whatever the parable's significance for modern civilization and its arsenals, it should help with this character.

Oh yes, we should not forget that cliff-like element. Think of it as an abbreviation of the primitive for *zoo* (the first and fourth strokes, actually), in order to fit the **tiger** somewhere into the picture. In fact, the abbreviation is perfectly logical, since the bottom elements usurp the room for the rest of the primitive for *zoo*. [8]

卜　广　虍　虎

❖ As a primitive element itself, the *human legs* are also swallowed up, but the meaning of *tiger* is kept, and the whole serves as a roof for what comes beneath, 虍, giving the *tiger* something else to eat.

1423	ponder
慮	*Tiger . . . consider.* [15]

1424	location
處	*Tiger . . . walking legs . . . wind.* [11]

1425	frolic
戲	*Tiger . . . beans . . . fiesta.* [17]

1426	drama
劇	*Tiger . . . sow . . . saber.* [15]

1427	certificate
據	*Fingers . . . tiger . . . sow.* [16]

1428	deer
鹿	Drawn on the walls of a complex of *caves* near Niaux in southern France are a number of animal likenesses dating from the Upper Paleolithic period. Among them we find pictures of **deer**, some of them showing men in **deer** masks. By *comparing* their drawings to real **deer**, Stone Age people hoped to acquire power over the animal in the hunt; and by *comparing* themselves to the **deer**, to take on that animal's characteristics. But time has locked with a "double-*key*" (the extra stroke through the element for *key*) the real secret of this art form from us, and we can only surmise such meanings. But more important than the enigmas of the troglodytic mind is the way in which *caves*, a double-*key*, and *compare* gives us the character for **deer**. [11]

广 戶 戶 庐 庐 鹿

❖ As a primitive, this character is abbreviated much the same as the *tiger* was: the lower element is dropped to leave room for a replacement: 庐. Its meaning, however, remains the same. There are a very few cases (see FRAME 1430) in which there is no abbreviation. When this happens, we may keep the image suggested by the above explanation: *painting of a deer.*

1429	dust (N.)
塵	*Deer . . . soil.* [14]

1430	lovely
麗	The painting of a *deer* itself with its form and color is enough to fill the bill for an image of something **lovely**. But to give a bit of contrast, we see two *ordinary* drawings from a later age on two patches of *ceiling* above. Note that the drop in *ordinary* has been lengthened somewhat and the second stroke drawn down straight. [19]

1431	bear (N.)
熊	*Elbow ... flesh ... spoon* atop a *spoon ... cooking fire.* [14]

1432	ability
能	Try relating this character to that of the previous frame. For instance, you might imagine that the test of **ability** envisioned here is removing the *bear* from the cooking fire. [10]

1433	attitude
態	*Ability ... heart.* [14]

LESSON 54

THE GROUPING of characters in this short lesson is based on primitives related to fantastical animals and beings. We begin with two animals belonging to the zodiac.

1434 寅	**sign of the tiger** *House . . . ceiling . . . sprout . . . animal legs.* [11]
1435 演	**perform** *Water . . . sign of the tiger.* [14]
1436 辰	**sign of the dragon** To keep the character for the astrological **sign of the dragon** distinct from the actual dragon, think of someone particularly draconic born in the year of the dragon (2000 and every year a multiple of 12 before and after it). The elements: *cliff . . . two . . . barrettes.* Here again, note that the first stroke of *barrette* doubles up with the second stroke of the primitive above it. [7]
1437 晨	**morning** *Sun . . . sign of the dragon.* [11]
1438 農	**agriculture** *Bent . . . sign of the dragon.* [13]
1439 濃	**concentrated** Among other things, the key word refers to the thick consistency of liquids. Its elements: *water . . . agriculture.* [16]
❖ 关	**golden calf** The story is told of the people of the Exodus who, dissatisfied with Moses' leadership, collected their gold ornaments and

melted them down to fashion a **golden calf** for an idol. The *animal horns* and *heavens* here represent that god of theirs. [6]

1440 送	**deliver** *Golden calf . . . road.* [9]
1441 鬼	**ghost** *Drop of . . . brains . . . human legs . . . elbow.* [10]
1442 魔	**demon** *Hemp . . . ghost.* [21]
1443 塊	**lump** (N.) *Soil . . . ghost.* [13]

1444 龍 **dragon**

This character will take a bit of time to learn, but only because of the final five strokes. Once you learn it, you will enjoy writing it for the great feeling you get from the flow of the strokes. In order not to confuse this character with the zodiacal *sign of the dragon,* learned earlier in FRAME 1436, you might think here of a parade **dragon.** [16]

立　育　䏍　䑽　龍　龍

1445 襲 **raid** (V.)

Dragon . . . clothing. [22]

LESSON 55

THIS FINAL LESSON, one of the longest in Book 1, is intended to complete this volume and prepare for the transition to Book 2. A number of characters have been reserved for this purpose and arranged into 21 groups, the last of which is a short assortment of stragglers.

❖ 臼	**mortar** The primitive element for a *mortar* (a vessel you use a pestle to crush or grind something in) should not be confused with that for *zipper*. [6]

ノ　亻　仟　臼　臼　臼

1446 兒	**youngster** This character is often used for small infants to young toddlers. It is composed of a *mortar* with *human legs*. [8]

1447 舊	**old** *Flowers . . . turkey . . . mortar.* [18]

1448 寫	**write** *House . . . mortar . . . bound up . . . fire.* [15]

1449 瀉	**diarrhea** *Water . . . write.* [18]

1450 兩	**dos** Assuming that everyone knows how to count at least uno-**dos**-tres in Spanish, we can use this key word to indicate the number "two" used before a classifier or measure word. The first four strokes can be thought of as a drawing of a yoke. Inside, we see the character for *enter* twice, clearly because one of the **dos** oxen of this team has to *enter* each side of the yoke. [8]

帀 帀 兩

❖ When used as a primitive, this character will mean a *yoke*, in line with the above explanation.

1451

duo

倆 *Persons . . . yoke.* [10]

1452

full

滿 *Water . . . twenty . . . yoke.* Note how the first stroke of *yoke* is shortened to double up with the final stroke of *twenty*. [14]

❖

stitching

爻 Think of these four xes as the cross-*stitching* you see on those old-fashioned "Home Sweet Home" embroideries. [8]

丿　爻　爻　爻　爻

1453

you (literary)

爾 This key word should be kept distinct from the characters we already learned for *you* and *you (respectful)*. It is drawn with a *tool*, a *towel*, and *stitching*. [14]

1454

fill (v.)

彌 This character, whose elements are *bow* and *you (literary)*, has the meaning of the verb **fill**, but it is also used as a surname or for its phonetic value. [17]

❖

saguaro cactus

 The meaning of **saguaro cactus** is chosen because of the shape of the primitive itself. If you aren't quite sure what one looks like, think of Snoopy's brother, Spike, and his friend the (**saguaro**) **cactus**.

　　When it appears under a pair of its *cocoon*-shaped fruits, we will treat the resulting primitive as *cactus fruit*, which in the case of the **saguaro cactus** is sweet and edible. [6]

L   ㄐ   ㄐㄧ   ㄐㄧ'   ㄐㄧㄈ   ㄐㄩㄈ

1455   **false**

虛   *Tigers . . . saguaro cactus.* [12]

1456   **unite**

聯   *Ear . . . cactus fruit.* [17]

耳   聯   聯   聯   聯   聯   聯   聯

1457   **shut** (v.)

關   *Gate . . . cactus fruit.* [19]

❖   **razor wire**

月   **Razor wire** refers to a type of fencing meant to keep people in
or out. It is represented by a *dagger* with two razor-sharp metal
barbs (the two horizontal strokes) attached to it. [4]

丁   丁   ヨ   月

1458   **that**

那   *Razor wire* and *pinnacle* suggest a high-security prison like the
famous Alcatraz. How do we associate this with the key word?
We suggest imagining yourself on a tour-guided cruise around
San Francisco Bay. At one point, one of the visitors points to a
small island and asks, "What's THAT?" The guide answers theat-
rically, "**That**, my friends, is the famous Alcatraz!" [7]

❖ The primitive meaning will be *Alcatraz*, from the above
explanation.

1459   **which?**

哪   "**Which** witch wishes?" This is a sentence you might have been
asked to pronounce in primary school holding a thin strip of
paper under your *mouth* so that it will flutter when the word
"**which**" is properly pronounced and remain still when the

words "witch wishes" are spoken. It's a bit of a tongue-twister, but the warden at *Alcatraz*, herself a former third-grade teacher, insisted that inmates pronounce it correctly three times in quick succession or face solitary confinement. [10]

1460 witch

巫 *I-beam . . . assembly line.* [7]

丁　叮　巫　巫

1461 spirit

靈 The three *mouths* indicate three *witches* who are invoking the weather **spirits** to send *rain*. [24]

1462 county

縣 When you draw the left side of this character think of a *small tool* (the element for *small* taking the place of the *animal legs*), perhaps a nano-wrench for tightening up a memory chip. The right side has the primitive for *yarn*. [16]

1463 suspend

懸 In the sense of "hang," not "interrupt." *County . . . heart.* [20]

1464 offer (v.)

與 If this tangle of primitives seems too much to manage, we would like to **offer** you a hint you can't refuse: Think of the short *walking stick* as combining with the final three strokes to make the character for *six*. That leaves only a *zipper* and a *slingshot*. [14]

1465 lift up

舉 *Offer . . . cornstalk.* [17]

❖ Farmer's Almanac

凶 The small box with an antenna coming out the top suggests a handheld electronic device. On the screen, we see only a *sheaf*, indicating that it is in fact a portable **Farmer's Almanac** that can be popped open for consultation as the need arises. [6]

´ 冂 內 囟

1466   brain

腦   *Part of the body . . . stream . . . Farmer's Almanac.* By now, you will have used the primitive for *brains* enough not to confuse it with the character for **brain** shown here. [13]

1467   annoyed (N.)

惱   *State of mind . . stream . . . Farmer's Almanac.* Since this character and that of the previous frame are the only occasions on which the elements for *stream* and *Farmer's Almanac* appear together, you might consider them as a unit and combine the images you use. [12].

1468   specialty

專   The first six strokes of this character are the same as the first six of *east*, and the last two the same as the last two of *insect*. Accordingly, we can think of the whole piece as a kind of oriental ladybug, perhaps with a kimono-like pattern on her back. The *glue* at the bottom shows us where she ended up: stuck to a board and mounted behind glass for the collection of an entomologist—someone whose **specialty** is abducting, torturing, and impaling innocent insects. Oh well, it's a living. [11]

串   車   車   專

1469   spread (V.)

傳   *Person . . . specialty.* [13]

1470   rotate

轉   *Car. . . specialty.* [18]

1471   troupe (N.)

團   *Pent in . . specialty.* The meaning of the key word can be extended to include groupings or concentrations of all sorts of things, not just organized **troupes**. [14]

1472 黃	**yellow** The only thing that distinguishes **yellow** from the *sign of the tiger* (FRAME 1434) is the top element: *twenty* instead of *house*. Think of the *sign of the tiger* as belonging to an astrological *"house"* and **yellow** as a Hawaiian lei made of *twenty* **yellow** hibiscus flowers. [12]
1473 廣	**extensive** *Cave ... yellow.* [15]
1474 橫	**horizontal** *Tree ... yellow.* [16]
❖ 囟	**GPS** The only difference between the *Farmer's Almanac* and this element is that the *sheaf* in the middle is replaced with a pair of *walking legs*. This gives us a handheld, portable Global Positioning System or **GPS**. [7]
1475 窗	**window** *Hole ... GPS.* [12]
1476 總	**general** (ADJ.) *Silk ... GPS ... heart.* [17]
1477 詹	**verbose** The first six strokes of the character show someone *bound up* by the *human legs* and suspended over the edge of a *cliff*. It is a picture of revenge for someone who squealed on his partners (*the words*) and hence was too **verbose** with the police when he should have remained silent. [13] ❖ As a primitive element, this character will mean a *snitch*, from the explanation above.

| 1478 擔 | assume |

Fingers . . . snitch. The sense of the key word **assume** is to take on or shoulder responsibility for something. [16]

| ❖ 婁 | Flying Dutchman |

The legendary ghost ship known as the **Flying Dutchman**, doomed to sail forever without ever coming to rest in port, is depicted in this character. It begins with the sails and crossed mast of the clipper ship. Below it we find the carved bust of a *woman* affixed to the prow of the ship. Take special care with the stroke order. [11]

冂 冄 冄 冐 串 婁

| 1479 數 | number (N.) |

Flying Dutchman . . . taskmaster. [15]

| 1480 樓 | multistory building |

Tree . . . Flying Dutchman. [15]

| ❖ 蜀 | butterfly net |

Net . . . bound up . . . insect. These elements should make the primitive meaning of a **butterfly net** simple to remember. [13]

罒 冎 蜀

| 1481 獨 | alone |

Pack of wild dogs . . . butterfly net. [16]

| 1482 屬 | belong to |

Flag . . . snowflake . . . butterfly net. [21]

| ❖ 闟 | gargoyle |

Think of a **gargoyle** in the form of a *horned toad* attached to the outer *gate* of a stately old Gothic mansion. [17]

| 1483 | spoiled |

爛 — *Fire . . . gargoyle.* The key word refers to food and other things that have **spoiled**, rotted, worn out, or otherwise gone bad. [21]

| 1484 | orchid |

蘭 — *Flowers . . . gargoyle.* [21]

| ❖ | footrace |

从 — Two *persons . . . trail of footprints.* [8]

| 1485 | follow |

從 — This character depicts an annual series of *footraces* that **follow** one after the other for an entire week. Each race pits two *persons* against each other. On the left you see the *queue* of the thousands of competitors awaiting their turn. As you watch the first two *runners* disappear into the distance, you see the *trail of footprints* they leave in the sand. [11]

彳　彳从　從

| 1486 | vertical |

縱 — *Thread . . . follow.* [17]

| 1487 | identical |

齊 — Think first of an **identical** image of yourself in a shiny surface, such as a mirror. Then take a pencil and draw this character very large on a piece of paper. Next, draw a thin line down the center. You should see how the right side is pretty much **identical** to the left, just reversed.

We still need to learn how to draw it. The *top hat* is no problem. After it, comes what looks like a pair of *animal horns* affixed to the head of a fashionable *walking stick*. To the left is the character for *dagger*, which is "mirrored" on the right. Take special care with this piece; it is the key to writing the whole character. If you have trouble with the final four strokes, you might think of them as a doodle of a *badminton net*, drawn in the order shown below. [14]

❖ When used as a primitive, this character will take the meaning of a *mirror image*, from the explanation above.

1488

濟

relieve

Water . . . mirror image. The sense of the key word is to "bring relief" to someone in need. [17]

1489

丑

clown

If you look closely at this character you will see a *needle* being used as a *key*—clearly the sign of a lock-picker at work. We leave it to you to associate this with the key word. [4]

７ 刀 丑 丑

1490

扭

twist (v.)

Fingers . . . clown. [7]

1491

卑

lowly

Think of someone of **lowly** origins who has submitted himself to scientific experiments to add a *drop of* income to his meager earnings. After that initial *drop,* we see what looks like *brains,* except that part of them are leaking out to the left—actually not the *brains* themselves, just the data that the *needle* has been stuck in to extract. [8]

1492	brand (N.)
牌	Slice . . . lowly. The **brand** this key word refers to is the trademark of a manufactured product, not the impression a hot iron makes on the backside of a cow. [12]

We conclude this lesson with a number of characters that fell between the cracks along the way.

1493	appellation
號	Mouth . . . snare . . . tiger. The key word is used for names or titles in general. [13]

1494	peculiar
怪	State of mind . . . crotch . . . soil. [8]

1495	crimson
赤	Soil . . . saber . . . animal legs. [7]

1496	likewise
亦	No doubt your imagination took you to a pretty bloody scene in the last frame for *crimson*. But there are other things that are **likewise** a shade of red—like a fresh, shiny apple. And this immediately conjures up the image of Johnny Appleseed, with his kettle for a *top hat* and surrounded by all the curious animals of the wilderness (the *animal legs*). Apocryphal accounts **likewise** identify him as a master swordsman, but we only know him after he took the biblical prophet's advice and turned his *saber* into a plowshare. [6]

1497	extreme (N.)
極	Tree . . . snare . . . mouth . . . crotch . . . floor. [12]

1498 雜	miscellaneous

The character for **miscellaneous** lives up to its name with the motley assortment of primitives used to make it up: *top hat . . . assembly line . . . tree . . . turkey.* [18]

1499 日	sayeth

Pent in . . . one. The key word refers to famous sayings of famous people, and is the origin for the primitive meaning of a *tongue wagging in the mouth* that we learned in FRAME 12.

The size of this character, a relatively rare one, distinguishes it from *day*, but we have used the primitive meanings of the two characters interchangeably. [4]

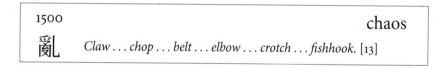

Finally, we bring Book 1 to a close with a Chinese character that will test all the skills you have learned so far, a character whose composition somehow seems to befit its meaning.

1500 亂	chaos

Claw . . . chop . . . belt . . . elbow . . . crotch . . . fishhook. [13]

Indexes

Hand-Drawn Characters

This Index presents all the characters in this book in the order of their appearance. They are printed in one of the typical type styles used to teach children how to draw characters with a pen or pencil—the same form used in this book to show proper stroke order. The pronunciation (Mandarin) of the character is given beneath. Some of the characters have multiple pronunciations, which can be found by consulting a dictionary under the pronunciation given here.

一	二	三	四	五	六	七	八	九	十
yī	èr	sān	sì	wǔ	liù	qī	bā	jiǔ	shí
1	2	3	4	5	6	7	8	9	10

口	日	月	田	目	古	胡	吾	朋	明
kǒu	rì	yuè	tián	mù	gǔ	hú	wú	péng	míng
11	12	13	14	15	16	17	18	19	20

唱	晶	品	昌	早	旭	世	胃	旦	凹
chàng	jīng	pǐn	chāng	zǎo	xù	shì	wèi	dàn	āo
21	22	23	24	25	26	27	28	29	30

凸	自	白	百	皂	中	千	舌	升	昇
tú	zì	bái	bǎi	zào	zhōng	qiān	shé	shēng	shēng
31	32	33	34	35	36	37	38	39	40

丸	卜	占	上	下	卡	卓	朝	嘲	只
wán	bǔ	zhān	shàng	xià	kǎ	zhuó	cháo	chǎo	zhǐ
41	42	43	44	45	46	47	48	49	50

貝	貼	貞	員	見	元	頁	頑	凡	肌
bèi	tiē	zhēn	yuán	jiàn	yuán	yè	wán	fán	jī
51	52	53	54	55	56	57	58	59	60

負	勻	句	旬	勺	的	首	直	置	具
fù	yún	jù	xún	sháo	de	shǒu	zhí	zhì	jù
61	62	63	64	65	66	67	68	69	70

真	工	左	右	有	賄	貢	項	刀	刃
zhēn	gōng	zuǒ	yòu	yǒu	huì	gòng	xiàng	dāo	rèn
71	72	73	74	75	76	77	78	79	80
切	召	昭	則	副	丁	叮	可	哥	頂
qiè	zhào	zhāo	zé	fù	dīng	dīng	kě	gē	dǐng
81	82	83	84	85	86	87	88	89	90
乙	子	孔	吼	了	女	好	如	母	貫
yǐ	zǐ	kǒng	hǒu	le	nǔ	hǎo	rú	mǔ	guàn
91	92	93	94	95	96	97	98	99	100
兄	克	小	少	吵	大	尖	夕	多	夠
xiōng	kè	xiǎo	shǎo	chǎo	dà	jiān	xī	duō	gòu
101	102	103	104	105	106	107	108	109	110
外	名	厚	石	砂	妙	肖	削	光	太
wài	míng	hòu	shí	shā	miào	xiào	xiāo	guāng	tài
111	112	113	114	115	116	117	118	119	120
省	奇	川	洲	順	水	永	求	泉	原
shěng	qí	chuān	zhōu	shùn	shuǐ	yǒng	qiú	quán	yuán
121	122	123	124	125	126	127	128	129	130
願	沖	泳	洲	沼	沙	江	汁	潮	源
yuàn	chōng	yǒng	zhōu	zhǎo	shā	jiāng	zhī	cháo	yuán
131	132	133	134	135	136	137	138	139	140
活	消	況	河	湖	測	土	均	肚	填
huó	xiāo	kuàng	hé	hú	cè	tǔ	jūn	dù	tián
141	142	143	144	145	146	147	148	149	150
吐	哇	寸	封	寺	時	火	灰	煩	炎
tǔ	wā	cùn	fēng	sì	shí	huǒ	huī	fán	yán
151	152	153	154	155	156	157	158	159	160
淡	災	照	魚	漁	堯	燒	曉	里	量
dàn	zāi	zhào	yú	yú	yáo	shāo	xiǎo	lǐ	liàng
161	162	163	164	165	166	167	168	169	170
埋	黑	點	墨	冒	同	洞	向	尚	字
mái	hēi	diǎn	mò	mào	tóng	dòng	xiàng	shàng	zì
171	172	173	174	175	176	177	178	179	180

守 *shǒu* 181	完 *wán* 182	實 *shí* 183	宣 *xuān* 184	宵 *xiāo* 185	安 *ān* 186	宴 *yàn* 187	寄 *jì* 188	富 *fù* 189	貯 *zhù* 190
木 *mù* 191	林 *lín* 192	森 *sēn* 193	植 *zhí* 194	杏 *xìng* 195	呆 *dāi* 196	枯 *kū* 197	村 *cūn* 198	相 *xiāng* 199	本 *běn* 200
案 *àn* 201	未 *wèi* 202	末 *mò* 203	沫 *mò* 204	味 *wèi* 205	妹 *mèi* 206	查 *chá* 207	渣 *zhā* 208	染 *rǎn* 209	李 *lǐ* 210
桌 *zhuō* 211	若 *ruò* 212	草 *cǎo* 213	苦 *kǔ* 214	寬 *kuān* 215	葉 *yè* 216	莫 *mò* 217	模 *mó* 218	漠 *mò* 219	墓 *mù* 220
苗 *miáo* 221	瞄 *miáo* 222	兆 *zhào* 223	桃 *táo* 224	犬 *quǎn* 225	尤 *yóu* 226	默 *mò* 227	然 *rán* 228	哭 *kū* 229	器 *qì* 230
臭 *chòu* 231	狗 *gǒu* 232	厭 *yàn* 233	壓 *yā* 234	牛 *niú* 235	特 *tè* 236	告 *gào* 237	浩 *hào* 238	先 *xiān* 239	洗 *xǐ* 240
介 *jiè* 241	界 *jiè* 242	茶 *chá* 243	會 *huì* 244	合 *hé* 245	哈 *hā* 246	塔 *tǎ* 247	王 *wáng* 248	玉 *yù* 249	球 *qiú* 250
現 *xiàn* 251	玩 *wán* 252	狂 *kuáng* 253	皇 *huáng* 254	煌 *huáng* 255	呈 *chéng* 256	全 *quán* 257	理 *lǐ* 258	主 *zhǔ* 259	注 *zhù* 260
金 *jīn* 261	銅 *tóng* 262	釣 *diào* 263	針 *zhēn* 264	釘 *dīng* 265	銘 *míng* 266	鎮 *zhèn* 267	道 *dào* 268	導 *dǎo* 269	迅 *xùn* 270
造 *zào* 271	巡 *xún* 272	逛 *guàng* 273	車 *chē* 274	連 *lián* 275	蓮 *lián* 276	前 *qián* 277	剪 *jiǎn* 278	輸 *shū* 279	逾 *yú* 280
各 *gè* 281	格 *gé* 282	客 *kè* 283	額 *é* 284	夏 *xià* 285	洛 *luò* 286	落 *luò* 287	冗 *rǒng* 288	沉 *chén* 289	軍 *jūn* 290

輝 huī 291	運 yùn 292	冠 guān 293	夢 mèng 294	坑 kēng 295	高 gāo 296	享 xiǎng 297	熟 shú 298	亭 tíng 299	亮 liàng 300
京 jīng 301	涼 liáng 302	景 jǐng 303	就 jiù 304	周 zhōu 305	週 zhōu 306	士 shì 307	吉 jí 308	買 mǎi 309	賣 mài 310
書 shū 311	畫 huà 312	劃 huá 313	攻 gōng 314	敗 bài 315	故 gù 316	救 jiù 317	敬 jìng 318	敞 chǎng 319	言 yán 320
警 jǐng 321	計 jì 322	獄 yù 323	討 tǎo 324	訓 xùn 325	話 huà 326	詩 shī 327	語 yǔ 328	讀 dú 329	調 diào 330
談 tán 331	這 zhè 332	式 shì 333	試 shì 334	戈 gē 335	或 huò 336	賊 zéi 337	載 zài 338	鐵 tiě 339	茂 mào 340
成 chéng 341	城 chéng 342	誠 chéng 343	威 wēi 344	滅 miè 345	咸 xián 346	減 jiǎn 347	單 dān 348	戰 zhàn 349	錢 qián 350
淺 qiǎn 351	賤 jiàn 352	止 zhǐ 353	步 bù 354	涉 shè 355	頻 pín 356	肯 kěn 357	企 qǐ 358	歲 suì 359	武 wǔ 360
賦 fù 361	正 zhèng 362	政 zhèng 363	定 dìng 364	走 zǒu 365	超 chāo 366	越 yuè 367	是 shì 368	題 tí 369	建 jiàn 370
延 yán 371	誕 dàn 372	楚 chǔ 373	礎 chǔ 374	衣 yī 375	裡 lǐ 376	哀 āi 377	袁 yuán 378	遠 yuǎn 379	壞 huài 380
初 chū 381	巾 jīn 382	布 bù 383	帽 mào 384	幕 mù 385	棉 mián 386	幫 bāng 387	市 shì 388	肺 fèi 389	帶 dài 390
滯 zhì 391	刺 cì 392	制 zhì 393	製 zhì 394	云 yún 395	雨 yǔ 396	雲 yún 397	雷 léi 398	電 diàn 399	霜 shuāng 400

冰	冬	天	夭	喬	橋	嬌	立	泣	站
bīng	dōng	tiān	yāo	qiáo	qiáo	jiāo	lì	qì	zhàn
401	402	403	404	405	406	407	408	409	410
章	競	帝	童	鐘	商	適	敵	匕	北
zhāng	jìng	dì	tóng	zhōng	shāng	shì	dí	bǐ	běi
411	412	413	414	415	416	417	418	419	420
背	比	昆	混	皆	此	些	它	旨	脂
bèi	bǐ	kūn	hùn	jiē	cǐ	xiē	tā	zhǐ	zhī
421	422	423	424	425	426	427	428	429	430
每	梅	海	乞	吃	乾	複	腹	欠	吹
měi	méi	hǎi	qǐ	chī	gān	fù	fù	qiàn	chuī
431	432	433	434	435	436	437	438	439	440
歌	軟	次	資	姿	諮	賠	培	音	暗
gē	ruǎn	cì	zī	zī	zī	péi	péi	yīn	àn
441	442	443	444	445	446	447	448	449	450
韻	識	幟	竟	鏡	境	亡	盲	妄	望
yùn	shì	zhì	jìng	jìng	jìng	wáng	máng	wàng	wàng
451	452	453	454	455	456	457	458	459	460
方	妨	放	激	於	旁	兌	脫	說	曾
fāng	fáng	fàng	jī	yú	páng	duì	tuō	shuō	céng
461	462	463	464	465	466	467	468	469	470
增	贈	東	棟	凍	也	她	地	池	蟲
zēng	zèng	dōng	dòng	dòng	yě	tā	dì	chí	chóng
471	472	473	474	475	476	477	478	479	480
蛇	蛋	風	諷	己	改	記	已	包	泡
shé	dàn	fēng	fěng	jǐ	gǎi	jì	yǐ	bāo	pào
481	482	483	484	485	486	487	488	489	490
起	家	場	湯	羊	美	洋	鮮	達	樣
qǐ	jiā	chǎng	tāng	yáng	měi	yáng	xiān	dá	yàng
491	492	493	494	495	496	497	498	499	500
差	集	進	準	誰	售	雖	確	午	許
chà	jí	jìn	zhǔn	shéi	shòu	suī	què	wǔ	xǔ
501	502	503	504	505	506	507	508	509	510

羽	習	翔	困	固	國	圓	因	園	回
yǔ	xí	xiáng	kùn	gù	guó	yuán	yīn	yuán	huí
511	512	513	514	515	516	517	518	519	520
迴	圖	店	庫	褲	廠	床	麻	心	忘
huí	tú	diàn	kù	kù	chǎng	chuáng	má	xīn	wàng
521	522	523	524	525	526	527	528	529	530
忍	認	志	誌	思	意	想	息	恐	感
rěn	rèn	zhì	zhì	sī	yì	xiǎng	xī	kǒng	gǎn
531	532	533	534	535	536	537	538	539	540
憾	憂	怕	忙	慣	懷	必	手	看	拿
hàn	yōu	pà	máng	guàn	huái	bì	shǒu	kàn	ná
541	542	543	544	545	546	547	548	549	550
我	義	議	蟻	抱	抗	批	招	打	指
wǒ	yì	yì	yǐ	bào	kàng	pī	zhāo	dǎ	zhǐ
551	552	553	554	555	556	557	558	559	560
持	括	提	揮	推	接	掛	按	掉	拉
chí	kuò	tí	huī	tuī	jiē	guà	àn	diào	lā
561	562	563	564	565	566	567	568	569	570
啦	找	研	弄	鼻	刑	型	才	財	存
lā	zhǎo	yán	nòng	bí	xíng	xíng	cái	cái	cún
571	572	573	574	575	576	577	578	579	580
在	乃	奶	及	吸	史	更	硬	又	友
zài	nǎi	nǎi	jí	xī	shǐ	gèng	yìng	yòu	yǒu
581	582	583	584	585	586	587	588	589	590
雙	隻	護	獲	觀	歡	投	沒	設	股
shuāng	zhī	hù	huò	guān	huān	tóu	méi	shè	gǔ
591	592	593	594	595	596	597	598	599	600
支	技	枝	叔	督	寂	反	板	返	派
zhī	jì	zhī	shū	dū	jì	fǎn	bǎn	fǎn	pài
601	602	603	604	605	606	607	608	609	610
脈	爪	抓	采	採	菜	受	授	愛	雄
mài	zhǎo	zhuā	cǎi	cǎi	cài	shòu	shòu	ài	xióng
611	612	613	614	615	616	617	618	619	620

台	治	始	去	法	至	室	到	互	充
tái	*zhì*	*shǐ*	*qù*	*fǎ*	*zhì*	*shì*	*dào*	*hù*	*chōng*
621	622	623	624	625	626	627	628	629	630
育	流	梳	山	出	擊	密	入	內	吶
yù	*liú*	*shū*	*shān*	*chū*	*jī*	*mì*	*rù*	*nèi*	*nà*
631	632	633	634	635	636	637	638	639	640
分	貧	公	松	谷	浴	欲	慾	容	溶
fēn	*pín*	*gōng*	*sōng*	*gǔ*	*yù*	*yù*	*yù*	*róng*	*róng*
641	642	643	644	645	646	647	648	649	650
當	檔	黨	常	堂	皮	波	婆	破	被
dāng	*dàng*	*dǎng*	*cháng*	*táng*	*pí*	*bō*	*pó*	*pò*	*bèi*
651	652	653	654	655	656	657	658	659	660
歹	列	烈	死	葬	耳	取	趣	最	職
dǎi	*liè*	*liè*	*sǐ*	*zàng*	*ěr*	*qǔ*	*qù*	*zuì*	*zhí*
661	662	663	664	665	666	667	668	669	670
聖	敢	嚴	曼	慢	漫	環	還	夫	規
shèng	*gǎn*	*yán*	*màn*	*màn*	*màn*	*huán*	*huán*	*fū*	*guī*
671	672	673	674	675	676	677	678	679	680
替	失	臣	臨	賢	堅	力	另	別	拐
tì	*shī*	*chén*	*lín*	*xián*	*jiān*	*lì*	*lìng*	*bié*	*guǎi*
681	682	683	684	685	686	687	688	689	690
男	功	奴	努	加	賀	架	協	行	律
nán	*gōng*	*nú*	*nǔ*	*jiā*	*hè*	*jià*	*xié*	*háng*	*lǜ*
691	692	693	694	695	696	697	698	699	700
復	得	待	往	德	聽	廳	微	街	禾
fù	*děi*	*dài*	*wǎng*	*dé*	*tīng*	*tīng*	*wēi*	*jiē*	*hé*
701	702	703	704	705	706	707	708	709	710
程	和	移	秋	愁	利	香	季	委	秀
chéng	*hé*	*yí*	*qiū*	*chóu*	*lì*	*xiāng*	*jì*	*wěi*	*xiù*
711	712	713	714	715	716	717	718	719	720
透	誘	歷	米	迷	謎	類	竹	笑	箱
tòu	*yòu*	*lì*	*mǐ*	*mí*	*mí*	*lèi*	*zhú*	*xiào*	*xiāng*
721	722	723	724	725	726	727	728	729	730

筆	等	算	答	策	人	囚	份	佔	傢
bǐ	děng	suàn	dá	cè	rén	qiú	fèn	zhàn	jiā
731	732	733	734	735	736	737	738	739	740
你	您	什	條	值	做	但	住	位	件
nǐ	nín	shén	tiáo	zhí	zuò	dàn	zhù	wèi	jiàn
741	742	743	744	745	746	747	748	749	750
仍	他	休	信	依	例	個	健	停	倒
réng	tā	xiū	xìn	yī	lì	gè	jiàn	tíng	dǎo
751	752	753	754	755	756	757	758	759	760
仁	優	傷	保	堡	付	府	俯	代	袋
rén	yōu	shāng	bǎo	bǎo	fù	fǔ	fǔ	dài	dài
761	762	763	764	765	766	767	768	769	770
化	花	貨	何	便	丈	使	久	畝	丙
huà	huā	huò	hé	biàn	zhàng	shǐ	jiǔ	mǔ	bǐng
771	772	773	774	775	776	777	778	779	780
柄	肉	腐	眾	坐	座	檢	臉	來	麥
bǐng	ròu	fǔ	zhòng	zuò	zuò	jiǎn	liǎn	lái	mài
781	782	783	784	785	786	787	788	789	790
喝	渴	任	廷	庭	以	似	併	拼	呂
hē	kě	rèn	tíng	tíng	yǐ	sì	bìng	pīn	lǚ
791	792	793	794	795	796	797	798	799	800
侶	榮	勞	營	善	年	夜	液	喚	換
lǚ	róng	láo	yíng	shàn	nián	yè	yè	huàn	huàn
801	802	803	804	805	806	807	808	809	810
旅	施	游	遊	勿	忽	物	易	賜	屍
lǚ	shī	yóu	yóu	wù	hū	wù	yì	cì	shī
811	812	813	814	815	816	817	818	819	820
尼	呢	泥	屋	握	居	鋸	層	局	戶
ní	ne	ní	wū	wò	jū	jù	céng	jú	hù
821	822	823	824	825	826	827	828	829	830
房	雇	顧	示	社	視	福	禁	襟	宗
fáng	gù	gù	shì	shè	shì	fú	jìn	jīn	zōng
831	832	833	834	835	836	837	838	839	840

崇	祭	察	擦	由	抽	油	甲	押	申
chóng	jì	chá	cā	yóu	chōu	yóu	jiǎ	yā	shēn
841	842	843	844	845	846	847	848	849	850
伸	神	果	課	顆	斤	所	近	斬	暫
shēn	shén	guǒ	kè	kē	jīn	suǒ	jìn	zhǎn	zhàn
851	852	853	854	855	856	857	858	859	860
漸	質	斥	訴	乍	怎	昨	作	雪	急
jiàn	zhí	chì	sù	zhà	zěn	zuó	zuò	xuě	jí
861	862	863	864	865	866	867	868	869	870
尋	婦	掃	錄	碌	爭	淨	事	唐	糖
xún	fù	sǎo	lù	lù	zhēng	jìng	shì	táng	táng
871	872	873	874	875	876	877	878	879	880
康	尹	伊	君	裙	群	而	需	儒	瑞
kāng	yǐn	yī	jūn	qún	qún	ér	xū	rú	ruì
881	882	883	884	885	886	887	888	889	890
端	曲	斗	料	科	用	昔	借	錯	散
duān	qū	dǒu	liào	kē	yòng	xī	jiè	cuò	sǎn
891	892	893	894	895	896	897	898	899	900
撒	備	廿	席	度	渡	半	伴	胖	判
sǎ	bèi	niàn	xí	dù	dù	bàn	bàn	pàng	pàn
901	902	903	904	905	906	907	908	909	910
眷	拳	勝	片	版	妝	壯	莊	裝	將
juàn	quán	shèng	piàn	bǎn	zhuāng	zhuàng	zhuāng	zhuāng	jiàng
911	912	913	914	915	916	917	918	919	920
之	乏	眨	不	否	杯	矢	族	知	智
zhī	fá	zhǎ	bù	fǒu	bēi	shǐ	zú	zhī	zhì
921	922	923	924	925	926	927	928	929	930
矛	柔	揉	務	霧	予	序	預	野	班
máo	róu	róu	wù	wù	yǔ	xù	yù	yě	bān
931	932	933	934	935	936	937	938	939	940
弓	引	強	弱	彈	佛	費	弟	第	巧
gōng	yǐn	qiáng	ruò	dàn	fó	fèi	dì	dì	qiǎo
941	942	943	944	945	946	947	948	949	950

身	射	謝	老	考	烤	孝	教	者	著
shēn	shè	xiè	lǎo	kǎo	kǎo	xiào	jiāo	zhě	zhe
951	952	953	954	955	956	957	958	959	960
豬	追	帥	師	獅	官	管	父	交	效
zhū	zhuī	shuài	shī	shī	guān	guǎn	fù	jiāo	xiào
961	962	963	964	965	966	967	968	969	970
較	校	足	跑	跳	路	露	骨	滑	過
jiào	xiào	zú	pǎo	tiào	lù	lù	gǔ	huá	guò
971	972	973	974	975	976	977	978	979	980
阿	啊	際	險	隨	陽	陳	防	附	院
ā	ā	jì	xiǎn	suí	yáng	chén	fáng	fù	yuàn
981	982	983	984	985	986	987	988	989	990
陣	隊	降	階	穴	究	突	空	控	邊
zhèn	duì	jiàng	jiē	xuè	jiū	tú	kōng	kòng	biān
991	992	993	994	995	996	997	998	999	1000
深	探	丘	兵	絲	線	維	羅	續	統
shēn	tàn	qiū	bīng	sī	xiàn	wéi	luó	xù	tǒng
1001	1002	1003	1004	1005	1006	1007	1008	1009	1010
給	結	終	級	紀	紅	約	細	緊	織
gěi	jié	zhōng	jí	jì	hóng	yuē	xì	jǐn	zhī
1011	1012	1013	1014	1015	1016	1017	1018	1019	1020
網	綠	彎	灣	戀	變	經	輕	後	幾
wǎng	lǜ	wān	wān	liàn	biàn	jīng	qīng	hòu	jǐ
1021	1022	1023	1024	1025	1026	1027	1028	1029	1030
機	斷	繼	顯	樂	藥	雞	麼	系	係
jī	duàn	jì	xiǎn	yuè	yào	jī	me	xì	xì
1031	1032	1033	1034	1035	1036	1037	1038	1039	1040
孫	卻	腳	服	命	留	溜	聊	柳	令
sūn	què	jiǎo	fú	mìng	liú	liū	liáo	liǔ	lìng
1041	1042	1043	1044	1045	1046	1047	1048	1049	1050
冷	零	領	通	勇	犯	危	脆	印	興
lěng	líng	lǐng	tōng	yǒng	fàn	wéi	cuì	yìn	xìng
1051	1052	1053	1054	1055	1056	1057	1058	1059	1060

酒	配	酉	尊	遵	豆	頭	短	禮	體
jiǔ	pèi	qiú	zūn	zūn	dòu	tóu	duǎn	lǐ	tǐ
1061	1062	1063	1064	1065	1066	1067	1068	1069	1070
鼓	喜	廚	樹	血	盡	儘	蓋	溫	監
gǔ	xǐ	chú	shù	xiě	jìn	jǐn	gài	wēn	jiān
1071	1072	1073	1074	1075	1076	1077	1078	1079	1080
籃	藍	銀	跟	很	根	即	節	退	腿
lán	lán	yín	gēn	hěn	gēn	jí	jié	tuì	tuǐ
1081	1082	1083	1084	1085	1086	1087	1088	1089	1090
限	眼	良	浪	娘	食	飯	餐	館	養
xiàn	yǎn	liáng	làng	niáng	shí	fàn	cān	guǎn	yǎng
1091	1092	1093	1094	1095	1096	1097	1098	1099	1100
既	概	平	評	坪	乎	呼	希	稀	學
jì	gài	píng	píng	píng	hū	hū	xī	xī	xué
1101	1102	1103	1104	1105	1106	1107	1108	1109	1110
覺	攪	凶	兇	胸	離	禽	辛	辦	辯
jué	jiǎo	xiōng	xiōng	xiōng	lí	qín	xīn	bàn	biàn
1111	1112	1113	1114	1115	1116	1117	1118	1119	1120
壁	避	新	薪	親	襯	幸	執	報	叫
bì	bì	xīn	xīn	qīn	chèn	xìng	zhí	bào	jiào
1121	1122	1123	1124	1125	1126	1127	1128	1129	1130
收	陸	勢	熱	藝	亥	核	孩	刻	該
shōu	lù	shì	rè	yì	hài	hé	hái	kè	gāi
1131	1132	1133	1134	1135	1136	1137	1138	1139	1140
述	術	殺	襄	讓	壞	寒	賽	毒	素
shù	shù	shā	xiāng	ràng	rǎng	hán	sài	dú	sù
1141	1142	1143	1144	1145	1146	1147	1148	1149	1150
青	精	請	情	晴	清	靜	責	績	積
qīng	jīng	qǐng	qíng	jīng	qīng	jìng	zé	jī	jī
1151	1152	1153	1154	1155	1156	1157	1158	1159	1160
表	錶	生	星	姓	性	害	割	慧	豐
biǎo	biǎo	shēng	xīng	xìng	xìng	hài	gē	huì	fēng
1161	1162	1163	1164	1165	1166	1167	1168	1169	1170

春	泰	奉	棒	勤	謹	僅	漢	難	攤
chūn	tài	fèng	bàng	qín	jǐn	jǐn	hàn	nán	tān
1171	1172	1173	1174	1175	1176	1177	1178	1179	1180
華	嘩	垂	錘	睡	今	含	念	陰	蔭
huá	huá	chuí	chuí	shuì	jīn	hán	niàn	yīn	yìn
1181	1182	1183	1184	1185	1186	1187	1188	1189	1190
西	要	腰	票	漂	標	賈	價	煙	南
xī	yào	yāo	piào	piào	biāo	gǔ	jià	yān	nán
1191	1192	1193	1194	1195	1196	1197	1198	1199	1200
門	們	閒	問	間	簡	開	聞	倉	槍
mén	men	xián	wèn	jiàn	jiǎn	kāi	wén	cāng	qiāng
1201	1202	1203	1204	1205	1206	1207	1208	1209	1210
創	非	排	罪	靠	侯	候	決	快	筷
chuàng	fēi	pái	zuì	kào	hóu	hòu	jué	kuài	kuài
1211	1212	1213	1214	1215	1216	1217	1218	1219	1220
韋	圍	偉	衛	干	岸	幹	旱	趕	于
wéi	wéi	wěi	wèi	gān	àn	gàn	hàn	gǎn	yú
1221	1222	1223	1224	1225	1226	1227	1228	1229	1230
宇	余	餘	除	途	束	速	辣	整	練
yǔ	yú	yú	chú	tú	shù	sù	là	zhěng	liàn
1231	1232	1233	1234	1235	1236	1237	1238	1239	1240
揀	重	懂	動	種	衝	病	痛	瘋	匹
jiǎn	zhòng	dǒng	dòng	zhǒng	chōng	bìng	tòng	fēng	pī
1241	1242	1243	1244	1245	1246	1247	1248	1249	1250
區	樞	歐	醫	仰	迎	登	燈	證	發
qū	shū	ōu	yī	yǎng	yíng	dēng	dēng	zhèng	fā
1251	1252	1253	1254	1255	1256	1257	1258	1259	1260
廢	形	影	彩	須	珍	參	慘	修	文
fèi	xíng	yǐng	cǎi	xū	zhēn	cān	cǎn	xiū	wén
1261	1262	1263	1264	1265	1266	1267	1268	1269	1270
蚊	彥	顏	產	率	摔	央	英	巴	把
wén	yàn	yán	chǎn	shuài	shuāi	yāng	yīng	bā	bǎ
1271	1272	1273	1274	1275	1276	1277	1278	1279	1280

爸	吧	色	絕	甘	某	其	期	基	斯
bà	*bā*	*sè*	*jué*	*gān*	*mǒu*	*qí*	*qī*	*jī*	*sī*
1281	1282	1283	1284	1285	1286	1287	1288	1289	1290

甚	貴	遺	舞	無	撫	且	姐	組	祖
shèn	*guì*	*yí*	*wǔ*	*wú*	*fǔ*	*qiě*	*jiě*	*zǔ*	*zǔ*
1291	1292	1293	1294	1295	1296	1297	1298	1299	1300

助	並	普	業	對	共	供	異	巷	港
zhù	*bìng*	*pǔ*	*yè*	*duì*	*gòng*	*gōng*	*yì*	*xiàng*	*gǎng*
1301	1302	1303	1304	1305	1306	1307	1308	1309	1310

選	井	亞	惡	角	解	嘴	再	稱	講
xuǎn	*jǐng*	*yà*	*è*	*jiǎo*	*jiě*	*zuǐ*	*zài*	*chēng*	*jiǎng*
1311	1312	1313	1314	1315	1316	1317	1318	1319	1320

構	扁	篇	編	論	輪	典	氏	紙	昏
gòu	*biǎn*	*piān*	*biān*	*lùn*	*lún*	*diǎn*	*shì*	*zhǐ*	*hūn*
1321	1322	1323	1324	1325	1326	1327	1328	1329	1330

婚	低	底	民	眠	甫	補	博	搏	都
hūn	*dī*	*dǐ*	*mín*	*mián*	*fǔ*	*bǔ*	*bó*	*bó*	*dū*
1331	1332	1333	1334	1335	1336	1337	1338	1339	1340

部	郎	鄉	響	段	鍛	幻	司	詞	舟
bù	*láng*	*xiāng*	*xiǎng*	*duàn*	*duàn*	*huàn*	*sī*	*cí*	*zhōu*
1341	1342	1343	1344	1345	1346	1347	1348	1349	1350

船	般	盤	搬	瓜	孤	益	假	蝦	氣
chuán	*bān*	*pán*	*bān*	*guā*	*gū*	*yì*	*jià*	*xiā*	*qì*
1351	1352	1353	1354	1355	1356	1357	1358	1359	1360

汽	飛	面	麵	革	鞋	馨	聲	吳	娛
qì	*fēi*	*miàn*	*miàn*	*gé*	*xié*	*xīn*	*shēng*	*wú*	*yú*
1361	1362	1363	1364	1365	1366	1367	1368	1369	1370

誤	承	蒸	牙	穿	呀	釋	番	翻	播
wù	*chéng*	*zhēng*	*yá*	*chuān*	*ya*	*shì*	*fān*	*fān*	*bō*
1371	1372	1373	1374	1375	1376	1377	1378	1379	1380

毛	尾	宅	託	為	偽	長	張	漲	套
máo	*wěi*	*zhái*	*tuō*	*wèi*	*wèi*	*cháng*	*zhāng*	*zhàng*	*tào*
1381	1382	1383	1384	1385	1386	1387	1388	1389	1390

髮	展	喪	雁	應	烏	鷹	鴨	島	遇
fǎ	*zhǎn*	*sàng*	*yàn*	*yīng*	*niǎo*	*yīng*	*yā*	*dǎo*	*yù*
1391	1392	1393	1394	1395	1396	1397	1398	1399	1400

萬	邁	岡	剛	缺	寶	遙	搖	兔	逸
wàn	*mài*	*gāng*	*gāng*	*quē*	*bǎo*	*yáo*	*yáo*	*tù*	*yì*
1401	1402	1403	1404	1405	1406	1407	1408	1409	1410

免	晚	象	像	馬	媽	罵	嗎	驗	騎
miǎn	*wǎn*	*xiàng*	*xiàng*	*mǎ*	*mā*	*mà*	*ma*	*yàn*	*qí*
1411	1412	1413	1414	1415	1416	1417	1418	1419	1420

驚	虎	慮	處	戲	劇	據	鹿	塵	麗
jīng	*hǔ*	*lǜ*	*chù*	*xì*	*jù*	*jù*	*lù*	*chén*	*lì*
1421	1422	1423	1424	1425	1426	1427	1428	1429	1430

熊	能	態	寅	演	辰	晨	農	濃	送
xióng	*néng*	*tài*	*yín*	*yǎn*	*chén*	*chén*	*nóng*	*nóng*	*sòng*
1431	1432	1433	1434	1435	1436	1437	1438	1439	1440

鬼	魔	塊	龍	襲	兒	舊	寫	瀉	兩
guǐ	*mó*	*kuài*	*lóng*	*xí*	*ér*	*jiù*	*xiě*	*xiè*	*liǎng*
1441	1442	1443	1444	1445	1446	1447	1448	1449	1450

倆	滿	爾	彌	虛	聯	關	那	哪	巫
liǎ	*mǎn*	*ěr*	*mí*	*xū*	*lián*	*guān*	*nà*	*nǎ*	*wū*
1451	1452	1453	1454	1455	1456	1457	1458	1459	1460

靈	縣	懸	與	舉	腦	惱	專	傳	轉
líng	*xiàn*	*xuán*	*yǔ*	*jǔ*	*nǎo*	*nǎo*	*zhuān*	*chuán*	*zhuàn*
1461	1462	1463	1464	1465	1466	1467	1468	1469	1470

團	黃	廣	橫	窗	總	詹	擔	數	樓
tuán	*huáng*	*guǎng*	*héng*	*chuāng*	*zǒng*	*zhān*	*dān*	*shù*	*lóu*
1471	1472	1473	1474	1475	1476	1477	1478	1479	1480

獨	屬	爛	蘭	從	縱	齊	濟	丑	扭
dú	*shǔ*	*làn*	*lán*	*cóng*	*zòng*	*qí*	*jì*	*chǒu*	*niǔ*
1481	1482	1483	1484	1485	1486	1487	1488	1489	1490

卑	牌	號	怪	赤	亦	極	雜	曰	亂
bēi	*pái*	*hào*	*guài*	*chì*	*yì*	*jí*	*zá*	*yuē*	*luàn*
1491	1492	1493	1494	1495	1496	1497	1498	1499	1500

INDEX II
Primitive Elements

This Index lists all the primitive elements used in this book. Characters used as primitives are only listed where the writing is significantly altered. The primitives are arranged according to the number of strokes. The number refers to the page on which the element is first introduced.

1 劃	′	丨	ㄴ	ㄴ	㇏	コ
	31	32	57	57	248	349

2 劃	八	儿	几	勹	⍩	ナ	⼃	刂	厂
	39	39	40	40	40	50	52	52	65
	冂	𠆢	冖	二	口	⼆	冫	乀	乂
	88	114	134	136	166	168	168	176	214
	厂	厶	亻	㇀	丂	与	卩	卩	マ
	217	219	240	248	276	278	292	293	293
	己	乄	凵	丩	𠃌	匚			
	294	303	303	306	323	329			

3 劃	𠫔	⺌	少	巛	川	氵	宀	犭	亼
	49	62	63	69	69	70	90	108	115
	辶	夂	弋	夊	巳	口	广	忄	扌
	128	131	147	158	194	202	203	204	209
	廾	开	彳	云	彳	尸	彐	厶	阝..
	211	211	212	220	233	253	263	282	289

17劃 闌
376

18劃 翟
216

19劃 孌
288

Characters by Number of Strokes

Here you will find all the characters treated in this book, grouped by the number of strokes. The ordering within each stroke-number group follows the standard dictionary practice of arranging the characters according to "radicals."

1 劃		丈	776	干	1225	勻	62	方	461
一	1	之	921	弓	941	勿	815	牙	1374
乙	91	久	778	才	578	化	771	曰	1499
		及	584			匹	1250	日	12
		丸	41			午	509	月	13
2 劃		乞	434	**4 劃**		廿	903	木	191
七	7	也	476	丑	1489	升	39	欠	439
丁	86	于	1230	不	924	反	607	止	353
乃	582	亡	457	中	36	友	590	歹	661
九	9	凡	59	乏	922	太	120	比	422
了	95	刃	80	云	395	天	403	毛	1381
二	2	勺	65	五	5	夫	679	氏	1328
人	736	千	37	互	629	夭	404	水	126
入	638	口	11	井	1312	孔	93	火	157
八	8	土	147	介	241	少	104	爪	612
刀	79	士	307	今	1186	尤	226	父	968
力	687	夕	108	什	743	尹	882	片	914
匕	419	大	106	仍	751	巴	1279	牛	235
十	10	女	96	仁	761	幻	1347	犬	225
卜	42	子	92	內	639	引	942	王	248
又	589	寸	153	予	936	心	529		
		小	103	元	56	戈	335	**5 劃**	
		山	634	公	643	戶	830	丘	1003
3 劃		川	123	六	6	手	548	且	1297
下	45	工	72	冗	288	支	601	世	27
三	3	己	485	凶	1113	文	1270	丙	780
上	44	巳	488	切	81	斗	893	主	259
		巾	382	分	641	斤	856		

乎	1106	巧	950	亥	1136	存	580	舟	1350
乍	865	左	73	交	969	安	186	色	1283
以	796	市	388	伊	883	宇	1231	血	1075
他	752	布	383	企	358	守	181	行	699
代	769	平	1103	休	753	宅	1383	衣	375
付	766	必	547	仰	1255	寺	155	西	1191
令	1050	打	559	件	750	尖	107	巡	272
兄	101	斥	863	全	257	州	124	迅	270
凸	31	且	29	任	793	年	806	臣	683
凹	30	本	200	份	738	式	333		
出	635	末	203	兒	1114	忙	544	**7 劃**	
加	695	未	202	光	119	成	341	佛	946
功	692	正	362	充	630	收	1131	位	749
包	489	母	99	先	239	曲	892	何	774
北	420	民	1334	兆	223	旭	26	作	868
半	907	永	127	共	1306	旨	429	似	797
占	43	汁	138	再	1318	旬	64	你	741
卡	46	犯	1056	冰	401	早	25	住	748
去	624	玉	249	刑	576	有	75	伸	851
可	88	瓜	1355	列	662	次	443	但	747
句	63	甘	1285	印	1059	此	426	低	1332
古	16	生	1163	危	1057	死	664	佔	739
只	50	用	896	各	281	每	431	伴	908
史	586	甲	848	吉	308	江	137	余	1232
司	1348	申	850	吃	435	池	479	克	102
召	82	田	14	吸	585	灰	158	兌	467
台	621	由	845	向	178	爭	876	免	1411
叮	87	白	33	合	245	百	34	兵	1004
叫	1130	皮	656	吐	151	竹	728	冷	1051
右	74	目	15	同	176	米	724	初	381
另	688	矛	931	名	112	羊	495	判	910
四	4	矢	927	因	518	羽	511	別	689
囚	737	石	114	回	520	老	954	利	716
冬	402	示	834	在	581	考	955	助	1301
外	111	禾	710	地	478	而	887	努	694
央	1277	穴	995	多	109	耳	666	即	1087
失	682	立	408	好	97	肉	782	呀	1376
奶	583			如	98	肌	60	含	1187
奴	693	**6 劃**		她	477	自	32	君	884
它	428	亦	1496	妄	459	至	626	吾	18
尼	821			字	180	舌	38		

吳	1369	投	597	辛	1118	周	305	拐	690
吼	94	把	1280	辰	1436	味	205	招	558
告	237	改	486	近	858	命	1045	抽	846
吵	105	攻	314	迎	1256	和	712	拉	570
吹	440	旱	1228	返	609	固	515	放	463
呈	256	更	587	那	1458	坪	1105	於	465
呐	640	肖	117	里	169	垂	1183	易	818
吧	1282	肚	149	防	988	夜	807	昆	423
否	925	杏	195			奇	122	昏	1330
呆	196	束	1236	**8 劃**		奉	1173	昇	40
呂	800	村	198			委	719	昌	24
困	514	李	210	並	1302	妹	206	昔	897
均	148	步	354	事	878	始	623	明	20
坑	295	求	128	亞	1313	姓	1165	育	631
坐	785	汽	1361	些	427	姐	1298	股	600
壯	917	決	1218	享	297	季	718	肯	357
妝	916	沙	136	京	301	孤	1356	服	1044
妨	462	沖	132	依	755	官	966	朋	19
妙	116	沉	289	供	1307	宗	840	果	853
孝	957	沒	598	使	777	定	364	采	614
完	182	災	162	併	798	尚	179	枝	603
局	829	狂	253	例	756	居	826	松	644
尾	1382	甫	1336	來	789	岸	1226	東	473
希	1108	男	691	兒	1446	岡	1403	杯	926
序	937	皂	35	兔	1409	幸	1127	板	608
床	527	社	835	兩	1450	底	1333	林	192
廷	794	秀	720	其	1287	店	523	武	360
弄	574	究	996	具	70	府	767	河	144
弟	948	系	1039	典	1327	延	371	泣	409
形	1262	良	1093	刻	1139	往	704	況	143
志	533	見	55	刺	392	忽	816	治	622
忍	531	角	1315	制	393	念	1188	沼	135
忘	530	言	320	到	628	怪	1494	注	260
快	1219	谷	645	協	698	性	1166	泳	133
我	551	豆	1066	卓	47	怕	543	泥	823
找	572	貝	51	卑	1491	或	336	波	657
技	602	赤	1495	受	617	所	857	法	625
抗	556	走	365	取	667	房	831	泡	490
扭	1490	足	973	叔	604	承	1372	沫	204
抓	613	身	951	呼	1107	抱	555	油	847
批	557	車	274	呢	822	押	849	炎	160

弱	944	真	71	高	296	康	881	涼	302
修	1269	眠	1335	鬼	1441	強	943	率	1275
恐	539	破	659			張	1388	球	250
息	538	陣	991	**11 劃**		彩	1264	現	251
拳	912	站	410			從	1485	理	258
拿	550	笑	729	乾	436	得	702	產	1274
效	970	紙	1329	假	1358	您	742	異	1308
料	894	素	1150	偽	1386	慾	648	眼	1092
旁	466	缺	1405	偉	1223	情	1154	眷	911
旅	811	臭	231	健	758	掛	567	祭	842
時	156	般	1352	做	746	控	999	票	1194
書	311	茶	243	停	759	採	615	移	713
胸	1115	草	213	剪	278	授	618	竟	454
脂	430	蚊	1271	副	85	接	566	章	411
脆	1058	袁	378	動	1244	掃	873	第	949
能	1432	被	660	務	934	探	1002	細	1018
脈	611	記	487	區	1251	推	565	終	1013
案	201	訓	325	參	1267	排	1213	組	1299
核	1137	託	1384	售	506	掉	569	眾	784
格	282	討	324	商	416	救	317	習	512
校	972	貢	77	唱	21	教	958	聊	1048
根	1086	財	579	啊	982	敗	315	船	1351
桌	211	起	491	問	1204	斬	859	莊	918
桃	224	速	1237	啦	571	族	928	莫	217
氣	1360	通	1054	國	516	晨	1437	菜	616
泰	1172	途	1235	執	1128	曼	674	華	1181
海	433	逛	273	培	448	晚	1412	著	960
浩	238	透	721	堂	655	脫	468	蛇	481
消	142	造	271	基	1289	望	460	蛋	482
浴	646	這	332	夠	110	條	744	術	1142
涉	355	連	275	婚	1331	梅	432	袋	770
流	632	酒	1061	婆	658	梳	633	規	680
浪	1094	配	1062	婦	872	欲	647	視	836
烤	956	針	264	寄	188	殺	1143	許	510
烈	663	釘	265	寂	606	液	808	設	599
特	236	關	1457	寅	1434	混	424	貧	642
班	940	院	990	密	637	淺	351	貨	773
留	1046	除	1234	將	920	渴	792	貫	100
畝	779	隻	592	專	1468	深	1001	責	1158
病	1247	馬	1415	崇	841	清	1156	軟	442
益	1357	骨	978	常	654	淡	161	逸	1410

筷	1220	零	1052	爾	1453	領	1053	歐	1253
節	1088	雷	398	獄	323	麼	1038	潮	139
經	1027	頑	58	瘋	1249	鼻	575	熟	298
罪	1214	預	938	盡	1076	齊	1487	熱	1134
置	69	鼓	1071	監	1080			盤	1353
義	552			瞄	222	**15 劃**		箱	730
群	886			確	508			篇	1323
聖	671	**14 劃**		稱	1319	價	1198	線	1006
腦	1466	像	1414	種	1245	劇	1426	編	1324
腳	1043	劃	313	端	891	嘲	49	罵	1417
腹	438	厭	233	管	967	增	471	蔭	1190
腰	1193	嘩	1182	算	733	墨	174	處	1424
腿	1090	團	1471	精	1152	嬌	407	蝦	1359
萬	1401	圖	522	維	1007	寫	1448	衛	1224
葬	665	境	456	網	1021	寬	215	衝	1246
葉	216	墓	220	緊	1019	導	269	褲	525
落	287	塵	1429	綠	1022	層	828	課	854
敬	318	夢	294	聞	1208	幟	453	誰	505
號	1493	察	843	腐	783	廣	1473	請	1153
裝	919	實	183	與	1464	廢	1261	誕	372
裡	376	對	1305	舞	1294	廠	526	談	331
解	1316	幕	385	蒸	1373	廚	1073	調	330
該	1140	態	1433	蓋	1078	彈	945	論	1325
試	334	慘	1268	蓮	276	影	1263	豬	961
詩	327	摔	1276	製	394	德	705	賣	310
詹	1477	慣	545	複	437	慧	1169	賜	819
話	326	慢	675	語	328	憂	542	質	862
誠	343	榮	802	誤	1371	慮	1423	賤	352
賈	1197	構	1321	誌	534	戲	1425	賠	447
資	444	槍	1210	說	469	撒	901	賦	361
賊	337	歌	441	認	532	撫	1296	賢	685
賄	76	漢	1178	誘	722	播	1380	趣	668
跟	1084	漠	219	趕	1229	敵	418	輝	291
跳	975	演	1435	輕	1028	數	1479	輪	1326
路	976	漁	165	辣	1238	暫	860	遺	1293
較	971	漸	861	適	417	樂	1035	遵	1065
載	338	漲	1389	銀	1083	樓	1480	選	1311
農	1438	漂	1195	銅	262	標	1196	隨	985
遙	1407	漫	676	銘	266	樞	1252	靠	1215
遠	379	滿	1452	際	983	樣	500	鞋	1366
電	399	熊	1431	需	888	模	218	餘	1233

Character Pronunciations

This Index lists alphabetically the pronunciations, with their respective frame numbers, of all the characters treated in this volume. Some of the characters have multiple pronunciations, which can be found by consulting a dictionary under the pronunciation given here.

chén	晨	1437	cuì	脆	1058	diǎn	點	173	**F**
chèn	襯	1126	cūn	村	198	diǎn	典	1327	
chēng	稱	1319	cún	存	580	diàn	電	399	fā 發 1260
chéng	呈	256	cùn	寸	153	diàn	店	523	fá 乏 922
chéng	成	341	cuò	錯	899	diào	釣	263	fǎ 法 625
chéng	城	342		**D**		diào	調	330	fà 髮 1391
chéng	誠	343	dá	達	499	diào	掉	569	fān 番 1378
chéng	程	711	dá	答	734	dīng	丁	86	fān 翻 1379
chéng	承	1372	dǎ	打	559	dīng	叮	87	fán 凡 59
chī	吃	435	dà	大	106	dīng	釘	265	fán 煩 159
chí	池	479	dāi	呆	196	dǐng	頂	90	fǎn 反 607
chí	持	561	dǎi	歹	661	dìng	定	364	fǎn 返 609
chì	斥	863	dài	帶	390	dōng	冬	402	fàn 犯 1056
chì	赤	1495	dài	待	703	dōng	東	473	fàn 飯 1097
chōng	沖	132	dài	代	769	dǒng	懂	1243	fāng 方 461
chōng	充	630	dài	袋	770	dòng	洞	177	fáng 妨 462
chōng	衝	1246	dān	單	348	dòng	棟	474	fáng 房 831
chóng	蟲	480	dān	擔	1478	dòng	凍	475	fáng 防 988
chóng	崇	841	dàn	旦	29	dòng	動	1244	fàng 放 463
chōu	抽	846	dàn	淡	161	dǒu	斗	893	fēi 非 1212
chóu	愁	715	dàn	誕	372	dòu	豆	1066	fēi 飛 1362
chǒu	丑	1489	dàn	蛋	482	dū	督	605	fèi 肺 389
chòu	臭	231	dàn	但	747	dū	都	1340	fèi 費 947
chū	初	381	dàn	彈	945	dú	讀	329	fèi 廢 1261
chū	出	635	dāng	當	651	dú	毒	1149	fēn 分 641
chú	廚	1073	dǎng	黨	653	dú	獨	1481	fèn 份 738
chú	除	1234	dàng	檔	652	dù	肚	149	fēng 封 154
chǔ	楚	373	dāo	刀	79	dù	度	905	fēng 風 483
chǔ	礎	374	dǎo	導	269	dù	渡	906	fēng 豐 1170
chù	處	1424	dǎo	倒	760	duān	端	891	fēng 瘋 1249
chuān	川	123	dǎo	島	1399	duǎn	短	1068	fěng 諷 484
chuān	穿	1375	dào	道	268	duàn	斷	1032	fèng 奉 1173
chuán	船	1351	dào	到	628	duàn	段	1345	fó 佛 946
chuán	傳	1469	dé	德	705	duàn	鍛	1346	fǒu 否 925
chuāng	窗	1475	de	的	66	duì	兌	467	fū 夫 679
chuáng	床	527	děi	得	702	duì	隊	992	fú 福 837
chuàng	創	1211	dēng	登	1257	duì	對	1305	fú 服 1044
chuī	吹	440	dēng	燈	1258	duō	多	109	fǔ 府 767
chuí	垂	1183	děng	等	732		**E**		fǔ 俯 768
chuí	錘	1184	dī	低	1332	é	額	284	fǔ 腐 783
chūn	春	1171	dí	敵	418	è	惡	1314	fǔ 撫 1296
cí	詞	1349	dǐ	底	1333	ér	而	887	fǔ 甫 1336
cǐ	此	426	dì	帝	413	ér	兒	1446	fù 負 61
cì	刺	392	dì	地	478	ěr	耳	666	fù 副 85
cì	次	443	dì	弟	948	ěr	爾	1453	fù 富 189
cì	賜	819	dì	第	949	èr	二	2	fù 賦 361
cóng	從	1485							fù 複 437

fù	腹	438	gū	孤	1356	hào	號	1493	huī	輝	291
fù	復	701	gǔ	古	16	hē	喝	791	huī	揮	564
fù	付	766	gǔ	股	600	hé	和	712	huí	回	520
fù	婦	872	gǔ	谷	645	hé	河	144	huí	迴	521
fù	父	968	gǔ	骨	978	hé	合	245	huì	賄	76
fù	附	989	gǔ	鼓	1071	hé	禾	710	huì	會	244

G

			gǔ	賈	1197	hé	何	774	huì	慧	1169
			gù	故	316	hé	核	1137	hūn	昏	1330
gāi	該	1140	gù	固	515	hè	賀	696	hūn	婚	1331
gǎi	改	486	gù	雇	832	hēi	黑	172	hùn	混	424
gài	蓋	1078	gù	顧	833	hěn	很	1085	huó	活	141
gài	概	1102	guā	瓜	1355	héng	橫	1474	huǒ	火	157
gān	乾	436	guà	掛	567	hóng	紅	1016	huò	或	336
gān	干	1225	guǎi	拐	690	hóu	侯	1216	huò	獲	594
gān	甘	1285	guài	怪	1494	hǒu	吼	94	huò	貨	773
gǎn	感	540	guān	冠	293	hòu	厚	113			
gǎn	敢	672	guān	觀	595	hòu	後	1029			
gǎn	趕	1229	guān	官	966	hòu	候	1217		**J**	
gàn	幹	1227	guān	關	1457	hū	忽	816			
gāng	岡	1403	guǎn	管	967	hū	乎	1106	jī	肌	60
gāng	剛	1404	guǎn	館	1099	hū	呼	1107	jī	激	464
gǎng	港	1310	guàn	貫	100	hú	胡	17	jī	擊	636
gāo	高	296	guàn	慣	545	hú	湖	145	jī	機	1031
gào	告	237	guāng	光	119	hǔ	虎	1422	jī	雞	1037
gē	哥	89	guǎng	廣	1473	hù	護	593	jī	績	1159
gē	戈	335	guàng	逛	273	hù	互	629	jī	積	1160
gē	歌	441	guī	規	680	hù	戶	830	jī	基	1289
gē	割	1168	guǐ	鬼	1441	huā	花	772	jí	吉	308
gé	格	282	guì	貴	1292	huá	劃	313	jí	集	502
gé	革	1365	guó	國	516	huá	滑	979	jí	及	584
gè	各	281	guǒ	果	853	huá	華	1181	jí	急	870
gè	個	757	guò	過	980	huá	嘩	1182	jí	級	1014
gěi	給	1011				huà	畫	312	jí	即	1087
gēn	跟	1084		**H**		huà	話	326	jí	極	1497
gēn	根	1086				huà	化	771	jǐ	己	485
gèng	更	587	hā	哈	246	huái	懷	546	jǐ	幾	1030
gōng	工	72	hái	孩	1138	huài	壞	380	jì	寄	188
gōng	攻	314	hǎi	海	433	huān	歡	596	jì	計	322
gōng	公	643	hài	亥	1136	huán	環	677	jì	記	487
gōng	功	692	hài	害	1167	huán	還	678	jì	技	602
gōng	弓	941	hán	寒	1147	huàn	喚	809	jì	寂	606
gōng	供	1307	hán	含	1187	huàn	換	810	jì	季	718
gòng	貢	77	hàn	憾	541	huàn	幻	1347	jì	祭	842
gòng	共	1306	hàn	漢	1178	huáng	皇	254	jì	際	983
gǒu	狗	232	hàn	旱	1228	huáng	煌	255	jì	紀	1015
gòu	夠	110	háng	行	699	huáng	黃	1472	jì	繼	1033
gòu	構	1321	hǎo	好	97	huī	灰	158	jì	既	1101
			hào	浩	238				jì	濟	1488
									jiā	家	492

jiā	加	695	jīn	斤	856	jūn	君	884	
jiā	傢	740	jīn	今	1186				
jiǎ	甲	848	jǐn	緊	1019	**K**			
jià	架	697	jǐn	儘	1077				
jià	價	1198	jǐn	謹	1176	kǎ	卡	46	
jià	假	1358	jǐn	僅	1177	kāi	開	1207	
jiān	尖	107	jìn	進	503	kàn	看	549	
jiān	堅	686	jìn	禁	838	kāng	康	881	
jiān	監	1080	jìn	近	858	kàng	抗	556	
jiǎn	剪	278	jìn	盡	1076	kǎo	考	955	
jiǎn	減	347	jīng	晶	22	kǎo	烤	956	
jiǎn	檢	787	jīng	京	301	kào	靠	1215	
jiǎn	簡	1206	jīng	經	1027	kē	顆	855	
jiǎn	揀	1241	jīng	精	1152	kē	科	895	
jiàn	見	55	jīng	睛	1155	kě	可	88	
jiàn	賤	352	jīng	驚	1421	kě	渴	792	
jiàn	建	370	jǐng	景	303	kè	克	102	
jiàn	件	750	jǐng	警	321	kè	客	283	
jiàn	健	758	jǐng	井	1312	kè	課	854	
jiàn	漸	861	jìng	敬	318	kè	刻	1139	
jiàn	間	1205	jìng	競	412	kěn	肯	357	
jiāng	江	137	jìng	竟	454	kēng	坑	295	
jiǎng	講	1320	jìng	鏡	455	kōng	空	998	
jiàng	將	920	jìng	境	456	kǒng	孔	93	
jiàng	降	993	jìng	淨	877	kǒng	恐	539	
jiāo	嬌	407	jìng	靜	1157	kòng	控	999	
jiāo	教	958	jiū	究	996	kǒu	口	11	
jiāo	交	969	jiǔ	九	9	kū	枯	197	
jiǎo	腳	1043	jiǔ	久	778	kū	哭	229	
jiǎo	攬	1112	jiǔ	酒	1061	kǔ	苦	214	
jiǎo	角	1315	jiù	就	304	kù	庫	524	
jiào	較	971	jiù	救	317	kù	褲	525	
jiào	叫	1130	jiù	舊	1447	kuài	快	1219	
jiē	皆	425	jū	居	826	kuài	筷	1220	
jiē	接	566	jú	局	829	kuài	塊	1443	
jiē	街	709	jǔ	舉	1465	kuān	寬	215	
jiē	階	994	jù	句	63	kuáng	狂	253	
jié	結	1012	jù	具	70	kuàng	況	143	
jié	節	1088	jù	鋸	827	kūn	昆	423	
jiě	姐	1298	jù	劇	1426	kùn	困	514	
jiě	解	1316	jù	據	1427	kuò	括	562	
jiè	介	241	juàn	眷	911	**L**			
jiè	界	242	jué	覺	1111				
jiè	借	898	jué	決	1218	lā	拉	570	
jīn	金	261	jué		1284	lā	啦	571	
jīn	巾	382	jūn	均	148	là	辣	1238	
jīn	襟	839	jūn	軍	290	lái	來	789	
						lán	籃	1081	

lán	藍	1082
lán	蘭	1484
làn	爛	1483
láng	郎	1342
làng	浪	1094
láo	勞	803
lǎo	老	954
le	了	95
léi	雷	398
lèi	類	727
lěng	冷	1051
lí	離	1116
lǐ	里	169
lǐ	李	210
lǐ	理	258
lǐ	裡	376
lǐ	禮	1069
lì	立	408
lì	力	687
lì	利	716
lì	歷	723
lì	例	756
lì	麗	1430
liǎ	倆	1451
lián	連	275
lián	蓮	276
lián	聯	1456
liǎn	臉	788
liàn	戀	1025
liàn	練	1240
liáng	涼	302
liáng	良	1093
liǎng	兩	1450
liàng	量	170
liàng	亮	300
liáo	聊	1048
liào	料	894
liè	列	662
liè	烈	663
lín	林	192
lín	臨	684
líng	零	1052
líng	靈	1461
lǐng	領	1053
lìng	另	688
lìng	令	1050
liū	溜	1047

zhāng	張	1388	zhī	隻	592	zhōng	鐘	415	zī	資	444
zhàng	丈	776	zhī	支	601	zhōng	終	1013	zī	姿	445
zhàng	漲	1389	zhī	枝	603	zhǒng	種	1245	zī	諮	446
zhāo	昭	83	zhī	之	921	zhòng	眾	784	zǐ	子	92
zhāo	招	558	zhī	知	929	zhòng	重	1242	zì	自	32
zhǎo	沼	135	zhī	織	1020	zhōu	州	124	zì	字	180
zhǎo	找	572	zhí	直	68	zhōu	洲	134	zōng	宗	840
zhǎo	爪	612	zhí	植	194	zhōu	周	305	zǒng	總	1476
zhào	召	82	zhí	職	670	zhōu	週	306	zòng	縱	1486
zhào	照	163	zhí	值	745	zhōu	舟	1350	zǒu	走	365
zhào	兆	223	zhí	質	862	zhū	豬	961	zú	族	928
zhě	者	959	zhí	執	1128	zhú	竹	728	zú	足	973
zhè	這	332	zhǐ	只	50	zhǔ	主	259	zǔ	組	1299
zhe	著	960	zhǐ	止	353	zhù	貯	190	zǔ	祖	1300
zhēn	貞	53	zhǐ	旨	429	zhù	注	260	zuǐ	嘴	1317
zhēn	真	71	zhǐ	指	560	zhù	住	748	zuì	最	669
zhēn	針	264	zhǐ	紙	1329	zhù	助	1301	zuì	罪	1214
zhēn	珍	1266	zhì	置	69	zhuā	抓	613	zūn	尊	1064
zhèn	鎮	267	zhì	滯	391	zhuān	專	1468	zūn	遵	1065
zhèn	陣	991	zhì	制	393	zhuàn	轉	1470	zuó	昨	867
zhēng	爭	876	zhì	製	394	zhuāng	妝	916	zuǒ	左	73
zhēng	蒸	1373	zhì	幟	453	zhuāng	莊	918	zuò	做	746
zhěng	整	1239	zhì	志	533	zhuāng	裝	919	zuò	坐	785
zhèng	正	362	zhì	誌	534	zhuàng	壯	917	zuò	座	786
zhèng	政	363	zhì	治	622	zhuī	追	962	zuò	作	868
zhèng	證	1259	zhì	至	626	zhǔn	準	504			
zhī	汁	138	zhì	智	930	zhuō	桌	211			
zhī	脂	430	zhōng	中	36	zhuó	卓	47			

Key Words and Primitive Meanings

This Index contains a cumulative list of all the key words and primitive meanings used in this book. Key words are listed with their respective character and frame number. Primitive meanings are listed in italics and are followed only by the number of the page (also in italics) on which they are first introduced.

O

oaken tub		*337*
obey	順	125
observe	觀	595
obvious	顯	1034
occasion	際	983
occupy	佔	739
ocean	洋	497
of	之	921
offend	干	1225
offer	與	1464
offer sacrifice	祭	842
office,		
government	府	767
official, feudal	臣	683
offshoot	支	601
often	常	654
oil	油	847
old	舊	1447
old man	老	954
Old West		*319*
old woman	婆	658
older brother	哥	89
older sister	姐	1298
once more	再	1318
one	一	1
one after another	連	275
one another	相	199
one of a pair	隻	592
oneself	自	32
only	只	50
only then	乃	582
ooh!	乎	1106
open	開	1207
opt for	揀	1241
or	或	336
orchid	蘭	1484
orders	令	1050
ordinary	凡	59
orientation	向	178
orifice	嘴	1317
orphan	孤	1356
ought to	應	1395
outhouse		*226*
outside	外	111
outstretched hands		*213*

overall	統	1010
overcome	克	102
overflow	漫	676
overly	太	120
overseer	尹	882
oyster		*41*

P

pack of wild dogs		*108*
page	頁	57
pagoda	塔	247
painting of a deer		*366*
pair	雙	591
pair, one of a	隻	592
papa	爸	1281
paper	紙	1329
paper punch		*285*
parade		*149*
park	園	519
part	分	641
part of the body		*23*
participate	參	1267
partition	壁	1121
partner	伴	908
party, political	黨	653
pass through	穿	1375
past, times	昔	897
paste	貼	52
patch	補	1337
path	路	976
patrol	巡	272
pattern	格	282
pavilion	亭	299
pawn	押	849
pay	付	766
peaceful	安	186
peach	桃	224
pebbles		*66*
peculiar	怪	1494
peel	削	118
pen	筆	731
pen, turkey		*199*
penetrate	透	721
pent in		*202*
people	民	1334
pepper plant		*305*
pepper, chili		*305*

peppery	辛	1118
perform	演	1435
perfume	香	717
perilous	險	984
period of time	期	1288
perish		*184*
permit	許	510
person	人	736
physician	醫	1254
pick	採	615
picture	圖	522
piece	件	750
piece of writing	篇	1323
piece together	拼	799
pierce	貫	100
piety, filial	孝	957
pig	豬	961
pigeon coop		*309*
piggy bank		*195*
Pigpen		*83*
pill	丸	41
pills, bottle of		*35*
pine tree	松	644
pinnacle		*282*
pipe	管	967
pit	坑	295
pit		*303*
place	所	857
plan	計	322
plank	板	608
plant	植	194
platform	台	621
play	玩	252
play with	弄	574
plentiful	豐	1170
plow		*248*
pluck	采	614
plum	李	210
plum, small	梅	432
(plural)	們	1202
poem	詩	327
poison	毒	1149
pole, wooden		*94*
police	警	321
political party	黨	653
politics	政	363
pond	池	479

swell	漲	1389	thin	淡	161	towel	巾	382
swim	泳	133	thing	物	817	*towel, white*		*164*
swimming, go	游	813	think	想	537	*trail of footprints*		*154*
sword	刀	79	third	丙	780	tranquil	泰	1172
system	制	393	thirsty	渴	792	transcend	超	366
			this	這	332	transform	化	771
T			this (literary)	此	426	transport	輸	279
table	桌	211	thorn	刺	392	trapped	困	514
table		*297*	*thorn*		*166*	travel	旅	811
table, small		*40*	thousand	千	37	tray	盤	1353
tail	尾	1382	*thread*		*286*	treasure	寶	1406
take	取	667	three	三	3	treat	待	703
take an exam	考	955	throw	投	597	tree	木	191
take charge of	司	1348	thunder	雷	398	*tree, family*		*101*
take out	抽	846	*tiara*		*137*	tremendously	甚	1291
talk	話	326	ticket	票	1194	tribe	族	928
Talking Cricket		*361*	tide	潮	139	tribute	貢	77
tall	高	296	tie	結	1012	troops	兵	1004
Tang	唐	879	tiger	虎	1422	troupe	團	1471
tanned hide	韋	1221	tiger, sign of the	寅	1434	trousers	褲	525
taskmaster		*142*	tight	緊	1019	true	真	71
tasks	務	934	timber	樹	1074	trunk	幹	1227
tea	茶	243	time	時	156	try	番	1378
teach	教	958	time, period of	期	1288	*tub, oaken*		*337*
teacher	師	964	times past	昔	897	tucked under		
team	隊	992	*tin can*		*362*	the arm		*214*
technique	藝	1135	tiny	微	708	tumble	摔	1276
teenager		*61*	tip	尖	107	tune	調	330
teepee		*331*	to the utmost	儘	1077	*turkey*		*198*
teeth, wind-up		*109*	*toad, horned*		*327*	*turkey house*		*199*
telescope		*311*	together	共	1306	*turkey pen*		*199*
tell fortunes	占	43	toil	努	694	turn	拐	690
temperature	溫	1079	*tomahawk*		*261*	turn into	成	341
temple, Buddhist	寺	155	*tomato seedling*		*103*	turn over	翻	1379
temporary	暫	860	*tome*		*344*	*tusk*		*355*
ten	十	10	tongue	舌	38	twenty	廿	903
ten thousand	萬	1401	*tongue wagging*			twig	條	744
territory	壤	1146	*in the mouth*		*23*	twist	扭	1490
test	試	334	tool	具	70	two	二	2
thank	謝	953	*tool*		*49*	*two hands*		*211*
Thanksgiving		*149*	tooth	牙	1374			
that	那	1458	*top hat*		*136*	**U**		
that's right	對	1305	*top hat and scarf*		*161*	*umbrella*		*114*
then, only	乃	582	topic	題	369	uncle	叔	604
theory	論	1325	tot	孩	1138	*underling*		*231*
thick	厚	113	tour	遊	814	understand	懂	1243
thigh	股	600	toward	往	704	undertake	承	1372